DREAMS THAT BUILT AMERICA

365 INSPIRING STORIES

OF GRIT, PURPOSE, AND TRIUMPH

ALAN ELLIOTT

W PUBLISHING GROUP

AN IMPRINT OF THOMAS NELSON

Dedication

For Corley, Wesley, Ethan, Emily, Caroline, and Susanne

STARTING OVER

You may have a fresh start any moment you choose, for this thing that we call "failure" is not the falling down, but the staying down.
MARY PICKFORD

The month of January was named after the Greek god Janus, who had two faces. One face looked back, and the other looked forward. The stories in this book are about people who chose to look forward. An ancient proverb says, "Fall down seven times, stand up eight." It's been the same for millennia. Accomplishments belong to those who, even though they fail repeatedly, brush themselves off and try again. Without the grit and determination of people who refused defeat, this book would have no stories to tell. There would be no Hershey chocolate, landable and reusable rockets, Dr. Seuss books, Disneyland, or television. Significant accomplishments require courage, ingenuity, and persistence.

For example, in 2005 Hurricane Katrina blew through New Orleans with 175-mile-per-hour winds, pounding rain, and rampant twenty-foot floods. More than twelve hundred lives were lost. More than a million people were displaced. After the storm, buildings, homes, and churches lay destroyed or damaged in muck and waste. But as evacuated residents returned to the city, a renewal began. People from all over the world donated goods, labor, and money. Little by little, New Orleans rose from the muddy disaster. It took years, but in time NOLA's streets danced again to the vibes of jazz music and the blues. Of course, everyone experiences setbacks at one time or another. It could be from a natural disaster, the loss of a loved one, a financial crisis, divorce, or severe illness. Historically, the year's beginning is a time to set aside the past's troubles and embrace the future. The following stories are designed to help you reflect, recharge, and renew.

Consider This: Life's challenges happen to everyone. But never let them conquer you. Instead, rise up and start over. There's always a new day and a new opportunity waiting.

LIN-MANUEL MIRANDA AND *HAMILTON*

> You may encounter many defeats, but you must not
> be defeated. In fact, it may be necessary to encounter
> the defeats, so you can know who you are, what you
> can rise from, how you can still come out of it.
>
> **MAYA ANGELOU**

Lin-Manuel Miranda was born in New York City to Dr. Luz Towns-Miranda, a clinical psychologist, and Luis Miranda Jr. The love of music consumed his heart. He listened to Broadway music constantly and went to Broadway shows when he could afford it. Then one day, after watching Disney's *Little Mermaid*, he sat down and began writing his own songs. He even named his son Sebastian after a character in the movie.

Then Lin took a bold and life-changing step. He entered Connecticut's Wesleyan University to pursue a major in theater and film. Using his unique artistic voice, a mixture of his Spanish and Anglo heritage, he wrote his first musical, *In the Heights*, from his experiences in Upper Manhattan. It bombed. Lin backtracked, put his musical ambitions on hold, and took a job writing jingles for political candidates. But fate, luck, or Providence intervened. With the help of some college friends (Thomas Kail and Quiara Alegría Hudes), he reworked his musical. It was produced off-Broadway in 2007 and jumped up to the big time (Broadway) in 2009. *In the Heights* won four Tony Awards, including Best Musical. Success breeds opportunities, so Lin wrote another show about the history of the American Revolution. *Hamilton* opened in 2015 and has become one of the most phenomenal Broadway successes the world has ever seen.

Consider This: For most, success is not a direct path. There are ups and downs. But those who keep their eyes on their dream often find their patience and persistence will pay off.

BEYONCÉ, THE DREAM GIRL

*A true diva is graceful, and talented, and strong, and
fearless and brave and someone with humility.*
BEYONCÉ

With a heritage traced back to slavery and French royalty, Beyoncé Knowles grew up in a proud Acadian Creole family. At the age of seven, she entered a talent contest. Going up against a cadre of fifteen-year-olds, Beyoncé outsang them, outperformed them, and outshined them—winning the competition. A lover of music from childhood, she attended Parker Elementary School (a magnet school in Houston) and excelled in choir and solo performance. At age eight, she joined a singing group called Girls Tyme. In one of their performances, they were noticed by R&B producer Arne Frage and were invited to appear on *Star Search*. Although they didn't win, the big-time performance bug had bitten (both Beyoncé and her parents). Her dad gave up his job to manage the girls and signed Girls Tyme with Elektra Records. But, after much rehearsal and preparation, they were cut by the company and had to start over. They later signed with the Grass Roots Entertainment Group, which produced an album distributed by Sony Music. This step led to a bigger and better opportunity with Columbia Records.

Changing the group's name to Destiny's Child, their song "Killing Time" was featured on the soundtrack of *Men in Black*. The hit song "No, No, No" followed, and their album *The Writing's on the Wall* went platinum. Other successful albums followed, and Beyoncé made her film debut as Foxxy Cleopatra in an Austin Powers movie. Her solo album *B'Day* sold over a half million copies its first week. Success piled upon success, Grammy upon Grammy. She soon became one of the world's top-selling performers.

Consider This: Many people have talent. But talent alone does not make a star. Hard work, vision, and commitment (and maybe a little luck) are required to move from the school stage to the bright lights of stardom.

PIXAR—TO INFINITY AND BEYOND

It's not the manager's job to prevent risks. It's the manager's job to make it safe for others to take them.
ED CATMULL OF PIXAR

Pixar might just be the most successful creative enterprise ever. Yet founder Ed Catmull claims that all of their initial tries at animation "sucked." But they didn't give up. It all started when Catmull was hired by George Lucas in 1979 to develop ways to create digital effects for films. (The first was the "Genesis Effect" for the *Star Trek II: The Wrath of Kahn* movie.) John Lasseter joined Catmull in 1983, and a series of short experimental films followed. Then, in 1986, Steve Jobs bought into Lasseter and Catmull's vision of a CG-animated film and purchased Pixar. Catmull, Lassiter, and their team stepped up to Jobs's vision. But, as Catmull pointed out, making great films is more than cartooning. Without a great story, no animation is good enough. So Pixar had to figure out how to turn the spark of an idea into a great story. It took a lot of time-consuming and laborious work to arrive at a product that didn't suck. And it took years to create their first viable (and successful) full-length movie—*Toy Story.*

How did Pixar (and Pixar/Disney) continue to create one smash hit after another? In his book, *Creativity, Inc.*, Catmull said it began with a fantastic team—one comfortable working on the cutting edge of technology. Second, the team had to learn to work together and support one another. This meant that any failure was a team failure, not an individual's mistake. Third, the team must work together to overcome failures. And last, Catmull and Lasseter gave each creative employee their own chance to shine. They encouraged associates to decorate their workplace, tinker with new ideas, and blow the lid off old ideas. Their plan resulted in a stream of successful movies: *A Bug's Life, Monsters, Inc., Finding Nemo*, and many other instant hits.

Consider This: The team is all-important. Create the right team first. Then the story, creativity, production, and success will follow. Allow each person to think, create, tinker, and shine, and the entire company will reap the benefits.

SARA BLAKELY ELIMINATES PANTY LINES

*Don't be intimidated by what you don't know. That
can be your greatest strength and ensure that you
do things differently from everyone else.*

SARA BLAKELY

Okay, women, you have a closet full of clothes but a big problem. Panty lines. Suffering the same issue, Sarah Blakely thought up a solution. She cut the feet off pantyhose, and voilà! No panty lines, but they rolled up her legs. Nevertheless, she knew she had a great idea. Using $5,000 from her savings, she started a company. She wrote her own patent application and played around with possible names. Believing memorable names have a *k* in them, she came up with "Spanks." But while setting up her website, she changed it to "Spanx" because she figured made-up company names were easier to protect.

Her next problem was finding someone to make her product. She personally visited every hosiery manufacturer in North Carolina, but none were interested. Until she got a callback. An owner had talked to his daughters, and they'd liked her idea. Now she needed to get it into stores. It took a while for Neiman Marcus, for example, to give Spanx a try, but when they did, they put it in the back where no one would see it. Blakely took action. She went to each store, pretended to be a salesperson (without permission), and sold Spanx herself. She put Spanx sales cards on counters and gave gifts to sales associates, from hosiery to gift wrap. In the process, they became her secret sales force. Neiman's found out about her stealthy plan. But when they looked at her great sales numbers, they urged her to continue. She also sent samples to Oprah, and—surprise! She was invited to appear on Oprah's "Favorites" show. In her first year, Sarah earned $4 million, and within fifteen years, she was a billionaire and sole owner of her company.

Consider This: There is no substitute for persistence, determination, and tireless work to get an idea off the ground and into the record books.

EDISON'S BRIGHT IDEA

Genius is 1 percent inspiration and 99 percent perspiration.
THOMAS EDISON

By 1878, Thomas Edison had an established reputation as a genius inventor. So when he announced he would have a working small electric light "in a matter of weeks," gas stocks plummeted. Because of his past accomplishments, Edison quickly raised money for his venture. He organized the Edison Electric Light Company, and set out to invent the electric light. The task seemed easy enough. He simply had to find the correct element for the light filament. He tested hundreds of possible filaments. They all lasted only a few seconds, then fizzled out. He tested hundreds more. Then thousands. After months of failure, Edison brought in an expert, a physicist named Francis Upton. With Upton's help, experimentation focused on a new set of filaments. A platinum filament showed some promise, but its light vanished too quickly to make it feasible. It was now 1879. Work began early each morning, and Edison spent most of the day flitting from workbench to workbench observing the trials. He played songs at his pipe organ at night while he mulled over the day's findings in his mind. By mid-1879, it was clear the platinum lamp would not work.

In October Upton and Edison's assistant, Charles Batchelor, began researching carbon. They devised a lamp with a short, carbonized thread in a vacuum. Starting on October 21, 1879, the carbonized lamp remained lit for forty hours. The process had been messy, discouraging, and very unromantic, but success was finally achieved. Edison believed electric lights could be produced. He placed his reputation on the line and endured more than a thousand failures before seeing that first successful lamp.

Consider This: If you have a good idea, diligently work toward its completion. The road may be difficult and discouraging, but the success will be sweet.

DAVE THOMAS

*Don't just study people who succeed, study
people who handle success well.*
DAVE THOMAS

Dave Thomas was adopted by a loving family, but his mother died when he was only five. His father remarried three times, and the family moved more than a dozen times before Dave reached his midteens. The only constant in his life was his grandmother, who gave him security and taught him the pleasure of hard work. Dave remembers first learning about restaurants because his father took him out to eat quite often. Since he liked to eat, Dave thought that owning a restaurant would be a great career. He took a job at a Hobby House restaurant as soon as they'd hire him. When his father moved again, Dave stayed behind. At age fifteen, he was on his own.

During the Korean War, Dave joined the army and attended its Cooks' and Bakers' School. Because of the training and experience he gained during his service, he was given the opportunity to manage four Kentucky Fried Chicken restaurants when he returned. Dave learned the business well, and in 1968 he sold his KFC stock to begin his own chain of restaurants named after his daughter Wendy. His concept was to create a better hamburger—from fresh meat, made to order, and served in a relaxed family atmosphere. Wendy's grew rapidly until Thomas stepped out of the leadership in 1982. Then, after several years of falling sales and declining quality, Thomas returned to the company as its "spokesman, in-house cheerleader, and roaming quality-control man." Once back under the founder's watchful eye, Wendy's rebounded and once again began to prosper.

Consider This: Continued success requires a long-term commitment. Neglect your vision, and success may vanish. Therefore, maintain constant attention to your vision to keep it from fading.

THE RISKS OF LEADERSHIP

When we think we lead, we most are led.

LORD BYRON

In difficult situations, some people rise to the occasion. They think fast, bark orders, and get people to follow their lead. But most people would rather be followers. To find out why some people are influential leaders, Dean Frost, Fred Fiedler, and Jeff Anderson studied risk-taking leadership in the military. Bravery and courage are not generally thought of when defining leadership qualities in business; however, there are parallels. In the armed forces, those in command who are willing to take personal risks by exposing themselves to danger in combat gain high esteem among the troops. In business, the "theater of combat" may be at the corporate office, where bosses fight on behalf of their employees.

The Israeli military, generally considered among the best in the world, requires its commanders to be the point men of an attack, where the danger is greatest. American general George S. Patton knew the value of having a leader in the thick of the action. During his World War II campaigns in North Africa and Europe, Patton's jeep often moved toward the fighting. Many times he joined his troops at the very point of attack. Patton understood that the soldiers under his command would interpret such action as a vote of confidence in them and thus would maintain good morale.

Abraham Lincoln stood alone for values he believed in and led the nation into a more civilized and honorable national character. Leadership even extends to the world of art and entertainment. Charles Shulz received backlash from an editor when he introduced a Black character named Franklin in the Peanuts comic strip. He responded, "Either you print it just the way I draw it, or I quit. How's that?" They printed it.

Consider This: Are you seen as a leader who goes to bat for your "troops"? When things are rough, do you take the heat yourself? If you desire to be a leader, you must expose yourself to risks and stand up for what you believe is right.

STEINWAY QUALITY

Music is the universal language of mankind.
HENRY WADSWORTH LONGFELLOW

Heinrich Steinweg was born in the small German Hartz Mountain hamlet of Wolfshagen. Beginning in 1806, young Heinrich experienced a series of tragedies that wiped out most of his family. Orphaned, he joined the Prussian army and became a bugler. Heinrich was an able musician, entertaining the troops on the zither and pianoforte despite having no formal training. After leaving the military, he became a church organist and built pianos in his kitchen at night. Although Heinrich worked in primitive facilities, people recognized the high quality of his work. But as his business prospered, a revolution forced Heinrich and his family to move to America.

Settling in New York City, the family name was anglicized to Steinway. Heinrich and his three sons took jobs with different piano makers to learn the details of doing business in the United States. After three years of working for others, they started their own company, Steinway & Sons, producing one piano a week. The Steinway piano soon became known for its quality and clarity of sound. Steinway was more concerned with building the best than making the most, and Steinway pianos soon began to win awards. In 1872, the company opened Steinway Village, a Long Island minitown that included employee housing, a school, a library, and a bathhouse. During tough economic times, companies offered Heinrich royalties to use the Steinway name on items such as radios. Since the Steinway family could not control the quality of those products, they refused to compromise the integrity of their name. As a result, the Steinway name continues to be associated only with the finest musical instruments in the world.

Consider This: A reputation built on quality must never be compromised.

PATTON'S MESSAGE OF MIND OVER BODY

Now, if you are going to win any battle, you have to do
one thing. You have to make the mind run the body.
Never let the body tell the mind what to do.
GENERAL GEORGE S. PATTON

In his book, *Patton's Principles*, Porter Williamson recalls several of General Patton's pronouncements concerning the value of a healthy mind and body. Twenty-five years before jogging became popular, Patton demanded that every soldier run a mile daily. He warned his officers to stay away from desks. Instead, he insisted that they go into the field daily and talk with their troops. Too much desk work, according to Patton, soured the brain. He taught that one must exercise beyond the point of exhaustion to gain superior strength and stamina. To overcome the weakness of one's body, the mind had to also be trained. Patton encouraged his troops to gain mental strength from daily readings of the Bible. He knew that when it was time for battle, the mind must be in charge of the body since the body would always give up first.

Patton led his troops into some of the most dangerous battles in World War II. Because he trained them better than any other battalion of soldiers, they became both feared and respected. And they took pride in being the toughest and the best. Often, enemy soldiers would purposely arrange to surrender to Patton's units since that was considered no disgrace. In addition, Patton's emphasis on health gave his soldiers advantages over enemy troops, who would become exhausted in battle. Today, we know that physical fitness is an essential component of our own ability to face the battles of daily life. Exercise, diet, and mental exercises directly influence our health and ability to effectively carry out our activities.

Consider This: Is your life controlled by aches, pains, and tiredness—or by a mental determination to reach your life goals?

BILLY SUNDAY SPEAKS PLAINLY

I have neither wit, nor words, nor worth, nor actions, nor utterance, nor the power of speech to stir men's blood: I only speak right on.

SHAKESPEARE

Billy Sunday was a premier baseball player. He was a man's man—tough, sweaty, and hard-drinking. One day in 1887, when Billy was out carousing with friends, he encountered a group of men and women from the Pacific Garden Mission playing gospel songs. They invited Billy and his friends to a meeting to hear alcoholics and prostitutes tell how their lives had been changed by faith in God. Something clicked inside Billy. At that moment, he turned to his friends and told them, "I'm through. I am going to Jesus Christ."

Billy not only went to Christ; he also became an evangelist. When he came to New York in 1917, the city had never seen such a religious frenzy. A huge tabernacle was built to seat twenty thousand, the structure being so large that it took four train carloads of sawdust to cover its floor. At the revival, Billy preached to over 1.5 million people. "I am the rube of rubes," he declared. "The odor of the barnyard is on me yet. I have greased my hair with goose grease and blacked my boots with stove blacking. I have wiped my proboscis with a gunnysack towel, I have drunk coffee out of my saucer and have eaten with my knife." Billy would prop his feet up on the pulpit, say "done it" when he should have said "did it" and "I have saw" when he should have said "I have seen." At the end of each message, Billy would call for the people to "walk the sawdust trail" to salvation. As a result, millions of lives were changed.

Consider This: Are you speaking the language of your clients? More people will understand what you are talking about if you communicate with them on their own level.

RAY KROC FOUND A WINNER AND MULTIPLIED IT

Common sense is instinct, and enough of it is genius.
GEORGE BERNARD SHAW

Ray Kroc wanted to be a winner. He made a good living as a salesperson for forty years but never hit the jackpot. But he always kept his eyes open for an opportunity. In 1954, it happened. As a salesman for a milkshake company, he was impressed by an order from a small hamburger stand in California that needed to make forty-eight shakes at a time. When he investigated, he found two brothers, Maurice and Richard McDonald, turning out hamburgers as quickly as they could be made. He took a close look at their operation. They'd simplified their restaurant. As one of the brothers recalled: "Out went dishes, glasses, and silverware. Out went service, the dishwashers, and the long menu. We served just hamburgers, drinks, and french fries on paper plates. Everything prepared in advance, everything uniform."

Kroc wanted a taste of the McDonalds' success and hounded the brothers until they agreed to allow him to sell franchises. During the next six years, Kroc sold two hundred McDonald's franchises. In only twenty-two years, McDonald's became a billion-dollar company. The ingredients that led to the success of McDonald's over all others are simple. The menu is brief, containing only items whose consistent quality can be maintained in thousands of stores. There are strict standards for service, cleanliness, and store operations—and the standards are enforced. The company constantly researches its market (primarily families with children) to determine what customers want and utilizes prolific and efficient advertising to carry its message to consumers.

Consider This: The plan is simple: quality, consistency, cleanliness, and good value. Most people will agree with these ideas, but only the winner will implement them with passion.

GIRL SCOUT COOKIES

My purpose . . . to go on with my heart and soul, devoting all my energies to Girl Scouts, and heart and hand with them, we will make our lives and the lives of the future girls happy, healthy, and holy.
JULIETTE GORDON LOW

The Girl Scouts were started by Juliette "Daisy" Gordon Low in 1912 after she met Sir Robert Baden-Powell, the founder of the Boy Scouts. Her idea spread all over the country, and various troops created ways to raise money for their activities. In Muskogee, Oklahoma, the Scouts made cookies and sold them in the school cafeteria. A few years later, *American Girl* magazine printed a recipe to make six dozen cookies for about thirty cents. They were then sold for twenty-five cents a dozen. That's entrepreneurship! In the early 1930s, the Scouts in Philadelphia started selling commercially baked and boxed cookies. By 1937, over 125 Girl Scout Councils were selling the yummy cookies. World War II put a damper on sales, but they roared back in 1948, with twenty-nine bakers making the crunchy confections across the country. By the 1950s, sales hit their stride with varieties that included a sandwich cookie, shortbread (Trefoils), and chocolate mints (Thin Mints.)

Besides raising money for programs, which is significant, why do the Scouts sell cookies? The sales fold in precisely with what Girl Scouts is accomplishing. The cookie entrepreneurs are learning how to run a business. They learn money management, taking and filling orders, and keeping customers satisfied. They learn goal-setting, business ethics, and decision-making. Finally they develop people skills—talking to people, presenting their sales pitch, and closing the sale. A fundamental part of building the American Dream is creating citizens who can imagine an idea, make a plan to accomplish it, and spend the necessary time and resources to make it happen. Girl Scout cookie sales do just that.

Consider This: Youth is a time to learn more than just academics. It's a time to learn life skills that create the leaders of tomorrow.

GETTING A FOOT IN THE DOOR

I can tell where my own shoe pinches me.
CERVANTES, *DON QUIXOTE*

Young Billy Scholl enjoyed working with leather and made harnesses for the family farm's horses. He also had a fascination with shoes. Because he had twelve brothers and sisters, he enjoyed making each a pair of custom shoes. Billy's parents apprenticed him to a local cobbler at sixteen in response to his interest. One year later, he went to Chicago to work as a cobbler and shoe salesman. The number of foot ailments he encountered concerned Billy. The big city and the fast pace of modern times were rough on people's feet. Customers suffered from bunions, corns, and fallen arches. Billy saw an enormous need and decided to become the "foot doctor to the world." He enrolled in the Illinois Medical College. By the time he had graduated in 1904, he had patented his first invention, an arch support called the Foot-Eazer.

Billy opened his own company and began producing arch supports. To sell his wares, he visited shoe stores across the nation and pulled a skeleton of a human foot out of his bag. He then proceeded to explain the ailments of the foot to the proprietor. Then, inevitably, he took an order for his product. Billy personally promoted his own products with flair and enthusiasm for more than sixty years. He established a correspondence course for shoe clerks. He hired consultants to crisscross the country, giving lectures on foot-care products. Billy Scholl's enthusiastic dedication to good foot care and his endurance as an able spokesman has made his name a household word.

Consider This: You are at your best when you promote something you really believe in—and when you promote it with enthusiasm, pizzazz, and knowledge.

MARTIN LUTHER KING JR.'S DREAM

*I have a dream that one day . . . people will be judged more for
the content of their character than the color of their skin.*
DR. MARTIN LUTHER KING JR.

Americans love to dream about peace and prosperity. Some people dream only for themselves. Other people dream for us all. So it's not surprising that a dreamer would come to the forefront of the civil rights movement in the 1960s. Dr. Martin Luther King Jr. was more than a gifted orator. His message of integrity, hope, and love was fuller, more thought out, and more potent than any other leader's in the movement. He had a vision of the future where all people would be given an equal chance for success regardless of race. In this world, every person would be treated with dignity and respect. He painted a picture of hope—an American future where all of God's children would live together in peace with one another. But not everyone appreciated his message.

Leadership can be dangerous. Leaders are often loved deeply by some and hated intensely by others. As a result, they sometimes pay the price for standing at the forefront of a cause. For his courage to stand against prejudice and hate, Dr. King was assassinated. Fortunately, dreams are more powerful than one person's life. Dreams based on truth, dignity, and righteousness somehow stand up against those who would destroy them. America will always need leaders with a strong enough character to stand for fairness, justice, and dignity. We will always need brave people to fight against tyranny, no matter its source. And we will always need patriots who will stand at the forefront of a righteous cause. Only then will America grow closer to its dream of peace and prosperity for all of its citizens.

Consider This: Open your eyes and determine where people are being mistreated. Step forward. Be quick to respond. Use your influence to bring about equality and integrity among those you deal with.

MAUGHAM WAITS FOR SUCCESS

A man will work and slave in obscurity for ten years
and then become famous in ten minutes.
BOB RIPLEY

W. Somerset Maugham graduated from medical college, but his heart was set on writing fiction. Time and again, he tried to get jobs as a writer and failed. He went hungry. For eleven long years, editor after editor ignored his writings. But Maugham kept sending his manuscripts to whomever he could. Like a fisherman with many lines in the water, he held on, hoping for that first bite. One of Maugham's plays was on the desk of the manager of a London theater when the venue's current production failed. The manager needed to come up with something quickly to fill a time slot and fished around on his desk, ultimately finding Maugham's *Lady Frederick*. Initially, the manager had not thought much of the play. It had remained on his desk for a year. But since the show must go on, he decided to use Maugham's play to fill the time.

Lady Frederick was a smash! Instantly every theater manager in London began clamoring for a Maugham play. Publishers wanted his works, and royalties came pouring in. Maugham was the toast of high society within a month, and along with that came money, prestige, and fame. The rest is history. To be in the right place at the right time, you or your work must be visible in the marketplace. Nothing sitting on the shelf can ever find success. It must be available, waiting for the public to try it, taste it, feel it. Good work will then be discovered and recognized for its quality.

Consider This: Are your ideas being presented to the public? Is your product being tried and tested by those who would use it? Are you sitting on something that could be a success?

MAE JEMISON IS FIRST IN SPACE

Hope is the thing with feathers that perches in the soul.
EMILY DICKINSON

When *Star Trek* took to the small screen in the 1960s, it not only introduced concepts of space exploration, but it also placed minorities in significant leadership roles aboard the starship *Enterprise*. For young Mae Jemison, Lieutenant Uhura, portrayed by Black actress Nichelle Nichols, was inspiring. As an African-American girl interested in science and space, she found no role models in the all-white and all-male astronauts going into space. Yet in the fictional world of *Star Trek*, she found a like mind. When Mae graduated from high school, she entered Stanford and received degrees in chemical engineering and African-American history. Following her undergraduate studies, she earned a medical degree from Cornell.

Mae's interests extended beyond the scientific. She served with the Peace Corps in Africa, learned three foreign languages (Russian, Swahili, and Japanese), and became an accomplished amateur dancer. In 1985 Dr. Jemison interviewed at NASA and received encouragement from Ronald McNair, one of the first Black astronauts. Mae was accepted as an astronaut candidate in 1987 and, in September 1992, became the first Black woman in space. She began her work shift each day quoting Lieutenant Uhura's words: "Hailing frequencies open!" After her 127 orbits aboard the space shuttle, Dr. Jemison often took time from her busy work schedule to speak to children and encourage them to follow their dreams. Later, she taught environmental studies at Dartmouth College and directed the Jemison Institute for Advancing Technology in Developing Countries. In 1994 she was invited to appear in a *Star Trek: The Next Generation* episode as a teacher at a space camp.

Consider This: America is a land of many opportunities, but they are not given to you without cost. As a result, you often must struggle, study hard, and overcome substantial obstacles to realize your own American Dream.

THE ELECTRIC CAR

Any sufficiently advanced technology is
indistinguishable from magic.
ARTHUR C. CLARKE

In 1900 there were three main types of cars in the US: gasoline, steam, and electric. Interestingly, the most popular was electric, with about 40 percent of the market. It was the easiest to drive, start, and control. One problem was the battery. It limited the cars to a short range. When Henry Ford introduced the Model T at an incredibly low price, the other problem with electric vehicles was made evident. They cost a lot more than a Model T (because of battery prices). And steam cars could take up to forty minutes to start (the water had to boil). So, by the 1930s, combustion (gasoline) car engines dominated. The battery issue remained for almost a century until new technologies, particularly lithium-ion batteries, were introduced. Along with a continued rise in gasoline prices and the problem with pollution, electric vehicles began a comeback.

Although there were other unsuccessful tries in the marketplace, the first successful hybrid car (part electric, part combustion engine) was Toyota's Prius (released in Japan in 1997 and the US in 2000). This step moved the world closer to an all-electric car. The next leap came from Tesla, a company started by Martin Eberhard and Marc Tarpenning. Its 2008 introduction of the Tesla Roadster (at $102,000) was a pivotal moment in electric car history, showing the possibilities of such a vehicle. In 2010 Elon Musk took over Tesla as CEO. He led the company with the introduction of the Model S in 2012. This was followed by other models designed to make electric cars affordable to the average buyer. Continued (and sometimes frantic) work toward cheaper and more efficient batteries will help the electric car regain its place as the dominant automobile in the US and the world.

Consider This: What new technologies will create the next revolution? Whatever it is, some insightful person will grab the opportunity and create a new industry or revive an old one.

DOLLY PARTON'S IMAGINATION LIBRARY

My daddy just loved it when all the little kids would call me "The Book Lady." That meant more to him than the fact that I had become a star and worked my butt off.
DOLLY PARTON

Dolly Parton grew up in a poor family in Appalachia. Her father couldn't read or write, and her parents struggled to provide for their twelve children. She first learned to love music at home and in church. After getting her own guitar as a gift, Dolly wrote her first song at age ten. She soon started performing professionally in local venues, as far away as Knoxville, and even on local television. These early successes solidified her ambition to pursue a music career. As soon as she graduated from high school, she moved to Nashville. Her first break was appearing on *The Porter Wagoner Show*. She became so popular that the two produced hit after country hit together. Although she was well known in the country music arena, Dolly's global star began shining brightest when she appeared in the movie *9 to 5* and sang the song by the same name. In 1999 she was inducted into the Country Music Hall of Fame.

Some people who make tons of money spend it on fancy cars, houses, and indulgences. Some give back. Remembering her father's lack of opportunity, she decided to help kids by giving them books. In 1999 her Imagination Library gave 1,700 books to children in East Tennessee. Then her vision grew. And grew. First to other places in America, then around the world. As of 2021 Dolly Parton now sends out over a million (free) books per month. In 2018 the Library of Congress honored Parton for providing over 100 million free books to children worldwide.

Consider This: You may or may not be rich, but whatever your standing, you can make a difference in your community and perhaps the world. Give of yourself. Give of your resources. Make your dream helping others find their own dreams.

GEORGE LUCAS CREATES A NEW UNIVERSE

I set out to make a film for a generation
growing up without fairy tales.
GEORGE LUCAS

Growing up in Modesto, California, George Lucas watched every adventure serial he could find. These short action films were stories of good versus evil, full of fights, chase scenes, and suspenseful cliffhangers. When George needed inspiration for his own films, he returned in his mind to the movies that had excited him during his youth. Lucas graduated from the University of Southern California. He formed the American Zoetrope production company with his friend Francis Ford Coppola. His first feature, a science-fiction story called *THX 1138*, was the origin of the now famous THX "the audience is listening" advanced theater sound logo. In 1973 Lucas's film *American Graffiti* was successful enough to give boosts to the careers of Ron Howard and Richard Dreyfus.

His third film catapulted Lucas to instant fame. Working with a brilliant team of up-and-coming special-effects wizards, Lucas's new company, Industrial Light & Magic, created the dazzling effects for *Star Wars*. The sci-fi fairy tale, which merged cutting-edge effects with a strong story of good versus evil inspired by the early serials, took the world by storm. Lucas followed with *The Empire Strikes Back* and *Return of the Jedi* and used the serial formula successfully in the *Indiana Jones* movies. In 1992 with six megablockbusters under his belt, he received a special Academy Award—the prestigious Irving G. Thalberg Memorial Award. But no one is perfect. Lucus stumbled with a few of his later productions. However he continued to do his best work when he told stories using the technique that first inspired his love of film.

Consider This: What makes you excited and passionate about your work? Use the energy you feel in your own life to get your message across to others.

PARKER PENS

Our pens will write in any language.
GEORGE S. PARKER

George Parker kept his eyes open for new opportunities. Of course, he had to make a living in the meantime, so he taught telegraphy. One day in 1892, George finally found an idea worth pursuing. He had come up with a concept for a fountain pen design that would eliminate an annoying leakage problem that had plagued pens for over fifty years. George knew that the market for his pen would be huge. Virtually every person in the entire world who wrote anything was a potential customer. His company prospered by selling pens in the United States. But Parker wanted to expand. He encouraged his associates to expand into new markets with the message, "Our pens will write in any language!" To that end, George began exporting his pens in 1903.

George was a meticulous manufacturer. Even though he had a great design, he insisted on spending plenty of time and money to make sure that the pen would write in all conditions. It had to write equally well when used left-handed, slanted forward, slanted backward, and so on. George insisted on innovation but was never too eager to bring a product to market until he was sure it was the best. When ballpoint pens were introduced, George continued to research for another nine years before introducing the "T-Ball Jotter." Always keeping Parker pens at the top of the price lists, George acquired Eversharp in 1957 to address the lower price market. Today, Parker is one of the best-known brands around the world.

Consider This: Someone will always be at the top of the heap, and it will probably be the company that pays the most attention to quality.

POWERFUL MOTTOES

Without a vision, the people perish.
PROVERBS 29:18

Many leaders have a trademark, which is usually one or more sayings that concisely describe that person's or company's beliefs or management style. For example, Harry Truman had his motto inscribed on a sign that sat on the presidential desk: "The Buck Stops Here." Ronald Reagan's desk had a sign saying, "It Can Be Done." Tom Watson of IBM used signs that simply said "Think" and placed them in all of IBM's offices. Ray Kroc of McDonald's constantly talked about QSC&V (Quality, Service, Cleanliness, and Value). Sysco, a Houston-based food wholesaler, lives by the motto, "Don't sell food, sell peace of mind." Carl Sewell preached the concept of "customers for life" to stress superior service at his auto dealership.

Mottoes don't mean anything unless management backs them up. Watson indoctrinated all new employees of IBM with an incredible amount of exposure to corporate beliefs. Kroc believed so strongly in his motto that he removed the McDonald's franchise from any restaurant that didn't fulfill QSC&V, as outlined in a detailed operating manual. Mottoes serve the purpose of crystallizing a complicated issue. The two-finger *V* for victory sign in World War II and the phrases "Remember the Alamo" and "Fifty-four forty or fight" were used to unite citizens for a cause. Most people want something to believe in to give them a feeling of pride and belonging. Mottoes can boil down a complicated issue to a short phrase or symbol that the masses can understand and rally around. Choose your motto carefully. Make it succinct. And back it up.

Consider This: What motto do you live by? Do you have the opportunity to solidify your group or organization by adopting a saying or symbol that describes your goals?

INTERNET STARS

Life is trying things to see if they work.
RAY BRADBURY

It's been said that children born today will have jobs that haven't been invented yet. A few years ago, who would have thought that internet personalities would earn millions of dollars? But it happened. It works like this. When people watch a video, they also watch an ad. The advertiser pays for that ad. The video's producer splits the money with the provider (such as YouTube or TikTok). For example, when the online personality MrBeast created a July 4 show that included blowing up a car, shooting off one hundred rockets, and other antics, he had twenty-three million (yes, that's right) viewers. At a few pennies a pop, that adds up to big bucks. (MrBeast earns about $3 million a month.) At age twenty-four, comedian David Dobrik has made over $15 million on YouTube. By age twenty, dancer Addison Rae Easterling had earned over $5 million on TikTok. And the list goes on.

How can you get in on this action? It's as easy as becoming an NFL quarterback—a very, very long shot. But you don't have to be a superstar to make a living online. Are you an expert in woodworking, quilting, crafts, home restoration, plumbing, pool repair, movie editing, or taking Disney vacations? Whatever your passion, there is probably a channel devoted to the subject. And a few people are making a decent living (or supplemental income) by sharing their knowledge. So if you're skillful and are willing to make hundreds of videos on the topic, you might be able to rake in enough followers to earn substantial cash.

Consider This: Don't get stuck in yesterday. New opportunities appear daily. To move ahead, see if one fits your abilities, interests, and talent. You don't have to wait for Hollywood or some megacorporation to give you the green light. Instead, jump in and see what you can accomplish.

ACRES OF DIAMONDS

He most lives who thinks most, who feels
the noblest, and who acts the best.
ACRES OF DIAMONDS

Could one person's talk save a dying church, begin a university, support a hospital, and change millions of lives? Yes! If that man was Russell Conwell. And he did it with a speech (and later a book) titled *Acres of Diamonds*. In 1870, Conwell heard a folk tale as he traveled in a camel caravan along the Tigris River as a young traveling reporter. The story was about a Persian farmer lured away from his ancestral home by the prospect of riches in faraway places. The farmer deserted his fruitful lands in search of immense wealth. As the years passed, the farmer's youth and health disappeared. He died far from his home, a disillusioned pauper. Soon after the farmer's death, acres of fabulous diamonds were discovered on the property he had abandoned.

That simple parable changed Conwell's life. He began telling the story to others. What it meant to him was simple: "Your diamonds are not in faraway mountains or in distant seas; they are in your own backyard if you will but dig for them." Other stories were added to the tale, and his reputation as a master storyteller grew. Soon Conwell became a sought-after speaker. He believed what he preached, which led him into a life of helping others. That included saving a dilapidated Massachusetts church, serving for forty-three years at Philadelphia's Grace Church, and founding Temple University and its hospital. Around the world Conwell inspired audiences with his speeches and raised money for his causes. By 1925 he had delivered the *Acres* speech more than six thousand times.

Consider This: People yearn for truths that will give them better and more satisfying lives. A message of inspiration, hope, and optimism never gets old. What messages are you sending to your employees, family, or customers?

FAMOUS AMOS COOKIES

It's important to start . . . start from right where you are.
WALLY AMOS

Wally Amos is one of the most renowned Black entrepreneurs in America. He calls himself the "Jackie Robinson of the theatrical business." As an agent of the William Morris Agency, he discovered rock-star legends Simon and Garfunkel in a Manhattan club. But before William Morris, he had another discovery. While still a teenager he moved to New York to live with his Aunt Della. One night she made a batch of freshly baked chocolate chip cookies. They were so tasty that Amos wanted to know how to make them himself. Simple—the recipe was on a bag of Nestlé's Toll House chocolate chips. But he wanted to do better. In fact, he was so serious about learning how to make better cookies that he attended the Food Trades Vocational High School and studied culinary arts. The idea stayed in his mind as he served in the US Air Force for two years. Then, after returning to New York, he earned his way up the ladder at William Morris, starting in the mail room and rising to become their first-ever Black talent agent. In 1967 he made another move.

It was opening day in Hollywood, California. Two thousand people had been sent elegant invitations. A red carpet decorated the sidewalk. Celebrities arrived in limousines. Music was playing, and champagne was flowing. The event announced the grand debut of "Famous" Amos's first chocolate chip cookie store. Amos promoted his cookies nationwide, marketing them to exclusive department stores and specialty shops. Within five years, annual sales of Famous Amos cookies reached $5 million. Not everyone can afford a Rolls-Royce, a penthouse, diamonds, or jewelry. But almost everyone can afford a good chocolate chip cookie.

Consider This: What's out there waiting to be discovered? Look around. It may be the most straightforward, everyday thing that you can make the "best in the world."

LEMONS TO LEMONADE

When fate hands you a lemon, make lemonade.
DALE CARNEGIE

Smooth sailing through life is not what most people experience. Realizing your dream on your first attempt is the exception rather than the rule. Almost everyone faces times of doubt, frustration, failure to accomplish a goal, sadness, depression, or financial or emotional ruin. Yet at these times, something extraordinary may happen. When we have nothing else to lose, we're often willing to take calculated risks that would otherwise seem extreme or foolish. Adversity often brings out the best in us. Some say problems are really opportunities in disguise. For example, Bethany Hamilton had her arm bitten off by a shark. Yet she came back and won a surfing championship. Franklin D. Roosevelt suffered from debilitating polio. Bill Gates's first company failed miserably. Stephen King threw away the novel that would make him famous (*Carrie*). If his wife hadn't dug it out of the trash can, we'd probably never have heard of him.

Yet these people's lives and accomplishments are now celebrated. They overcame tragedies, limitations, and bad luck. Life gave them adversity, but they made the most of what they had. Perhaps you've been fired or laid off. You lost a loved one, your job, or you failed. Perhaps you're physically or emotionally drained or suffer from a debilitating disease. It's like the power went off in your life. Everything's dismal and dark. Some people give in and give up. Others get up and get going. The history of accomplishment is written by those who marched forward in the face of misfortune. If you need help, find someone who'll rescue your hopes and dreams out of life's trash can and show you how valuable your contributions can be. Or if you know someone facing difficulties, become the one who rescues them.

Consider This: Look straight ahead. Focus on your goals. Steadfastness overcomes tragedy. Diligence overcomes limitations. Hope overcomes doubt.

EDWIN LAND'S BETTER PHOTOGRAPHY IDEA

The stoical scheme of supplying our wants by lopping off our
desires is like cutting off our feet when we want shoes.
JONATHAN SWIFT

The golden age of photography provided a new way to take pictures. You loaded your Brownie camera with film and snapped photos of the new baby. You then processed the film in your own darkroom or took it to a local camera shop, who had your pictures ready a week later. Or, if you were patient, you sent it off by mail and waited a couple of weeks. (We're talking quite a few years ago!) Edwin Land had a better idea. What if it were possible to take a picture and, within seconds, have the developed photograph in your hands? The marketplace was not clamoring for this capability. In fact, very few people had probably even thought of the idea. Nevertheless, Land developed the technology and stimulated consumers' desires to "need" this convenience.

The instant Polaroid Land camera exemplifies how a breakthrough technology can change consumer behavior. It was serendipity. No one knew such technology was needed or wanted. Similarly, who would have thought that photography would take another leap within a few decades—this time into digital photography? Other innovations that defined a new (previously unknown) need include the microwave oven, 3M's Post-It Notes, sport watches, streaming movies, lasers, flat-screen TVs, and the internet. At the turn of the twentieth century, there were proposals to close the US Patent Office because "everything has been invented!" If those people could see us now! There are still thousands, maybe millions, of products and services that no one has thought of yet. When a new idea hits the market, everyone always says, "What a great idea. Why didn't someone think of that sooner?"

Consider This: Think beyond needs. Examine a new technology and consider how it might be applied in areas where no one has used it before.

ATTITUDES

For they can conquer who believe they can.

VIRGIL

We are what we think. Our mind is much more powerful than we know. It can cause us to be sick (it is a well-known fact that a vast amount of illness is caused by emotional stress), and it can bring us back to health (which is why placebos often work so well). Our mind can give us an attitude of failure or provide us with an attitude of success. Sports commentators often discuss the "mental" game taking place on the field of play. Talent and training will only get us so far. We must have the mental attitude to push us into the winner's circle.

In his book *Secrets of Successful Selling,* John Murphy relates the story of a man who could make only $5,000 a year. No matter the situation, he believed he was a $5,000-a-year employee. When he was given a good sales territory, he made $5,000. In a bad territory he made $5,000. In every place he was assigned, he made $5,000. He mentally believed he could make only $5,000 a year—no more, no less—and worked hard enough to prove himself right. Once, he made $5,000 early in the year and was sick for the rest of the year, although doctors could not determine why. Luckily, the salesman finally got the message that his limited belief in himself was holding him back. He needed to raise his expectations and have a more positive dream of what he could accomplish. Once on track, he lived up to his new image of himself and proved to be a stellar salesman.

Consider This: Are your attitudes and a poor opinion of your abilities holding you back from accomplishing great things?

EISENHOWER'S MENTOR

*You cannot teach a man anything; you can
only help to find it within himself.*

GALILEO

Dwight Eisenhower was a mediocre student at West Point. During World War I, he missed seeing any action, although many of his classmates were in the thick of the fighting. After the war, Eisenhower was transferred to Panama, where he wanted to work under General Fox Conner, whom he admired. General Conner was a father figure and mentor to Eisenhower, and the relationship was a turning point in Eisenhower's career. He later reflected, "Life with General Conner was a sort of graduate school in military affairs and the humanities, leavened by a man who was experienced in his knowledge of men and their conduct. I can never adequately express my gratitude to this one gentleman. In a lifetime of association with great and good men, he is the one more or less invisible figure to whom I owe an incalculable debt."

Unlike his previous lackluster performance at West Point, Eisenhower became a different student when he was selected to train at the Command and General Staff College. His learning experiences as a student of this great mentor made an enormous difference in his self-confidence and determination to succeed. As a result, Eisenhower ranked first in his class in a challenging and competitive school. He then became one of the most influential leaders of the twentieth century. During World War II, he served as a five-star general, became Supreme Commander of the Allied Expeditionary Forces, and was responsible for planning and executing the D-Day invasion. Without his experience of being mentored by Conner, one cannot speculate if Eisenhower ever would have found that capability within himself.

Consider This: Who around you can you learn from? Have you submitted yourself to a mentor? Are you a mentor to someone else?

WRIGLEY DIDN'T OVERLOOK THE LITTLE THINGS

When business is good, it pays to advertise; when
business is bad, you've got to advertise.

ANONYMOUS

Bill Wrigley was a problem child. He was thrown out of school and was always "up to no good." Finally, at age thirteen, he was taken out of school and put to work stirring pots of boiling soap at his father's factory. His father later decided to try the boy as a salesman and sent him to the small towns of New England. Bill soon demonstrated that he could sell. He readily made friends on the road and made it a point "to be always polite, always patient, and never to argue." At the age of twenty, in 1891, Bill struck out on his own. He moved to Chicago and became a sales representative for a baking powder company. As an incentive to those buying his product, he included two sticks of chewing gum with every package. It was just a sales gimmick, but he kept getting requests for more gum. The requests increased to the point that Wrigley was selling more gum than powder. He eventually dropped all other products and concentrated on promoting the gum.

By 1910 Wrigley's Spearmint was the top-selling gum in the country, and his Juicy Fruit gum was not far behind. In 1915 Wrigley sent free sticks of gum to one and a half million telephone subscribers. Later he repeated the mailout to seven million people. Wrigley dedicated more marketing resources into advertising his gum than any other product of the era had received. Even though a pack of gum sold for only five cents, Wrigley amassed a fortune and used it to create a giant financial empire.

Consider This: Look for clues about what you are doing now that could become a substantial business if you gave it a chance.

MILLION-DOLLAR PHRASES

You'll wonder where the yellow went when
you brush your teeth with Pepsodent.
PEPSODENT ADVERTISING SLOGAN

Why are some companies more memorable than others? Why do some climb to the top of the heap while others lag behind? One factor is how a brand pops into the public's mind. If asked to name a computer operating systems brand, most people would say Apple or Microsoft. Who offers Happy Meals and chicken nuggets? McDonald's. What's the "happiest place on earth"? Disneyland. That sought-after position with the public can often be summarized in a catch-phrase. When you hear "the real thing," you think of Coca-Cola. "When it absolutely, positively has to be there overnight" means FedEx. Even a common phrase such as "pizza delivery" has meaning—people often think of Domino's Pizza because of its original thirty-minute delivery guarantee. "May the Force be with you" will always be associated with *Star Wars*. "You're in good hands" with Allstate. "Just do it" belongs to Nike.

A politician who can sell a catchphrase to the public wins people's senti-ments. "Give me liberty, or give me death!" "I like Ike." "Make love, not war." "The buck stops here." Such phrases are worth millions of dollars because they are quickly and effectively locked into consumers' minds. Still, it seems that memorable phrases are elusive. Amazingly, companies sometimes abandon their million-dollar mottos, such as "Plop, plop, fizz, fizz. Oh, what a relief it is." When a company abandons a well-known motto, it may never recapture that magic.

Consider This: What catchy phrase describes your product's primary benefit or feature? Do you have one that sets your product apart from the rest? If not, search for one. If you have one, recognize it as a treasure, and abandon it at your own risk.

HARRIET TUBMAN

That this nation, under God, shall have a new birth of freedom.
ABRAHAM LINCOLN

Without freedom, there would be no American Dream. The freedom that allows us to have such a dream has been secured by many great Americans. Many risked their own lives for the benefit of others. Harriet Tubman, born into slavery in Maryland in 1822, became one of America's fighters for freedom. She had heard stories about a land in the North where Black people could be free. She dreamed of that land at night and looked into the deep night sky to find the North Star. That was the star that would lead to "the promised land." Other slaves talked about an "underground railroad," a network of people who would help enslaved people find freedom. Harriet knew she had to find that railroad before it was too late. One day she learned that she was to be sold away from her husband and sent farther south, where it was much more difficult to escape. That night, Harriet made her move.

She escaped first to the house of a woman she knew was a member of the Underground Railroad. From that point, Harriet was led farther and farther north, from station to station, until she walked into Pennsylvania and freedom. Former slaves worked as conductors on the railroad and would return to the South to lead others out. Harriet joined the railroad and risked her life to lead over three hundred people to freedom. She became known as Moses, after the biblical figure who cried, "Let my people go." After the Civil War, Harriet tended to the poor in Albany, New York, until she died in 1913. In 2022 a nine-foot statue named "Harriet Tubman: Journey to Freedom" was erected in her honor in Philadelphia.

Consider This: Freedom is the first and necessary step in realizing our dreams. And it often does not come easily or without a fight.

THE BAND-AID

To accept good advice is but to increase one's own ability.

GOETHE

Even when hundreds or thousands of people hear about a good idea, only the rare individual does something about it. Robert Johnson was a co-owner of the Seabury & Johnson company when he attended a meeting given by Joseph Lister. In it, Lister described the science of bacteriology and pleaded for sanitary conditions in hospitals. The year was 1876, and most of those in attendance listened with skepticism. It was hard to imagine tiny "bugs" causing problems. They believed in common sense more than science. But Johnson was convinced that Lister was on to something. So he talked his brothers Edward and James into developing products that would help make hospitals more sanitary. In 1886 the brothers formed their own company, Johnson & Johnson, and began promoting their sterilized gauze. By 1910 the company needed forty buildings to produce a growing line of medical products.

Another good idea that helped the company came from an employee, Earle Dickson. One day Dickson showed a coworker a self-stick bandage he had developed and used at home. Dickson put a dab of sterile cotton and gauze on a strip of surgical tape to create a bandage he could use to take care of his family's cuts and scrapes. Next he placed a crinoline fabric on the sticky parts of the tape. James Johnson saw one of the bandages and immediately recognized its potential in the marketplace. The invention was dubbed the "Band-Aid" and soon became one of the world's most recognized trademarks.

Consider This: Listen to the ideas of those around you. New ideas are often the basis of new products and perhaps new companies.

ACHIEVEMENT TAKES MORE THAN TALENT

Talent is cheaper than table salt. What separates the talented
individual from the successful one is a lot of hard work.
STEPHEN KING

Every person is as unique as their fingerprints. Some people are natural athletes, musicians, or scientists. Yet studies show that talent is not the determining factor in success or achievement. Even people with only moderate talent can often achieve gold through resolute practice. In her book *Grit: The Power and Passion of Perseverance*, author Angela Duckworth concludes, "As much as talent counts, effort counts twice." And, "Without effort, your talent is nothing more than unmet potential." Similarly, in his book *Peak Performance*, Brad Stulberg writes, "It isn't experience that sets top performers apart but the amount of deliberate practice they put in."

Many talented people do great in certain school subjects without studying. They enjoy figuring out algebraic equations, or they quickly learn to play songs on the piano. They can hit a baseball almost from birth or swim before walking. Using talent alone, they become pretty good, maybe outstanding. But rarely, without deliberate effort, will they reach any pinnacle of achievement. One of the most exceptional pianists of the twentieth century, Van Cliburn, practiced more than any other student at Juilliard. In fact, he often had to close the buildings at night because everyone else had already gone home. Larry Bird had athletic talent but became the best shooter in the NBA because of his practice ethic. His daily regimen included a long run, team practice, many sit-ups, a few more short-distance runs, and shooting drills. Before every game, with no other teammates around, he took three hundred practice shots. No one out-practiced Larry Bird, and his reward was a stellar career.

Consider This: Talent is only a starting point. If you want to achieve anything, you must put in the time and effort. Commit yourself to a deliberate and long-term learning regimen, and follow it with passion.

FACE YOUR TROUBLES SQUARELY

Three things give hardy strength: sleeping on hairy mattresses, breathing cold air, and eating dry food.
WELSH PROVERB

Many people remember Teddy Roosevelt riding on a horse in his Cavalry uniform, brandishing a sword. In the early 1900s he was a quintessential tough-guy leader to the American public. But that's not how he started out. As a kid, Theodore Roosevelt was a weakling. He was thin, in poor health, timid, and afraid of getting hurt. So the Roosevelt family took trips to find places more amenable to young Teddy's ailments. Finally, Teddy decided to conquer his frailty when he became a teenager. After traveling to parts of America and Europe, he realized that a simple change of climate would not cure his health problems, and he decided to immerse himself in physical activity.

The formula was to do things he was afraid of doing, so he became a cowboy in the Dakotas. In the process of improving his strength and courage, Teddy, at one time or another, broke his wrist, his arm, his nose, his ribs, and his shoulder. When he returned to school at Harvard, he took up boxing. Although Teddy was often "beat to a pulp," he became a good fighter and even fought in a championship match. (He lost.) In the Spanish-American War, Teddy was a lieutenant colonel in the Rough Riders, where he became a hero for his exploits at the Battle of San Juan Hill. Because of his Rough Rider image, Roosevelt became a famous military and political figure. He won an election for governor of New York in 1898. He was elected vice president of the United States in 1900, and after President McKinley died in 1901, Roosevelt became president.

Consider This: Struggle often provides us with our most productive times of growth. The caterpillar gains strength in its fight to tear out of its cocoon. Without the exercise provided by the struggle, it would not have the power to fly. When you are in the midst of a battle, step back and consider how this struggle might provide strength and insight for the future.

OLE EVINRUDE

Everything that is new or uncommon raises a pleasure in the imagination, because it fills the soul with an agreeable surprise.
JOSEPH ADDISON

One hot, lazy August afternoon, Bess Cary, Ole Evinrude, and friends picnicked on an island two miles from a Lake Michigan shore. The sweltering heat made Bess think about one thing: ice cream. Ole was deeply in love with Bess and would do anything for her. Jumping into the rowboat, he made it to shore quickly. But the breeze was against him on the way back, and the ice cream melted fast. When Ole finally returned, he had to serve his friends the melted ice cream. As they were drinking it, his mind started thinking about something else. The big Norwegian had owned a company that made small gasoline engines, but the enterprise had failed. He had also helped Harley-Davidson develop an air-cooled engine. Now Ole began to consider building a small motor to propel a rowboat.

Bess and Ole were married in 1906, and after that Ole continued to work on his project. In 1909, he built his first outboard motor. Bess thought it looked like a coffee grinder, but when Ole took it down to the river, he amazed the deckhands by skimming around the water at five miles per hour. Confident in his design, Ole made a few cosmetic changes and built engine number two. This time he loaned it to a friend, who promptly ordered ten and paid in cash. Bess and Ole went into business, with Bess handling the correspondence. She analyzed the market and wrote an advertisement that began, "*Don't row*, use the Evinrude Detachable Rowboat Motor." With Ole in the shop and Bess in the office, the Evinrude outboard motor became successful.

Consider This: How often has a product been made that lessens drudgery? If you can create one, that's what Americans want.

SEWELL'S CUSTOMERS FOR LIFE

*Keeping your word is worth more than all the empathy,
smiles, and chocolates on your pillow in the world.*
CARL SEWELL

Almost every customer would rather shop and buy goods in a clean, well-lighted, and friendly place than in a trashy store or a dump. For example, a customer entering a Sewell automobile dealership may be impressed by the atmosphere of the showroom—antique furniture, fresh flowers, and soothing music. But it takes more than good looks to entice and keep the car-buying public. Sewell's goal was not only to make a sale but to create "customers for life." Sewell wanted his business to stand out above the crowd. He wanted his car company to earn a reputation for taking care of more details than any other dealership. To create such a business, he knew he had to keep promises to fix problems the first time, never exceed an estimated price for a repair, and provide exceptional customer service where "yes" was always the answer. Therefore, when a Sewell customer needed help, they knew they would get quick and efficient service.

Carl Sewell Sr. learned selling from his family's first "dealership," a livery stable and movie theater. When the Sewell family began selling Model T's, the cars arrived in crates. The final assembly was done at the dealership. Since cars were new devices, they had to teach customers how to drive. Like many other families with thriving businesses, the Sewells adopted the motto: "Treat people like you want to be treated." It served them well. Today, Sewell's relentless and systematic demand for employee excellence results in the highest service, sales, and friendliness standards. And it has made his dealerships among the most successful and emulated in the country.

Consider This: Quality is difficult to obtain, and it will never develop by chance. Superior service requires a powerful commitment to a systematic plan of constant and long-term improvement.

POCKETS OF GENIUS

Great things in business are never done by one
person. They're done by a team of people.
STEVE JOBS

Throughout history many significant advancements and movements can be traced to teams of individuals supporting one another. After all, "two heads are better than one." These teams could be a married couple, friends, coworkers, or like-minded hobbyists. Perhaps they gathered together to share new ideas and discoveries or solve a problem. More likely than an individual, a well-chosen group can produce new and innovative ideas that will change the world. Examples included religious (Jesus and the disciples), political (the framers of the Constitution), literary (the British writer's group called the Inklings that included C. S. Lewis, J. R. R. Tolkien, and others), scientific groups (the Manhattan Project), and TV stars (Chip and Joanna Gaines).

In the mid-1970s, in an area between San Francisco and San Jose, California, a small group known as the Homebrew Computer Club was organized. The bearded and blue-jeaned members were some of the day's best computer hackers and engineers. Most worked in the emerging high-tech companies in Silicon Valley. Trade secrets were openly discussed within the group, and fellow members advised anyone attending their meetings of this. Notable among the members of the Homebrew Computer Club was Steve Leininger. He went to work for Tandy RadioShack and developed the TRS-80 Model I computer. Two other Steves (Wozniak and Jobs) were also club members. They created a computer board called the Apple I and showed it to the group. With the group's help and encouragement, they improved their ideas. Soon they had a full-fledged microcomputer and dubbed it the Apple II computer.

Consider This: Discoveries are seldom made in isolation. Progress often comes after many people have contributed. Find a group of trusted individuals who will provide input, criticism, and encouragement for your ideas, and build something new.

BABE, THE WORLD'S GREATEST ATHLETE

*The formula for success is simple: practice and concentration
then more practice and more concentration.*
BABE DIDRIKSON ZAHARIAS

Many sports historians consider Babe Didrikson Zaharias the greatest modern-day multisport athlete, male or female, bar none. Born Mildred Ella Didrikson in 1912, she took to sports with a passion. As a kid, after hitting five home runs in one baseball game, her friends started calling her "Babe" (after Babe Ruth). In high school she added the sport of basketball. After graduation she played on many of the era's women's teams (sponsored by local businesses) all over Texas. In the 1932 Olympics she won gold medals for the 80-meter hurdles and javelin. Then she took up golf. In 1935, playing in her second tournament, she won first place. In 1943 she won seventeen matches, including the British Women's Amateur Championship. In 1945 she played in a (men's) PGA tournament and made the 36-hole cut (not accomplished again until 2003 by Annika Sörenstam).

Golf is where Babe made her mark. In 1947 she turned professional and, with several other women golfers—Hope Seignious, Betty Hicks, Ellen Griffin, Peggy Kirk, Bettye Danoff, Patty Berg, Louise Suggs, Marilynn Smith, and Betsy Rawls—founded the Ladies Professional Golfers Association (LPGA.) Babe led the LPGA pack in money winnings between 1949 and 1951 and was named the Associated Press Woman Athlete of the Half-Century in 1951. Then, she faced a new obstacle. Cancer. She had a colostomy in 1953, and doctors said she'd have to retire. Instead, Babe prayed, "Please God, let me play again." With all her grit and guts, she came back. In 1953 she won five more tournaments. But her recovery was short-lived. She died in 1956, and one paper's headline read, "Death of the World's Greatest Athlete."

Consider This: Passion will help you rise above the crowd. Practice, persistence, and determination will help you become the best in your field. And when life happens, as it always does, go out in flames, doing what you do best.

MARION LABORATORIES

Those who apply themselves unswervingly
to a task are amply rewarded.
EWING M. KAUFFMAN

Ewing M. Kauffman had been described as "too friendly, too eager to accept challenges." This poor Missouri farm boy decided from the start that when he was faced with a task, he had better give it his all. His creed helped him excel in everything he did, particularly in sports. But in 1908, at the age of eleven, Ewing was stricken with a severe illness that left him with a faulty heart valve. The doctor prescribed a year in bed, flat on his back. He could not leave his bed for any reason and could not even sit up. The once-active Ewing did not violate his doctor's orders for a year. But his time wasn't wasted. He began devouring books at the rate of one hundred per month. He read the entire Bible several times. He read adventures such as *Tom Sawyer* and *Huckleberry Finn*. He also learned about astronomy, mathematics, and medicine. All of the positive input from his reading had a powerful impact on Ewing's future.

After his recovery Kauffman finished high school and spent two years in junior college. He excelled in the navy and later as a salesman with a Kansas pharmaceutical company. But when he began drawing commissions higher than the president's salary, his commission was cut. So Kauffman quit and formed his own business, Marion Laboratories. He packaged vitamin pills at night and sold them during the day. As he recruited employees, he promised them a bright future. Once Marion Laboratories passed $100 million in sales, those early employees reaped huge rewards.

Consider This: Use every opportunity to read, study, and learn. Put your knowledge to work for you, and allow those who help you to share in your success.

JEFF KINNEY IS NO WIMPY KID

*See, when you're a little kid, nobody ever warns you
that you've got an expiration date. One day you're hot
stuff and the next day you're a dirt sandwich.*
JEFF KINNEY, *DIARY OF A WIMPY KID: THE UGLY TRUTH*

If you see eleven-year-old kids huddling around a book and laughing, they're probably reading Jeff Kinney's *Diary of a Wimpy Kid*. More than 250 million copies of this title and the follow-up books have sold worldwide. Kinney's *Diary of a Wimpy Kid* books tell stories about a kid's antics that are sane enough to be printed, absurd enough to be hilarious, and crazy enough to be slightly uncomfortable to parents. Exactly what kids want to read. Kinney admits, "Greg is a fun house mirror version of myself. I took some of my more ignoble qualities and put them into this character . . . he's got my DNA."

Kinney initially released his *Wimpy Kids* stories as daily entries to the Funbrain website. He thought viewers would get a kick out of remembering their own elementary school antics. In 2007, after twenty million views, the stories were published into a book by publisher Harry N. Abrams. The first *Diary of a Wimpy Kid* book became an instant bestseller with more than 100,000 copies printed in the US alone. Today, the *Wimpy Kid* books are among the top five most popular series ever. In fact, in 2009 *Time* magazine listed Kinney as one of the world's one hundred most influential people. So how does Kinney do it? To generate his material, he uses a technique outlined in the book *Inside the Box: A Proven System of Creativity for Breakthrough Results* by Drew Boyd and Jacob Goldenberg. This book describes a method for generating new ideas using a series of time-tested templates to reshape old ideas into something new. Whatever his approach, Kinney has struck a chord with kids worldwide—from Manhattan to Shanghai.

Consider This: Reshape what you do best into new products, ideas, or services. Once you've found a popular concept, it is more efficient to reshape the old idea into a new product than to come up with a completely new idea.

MERCK'S RESEARCH QUALITY

Do few things, but do them well.
ST. FRANCIS OF ASSISI

Finding a new drug is often like taking your chances on a roll of the dice: you mix up several compounds and see if any of them do anything. That's how most of the drugs manufactured today got their start. It seems crude, and it is. Under the leadership of CEO John Horan, Merck & Co. decided to do something about the situation. In the early 1980s, Merck began looking for effective drugs by pouring millions of dollars into basic research. The research was meant to discover how life worked. The company believed that if this could be understood, perhaps its scientists would be more innovative in formulating drugs. Merck refused to diversify as other drug companies had done. Focusing 100 percent of its energies on the discovery of drugs had enormous positive consequences. As a result, research scientists found the corporate atmosphere at Merck academic heaven. They were permitted to use the latest equipment in their research, publish, confer with colleagues, and participate in creating products that would help the world.

In 1982 a third of Merck's sales were comprised of older, more established drugs. By 1987, however, because of new introductions created through Merck's innovative research, old drugs represented less than 10 percent of the company's sales. Moreover, the new drugs produced due to Merck's commitment to research garnered notice on Wall Street. Because of these successes, Merck became one of *Fortune* magazine's most admired companies. Merck merged with Schering-Plough in 2006 and has continued to produce world-renowned drugs, such as a treatment to combat Ebola on the African continent in 2019.

Consider This: Diversification's lure is to minimize risk. But diversification can destroy your primary focus. So keep your eyes focused on your main business, and stay away from enticing sidelines that can sap your energy.

COMING BACK AFTER FAILURE

*The only man who never makes a mistake is
the man who never does anything.*
THEODORE ROOSEVELT

Many people hide their failures. After one or two failures, they may be so ashamed that they will quit trying to do anything challenging. Successful people usually fail, too. They often leave a trail of "could have been successes" on their journey to real success. To some, failure is a stopping point. For those with the character to persevere, failure provides a chance to gain knowledge that can be applied to their next attempt. Babe Ruth failed many times at home plate, recording more strikeouts than home runs. Yet he is remembered as the "Sultan of Swat," one of baseball's most incredible batters. The British army suffered a staggering defeat at Dunkirk but went on to win the war. Abraham Lincoln was born to a poor family. He started life in a dirt-floor log cabin on the outskirts of pioneer America. He failed in business. He was defeated more than once while running for Congress. He lost his sweetheart, suffered a nervous breakdown, lost two bids for the Senate, and was defeated in a run for the vice presidency before being elected president of the United States in 1860.

Many people suffer a defeat and then lower their expectations or abandon their dreams. Leaders must help others learn to fail without fear. They must teach by example that it is right and good to dream, seek, fail, and try again. In his book *Bringing Out the Best in People*, Alan Loy McGinnis said, "If leaders can teach people how to handle failure creatively, it may be the most important contribution they can make."

Consider This: Don't be disheartened if your life has been riddled with temporary failures. Success favors those who persist.

TABITHA BABBITT SAW AN IDEA

No one is useless in this world who lightens the burdens of another.
CHARLES DICKENS

Tabitha Babbitt lived in an era when women weren't expected to do any inventing. Born in 1779, she grew up in a Shaker community in Harvard, Massachusetts, and became an expert weaver. The Shakers originally emigrated from England to New York in 1774 to escape religious persecution. Their leader, Ann Lee, set up several communities, the first one in New York. Then, in the 1880s, some of the group migrated to Massachusetts. As a farming community, they grew what they needed, built homes using their own hands, and sold what they could. One of their workplaces was a sawmill. Young Tabitha spent part of her childhood watching the men use a two-man whipsaw to cut logs into boards. It was a tedious and backbreaking job. Then she noticed that half of their sawing motion was wasted, as the blade cut only one way.

After mulling the problem over, she came up with a solution. If the saw were circular and could be turned like a wheel, it could cut logs in a single motion. The idea had merit. Soon a blade was forged, and a water-powered machine was devised to turn it. Cutting logs became quicker and took less labor. Her invention revolutionized an entire industry. Her concept can be seen today in the circular saws you probably have in your garage. It also made possible the proliferation of sawmills throughout America. Because Shaker law forbade applying for patents, others seized and patented the idea. Tabitha never received any money for her invention, and the little credit she received is known only through Shaker history.

Consider This: Not every invention makes a genius rich. Some inventors choose to give their creations to the world, either because of cultural conviction or wanting to get it to the masses without restriction. Other nonpatented innovations include the internet, matches, the computer mouse, and LED bulbs. What gift can you give to the world?

HERB KELLEHER AND SOUTHWEST AIRLINES

You must be very patient, very persistent. The world isn't going to shower gold coins on you just because you have a good idea. You're going to have to work like crazy to bring that idea to the attention of people.

HERB KELLEHER

In 1966 Rollin King met a lawyer friend named Herb Kelleher for lunch. King drew a sketch of a triangle on a cocktail napkin with the cities of Dallas, San Antonio, and Houston at the corners and used it to describe the opportunity for creating an inexpensive commuter airline between the cities. The conversation went something like this:

"Herb, let's start an airline."

"Rollin, you're crazy. Let's do it."

And Southwest Airlines was born. Well, it wasn't exactly that easy. The big problem was competition. Other airlines (notably Braniff International) didn't want Southwest to fly—and they had lots of lawyers and money. They waited a few days before the inaugural flight, then pounced with legal maneuvering to delay it.

Kelleher flew to Washington to convince the Civil Aeronautics Board (CAB) to reject the complaint. A few hours before the flight, the CAB ruled that Southwest could fly. Instantly, Braniff and Texas International filed another complaint in Texas and received a restraining order. Kelleher sprang into action in Austin and got the order rescinded in an emergency meeting of the Texas Supreme Court. On June 18, 1971, the inaugural Southwest flight took off from Love Field and into aviation history. Today Braniff and Texas International Airlines are gone, and Southwest is one of the most profitable airlines in the world.

Consider This: Good ideas don't spring into action by themselves. Instead, they often require a heavy dose of inspiration and perspiration to get off the ground.

WINCHESTER'S SECOND EFFORT

Take calculated risks. That is quite different from being rash.
GENERAL GEORGE S. PATTON

There was no shining future for orphans born in Boston in 1810. But Oliver Winchester didn't let that stop him. He pulled himself out of poverty with hard work. His enthusiasm, honesty, and determination allowed him to work his way into owning a small Baltimore clothing store. Although he was successful, he wasn't satisfied. He enjoyed the journey toward success too much to be content once he had achieved it. So in 1847 he decided to sell his store and move to more profitable ventures. His ambition took him to New York, where he believed a bigger market and more opportunity awaited. Using his expertise in the clothing industry, he patented a new shirtmaking method and made reasonable royalties from its use.

Not content with that success, Winchester used the profits from his invention to buy another company. This time his interests turned to a rifle manufacturing business named the Volcanic Repeating Arms Company. He bought the company, but sales were poor because the quality of the rifle was shoddy. To improve on the design, he acquired the patents of Hotchkiss, Browning, and other weapons builders. He hired great engineers and developed a state-of-the-art rifle. As a result, in 1860 Winchester introduced the Henry repeating rifle, which was used extensively during the Civil War and, in 1866, was renamed the Winchester. That weapon became the settlers' and cowboys' rifle of choice in opening up the American West. With his firearms company, Winchester finally found the industry that intrigued him enough to satisfy his ambition to succeed.

Consider This: Do you have too much energy to be satisfied with just an initial success? Instead, use one victory to finance your next adventure and continue the journey toward your dream.

HOWARD CORBIN'S TROUSERS

Thinking is like living and dying. Each of us has to do it for himself.
JOSIAH ROYCE

At the age of twenty-one, Lieutenant Howard J. Corbin left the air force to enroll in New York's Columbia Business School. Howard had been a bombardier/navigator aboard a B-25 during World War II, flying out of North Africa and Italy. He got used to his trimly cut officer's uniform in the service. But in the civilian market, pants were baggy and presented an unkempt appearance to Corbin. During his college years, Corbin worked with his brother and father. They operated a small pants factory in Brooklyn to design and tailor a "natural shoulder" jacket and pants. The style was soon called the Ivy League look. Corbin figured that many other ex-GIs would be interested in that kind of design. By the time Corbin was completing his bachelor of science degree in 1947, he was producing his line of Ivy League clothing. He must have been right about what men wanted, because within a few years his fashion caught on throughout the nation.

Corbin is also famous for popularizing khaki trousers as business casual menswear. Until he introduced them to the general public, they were worn only in the military. Now khaki trousers fill an important middle ground between jeans and formal wear. Corbin's family business developed a reputation that enabled it to sell its trousers and suits under the labels of the best clothiers in the world. Once the company's reputation was firmly established in men's clothing, Corbin introduced a line of women's apparel in 1982. Even after Howard Corbin retired, he continued to help other entrepreneurs discover their American Dream by serving as an executive-in-residence at Columbia University.

Consider This: Trust your own tastes. If they are different from what the market is promoting, maybe others share your ideas. Can you use this to develop new ideas for products?

HOW KODAK GOT ITS NAME

Man's distinction is his determination to think for himself.
ADMIRAL HYMAN G. RICKOVER

"What's in a name?" William Shakespeare's question has echoed down through the centuries, haunting everyone whose job was to choose a company, team, or organizational name. The Eastman Kodak Company is an example. It calls its name one of its most valuable assets. So how did the Kodak name come into being? According to George Eastman, the company's founder, he purposely invented the unique name out of thin air. In a 1920s article from *System Magazine*, Eastman is quoted as saying, "I devised the name myself . . . the letter K had been a favorite with me. The letter seemed like a strong, incisive sort of letter." Once he'd made that decision, he tried out combinations of words that started and ended with K. "Kodak" was settled upon after a considerable search. It was short, unique, easy to spell, and met the requirements of the trademark law. Eastman wrote, "There is, you know, commercial value in having a peculiar name; it cannot be imitated or counterfeited."

Kodak was first registered as a trademark in 1888. The first Kodak camera sold for twenty-five dollars and came loaded with film for one hundred exposures. Owners would return the entire camera for processing, and for ten dollars it was filled with a new roll of film. The pictures were good quality, and the easy-to-use camera brought photography to the masses. Since that time, the Kodak name has served the company well. Because "Kodak" had no meaning of its own, it could only be associated with the company. It was also almost impossible to misspell. As a result, the Kodak name has become a unique and distinctive trademark known worldwide.

Consider This: A unique and distinctive name or symbol helps your company establish recognition. What distinctive traits do people see in you—and remember you by?

WITH A NAME LIKE SMUCKER'S

Small opportunities are often the beginning of great enterprises.
DEMOSTHENES

Jerome Smucker was born in 1858. By the late nineteenth century, he and his wife, Ella, had developed a good business making apple cider in Orrville, Ohio. Smucker transformed his mill during the off-season and made apple butter for the local farmers, who supplied their own apples. Jerome also made his own apple butter using a recipe developed by his family. Everyone in the family helped in the business. The apple butter was first sold door-to-door for twenty-five cents per half-gallon crock. By 1900 word of the apple butter had spread, and Smucker began selling the crocks to local grocery stores.

The apple butter business became a major part of Smucker's production, and by 1920 the company had added a line of jams and jellies. Smucker's quality quickly became known, and soon the enterprise was the largest independent producer of preserves in the country. Jerome had four children, and one of them, Willard, took over the company's reins when Jerome died in 1948. Willard's son, Paul, was named CEO in 1970. Under the family leadership, the company continued to prosper. It introduced new ways of shipping fruit in steel drums rather than the older wooden barrels. It also became the first preserves maker to use essence recovery, a technique that captures fruit essence during cooking and then returns it before bottling. Although Smuckers still makes apple butter, now their most popular jelly products are strawberry preserves and grape jelly. Today Smucker's is one of the most recognized names in the jelly industry.

Consider This: Keep an eye out for those side opportunities that may turn into a gold mine.

HEWITT HIRES CHEMISTRY

*An industrial family should be united in purpose, as well
governed, contented, and peaceful, and the members
as courteous to one another as a domestic family.*

C. W. POST

In 1940 insurance salesman Edwin "Ted" Hewitt started a business. He made precise plans about the company's structure, the kinds of people he would hire, and the business principles he would instill in the new company. On October 1 of that year, he opened Edwin Shields Hewitt and Associates as a brokerage house focusing on insurance and personal financial services. In the 1960s, because of Hewitt's growing reputation in employee benefits, his company was chosen by the US government to help design and implement a new Employee Retirement Income Security Act. Hewitt continued to introduce innovative benefits products in the 1980s and '90s to address rising health-care costs.

The basic structure and philosophy of the company as defined by its founder still provides it with direction and identity today. One of the company's secrets is its hiring practices. Because the firm is very picky, only five applicants in every hundred are offered positions. The process used to choose employees is critical. The company looks for people who are bright, hardworking, and ambitious. But it avoids individuals who are so ambitious that they might try to succeed at the company's expense. Associates must be team players, possessing the right chemistry to consult within the model used throughout the company. Few titles are used, and the only real promotion is to be made a partner. Even then, everyone is treated the same, from secretaries to senior partners. As a result, it has a low (5 percent a year) turnover, and many associates become partners. Today Hewitt Associates is a Fortune 500 company and is often rated as one of America's best 100 companies to work for.

Consider This: Each business must take special care in curating a family of employees who create a fabric of cooperation and support corporate goals. Create a family that will help one another reach for their dreams.

MCMANUS'S TEN COMMANDMENTS OF BUSINESS

*When we do the best that we can, we never know what
miracle is wrought in our life, or in the life of another.*
HELEN KELLER

James McManus prepared for business at the University of Wisconsin (BBA
'55) and Northwestern (MBA '56) before gaining experience at Procter
& Gamble and Glendinning Products. In 1971 he started the successful
Marketing Corporation of America. MCA analyzes consumer behavior and
sells its knowledge and ideas to some of the nation's largest corporations. One
such idea was that Ralston Purina distribute, through veterinarians, puppy care
kits containing food samples and a pet-care booklet. It proved so successful
that Purina started charging the vets for the kits. In a speech for University of
Wisconsin–Madison business alumni, McManus outlined his ten commandments of business:

1. "With whom you go" is more important than where.
2. Execution is critical, how you do what you do.
3. Pay attention to the product before the profits, or "make sure the
   product works."
4. You have to spend money to make money.
5. It is important to plow back some of your profits into research and
   development.
6. Don't be afraid to fail. That's how you learn.
7. Provide your future employees with an environment that stresses
   individual accountability and rewards.
8. Share the rewards. Power and profits for the people!
9. Be the best that you can be.
10. Have fun!

*Consider This: The basics of business are doing your best and treating other
people with respect. Develop your own rules for success and stick to them.*

STAN LEE—THE GUARDIAN OF THE MARVEL GALAXY

The only advice anybody can give is if you want to be a writer,
keep writing. And read all you can, read everything.

STAN LEE

No recent movie franchise has captured theatergoers as much as the Marvel Cinematic Universe. And the spark for the characters and stories was in the imagination of Stan Lee (born Stanley Martin Lieber) from a young age. Lee went to work for Timely Comics right out of high school at age sixteen. He soon became editor and was writing his own stories. The company struggled to stay afloat and renamed itself Atlas. Lee constantly wrote and created. During the 1950s he came up with comic book series that included *The Witness*, *The Destroyer*, *Jack Frost*, and *Black Marvel*. In 1961 he created *The Fantastic Four*. By that time, every kid with a dime in their pocket could hardly wait to visit the drugstore and pull the latest Stan Lee comic off the rack.

Jump forward a few years, and Lee's characters landed on the big screen. Starting in 2000 with *X-Men*, a new universe appeared in theaters (and on TV). *Spiderman*, *The Hulk*, and *Iron Man* led the movie franchise into the billion-dollar territory. In every movie Lee portrayed some minor character in a cameo appearance. He once summarized his life like this: "I've been the luckiest man in the world because I've had friends, and to have the right friends is everything: people you can depend on, people who tell you the truth if you ask something." In 2009 Disney acquired Marvel, and the universe kept exploding. Today Lee's legacy lives on, not only in comic books but also in hit movies and in rides, buildings, and shows in Disney parks.

Consider This: Some people find their calling at a young age, like Stan. For others, it takes a while. But know that a universe of opportunities is out there waiting to be discovered and embraced. Step forward. Find what you do best and stick with it.

GEORGE WASHINGTON

The test of the progress of mankind will be their
appreciation of the character of Washington.
LORD BROUGHAM

The ideals of American character and integrity were initially established by
the examples set by our Founding Fathers. We have indeed become children
of their beliefs and the principles they honored. George Washington is perhaps
the most prominent. Even during his own lifetime, Washington symbolized
the character qualities that Americans look up to today. Daniel Webster called
George Washington a great example of American leadership with character
that rivaled any hero from the Old World. "If our American institutions had
done nothing else, that alone would entitle them to respect." Even the fab-
ricated cherry tree story by Mason Locke Weems, more commonly known
as Parson Weems, shows the kind of mystical respect Washington's integrity
commanded. In the story, young George says, "I cannot tell a lie, Pa; I cut
it down with my hatchet." Of course, we know Washington was flawed like
all of us. But America needed a hero, and Washington's selfless service to the
fledgling country put him at the top of the list.

In his time, Washington could have chosen to become a king. But he
refused that title. Instead, his powerful example as our nation's first president
gave America its respect, stability, and unique flavor of democracy. Henry Lee
called Washington "first in war, first in peace, and first in the hearts of his
countrymen." Other heroes have used their popularity to benefit their own
kingdoms. Washington used his popularity to establish a code of conduct in
which the welfare of the people came first. Because of Washington's example,
later American leaders have had a superior model to emulate.

*Consider This: No person is flawless, but a leader needs to strive to set a strong
example of character and integrity.*

LEVI STRAUSS INVENTS BLUE JEANS

Study how to do the most good, and let the pay take care of itself.
LYMAN ABBOTT

In 1853 Levi Strauss was invited by his brother-in-law David Stern to help start a dry goods store in San Francisco during the gold rush. Levi packed goods onto a ship that sailed seventeen thousand miles from New York to California. During the trip he sold most of his goods to the passengers. In fact, the only item he had left was canvas material used to make tents. Levi was told, "You shoulda brought pants" upon his arrival in California. All the prospectors were wearing out their pants almost faster than they could dig. Levi immediately went to a tailor and had the man make pants from the remaining canvas in stock. Word spread about the sturdiness of Levi's pants, and his inventory was soon sold out.

Levi was then able to get some heavy cloth from France called serge de Nîmes, which was Americanized to "denim." The original fabric was brown, but Levi dyed it indigo to make the deep color purple. Since the weight of their gold often ripped the prospectors' pockets, Levi began riveting the pockets to the pants to give them added strength. Levi and tailor Jacob Davis patented the innovation in 1873. Levi's business flourished, and he became a wealthy man. Until his death in 1902, Levi Strauss spent much of his wealth helping others, including the California School for the Deaf. He also provided scholarships to the University of California. Because Strauss was a bachelor when he died, he willed a considerable portion of his estate to orphanages and benevolent associations. Today relatives descended from Strauss's brother-in-law own the apparel company.

Consider This: Look at your resources. No matter how limited they seem, you may have just what it takes to meet the needs of the people around you.

PHILIP CALDWELL AT FORD

It is good to rule and polish our brains against those of others.
MICHEL DE MONTAIGNE

Philip Caldwell took over as chief executive officer of Ford Motor Company during a bleak period in 1979. The oil crisis and the growing importation of foreign cars had stunned the unprepared American automobile market. Sales plummeted. Ford's costs skyrocketed, and its vehicles were rated poor in quality and design. Caldwell remembered the temptation to cut all expenses to save what little was left. But he added, "That would have given away our future . . . we didn't even give it serious consideration." So instead Caldwell and other leaders at Ford went on an unprecedented spending spree. They poured over $13 billion worldwide into new products, processes, machinery, and equipment and spent another $9 billion on research and development. Company management agreed that "quality was our primary objective," said Caldwell.

Everyone at Ford seemed to get the message. By 1984 Ford had reduced its operating costs, introduced higher-quality cars, and posted a record profit of $2.9 billion—one of the most significant turnarounds in American corporate history. Caldwell gave much credit to Ford's employees, who originated many ideas that set the company back on the right course. As a result, there was a significant change in attitude. Workers felt they were being heard and their talents were being put to good use. Management and workers alike wanted to produce high-quality products—it was a matter of pride. Caldwell opened the doors of communication, and everyone, from assembly-line personnel to top management, listened to each other. That is what makes a business successful.

Consider This: Do you make it profitable for employees and management to communicate? Does everyone have the same goal of making your organization the best it can be?

ALEXANDER GRAHAM BELL'S TELEPHONE

Attempt the end, and never stand in doubt;
nothing's so hard, but search will find it out.

ROBERT HERRICK

Alexander Graham Bell was the son of a speech teacher from Scotland. In fact, both his father and grandfather made careers of elocution—teaching people how to speak correctly. Their interest was partly because Bell's mother and wife were deaf. Thus the family also developed methods for teaching the deaf to speak.

Tuberculosis in the family triggered the Bells' move from England to Canada. An offer to present teaching methods for the deaf in Boston brought young Alexander to the United States. During his study of speech, he read a German article titled "The Sensations of Tone as a Physiological Basis for the Theory of Music." Since he could barely read German, he mistakenly thought the report said vowel sounds could be produced by electricity and tuning forks.

Alexander's experiments with electricity and vibrations led to a "phonautograph" device that could draw sound waves on smoked glass. He thought this idea might be the beginning of a machine that could send multiple telegraphs. While attempting to perfect his machine, he realized that vibrations made by the voice could be picked up and changed into electrical pulses. His assistant, Thomas Watson, helped in the breakthrough by connecting some vibrating reeds too tightly. Alexander heard the sound emanating from another reed attached to the wire when plucked. Something important was happening. Bell studied the situation for several days, making various changes. Finally, on March 7, 1876, Alexander shouted, "Mr. Watson, come here, I want you!" In another room, Watson heard the message transmitted over the wire. The apparatus was the first working telephone.

Consider This: There is no telling what can be accomplished once you think it is possible.

TOM LANDRY LEARNS FOOTBALL

Coaching: To get people to do what they don't want to do in order to achieve what they want to achieve.

TOM LANDRY

In the small town of Mission, Texas, during the Great Depression, a scrappy boy named Tommy Landry began learning about football. There were no organized football leagues for kids, so Tommy and his friends would stage their own games on a field near his house. They played thousands of football games, often stopping only when their moms demanded that they come home for supper. Tommy played center and quarterback, coached, and organized the games. But he needed more than a small-town sandlot league to set him on the track to becoming one of America's greatest sports legends. He needed a coach.

When young Tom entered Mission High School, he was fortunate to be a member of Bill Martin's junior varsity team. Tom thrived on the competition provided by football. The fanaticism of Friday night football in Texas, combined with the increasing success of the Mission team under Coach Martin, ignited a blaze of enthusiasm throughout the entire community. During Mission's 1941 championship season, Tom experienced what he still remembers as his most memorable and sweetest victories. After World War II he became a gridiron star at the University of Texas, then went on to play and coach in the National Football League. Landry's successful reign as coach of the Dallas Cowboys from 1960 through 1988 led to his enshrinement in the Pro Football Hall of Fame in 1990. Chances are, he never would have achieved this honor had it not been for the experience he gained under Coach Martin as a youngster in Mission, Texas.

Consider This: Raw talent plus effective coaching equals success. Seek and hire the most talented people possible, then train them to be their best.

JAY LENO'S BIG BREAK

You can't stay mad at somebody who makes you laugh.
JAY LENO

Jay Leno was headed for a career of flipping burgers. He brought home poor grades and was known as the class clown. Even when slicing potatoes into fries at McDonald's, he earned a reputation as a "cutup." Jay remembered hating homework until his English teacher, Mrs. Hawkes, encouraged him to write down some of his funny stories as a creative writing assignment. Suddenly Jay was spending hours writing and rewriting his stories. When he read them in class, he got laughs, which encouraged him to create more funny stories.

Jay spent plenty of time in detention. Luckily, the overseeing teacher, Mr. Walsh, liked his stories. One day he asked Jay, "Why don't you go into show business?" That was a new concept for Jay—and it was the beginning of a dream. He got his first break as the French-Fry Cut-Up in a McDonald's talent show and won $150. While in college Jay began learning the comedy craft by performing in nonpaying, low-paying, and often sleazy joints. After spending years in New England, he decided to try his act in California. Jay played comedy clubs and began to land minor roles on TV sitcoms and in movies. A successful appearance on *The Tonight Show* is the ultimate break for a comedian. But it eluded Jay until one night when Steve Martin dropped by the club where he was performing. Martin liked what he saw and talked to the people at *The Tonight Show*, and Jay got his chance on March 2, 1977. His first *Tonight Show* performance drew big laughs and a "wink" from Johnny Carson, and Jay was on his way to stardom.

Consider This: Big breaks come to those whose hard work and talents prepare them for their "moment of judgment."

THE PLASTICS REVOLUTION

Every addition to true knowledge is an addition to human power.

HORACE MANN

Recent technological inventions and discoveries have caused an explosion of businesses and products, changing our everyday lives. Similarly, plastics were the technological marvel of a previous era. Although celluloid, the first plastic, was invented in England around 1850, it was an American who recognized plastic's commercial potential. In 1868 an ivory shortage prompted a New England manufacturer of billiard balls to offer a $10,000 prize for a suitable substitute. John Wesley Hyatt purchased the British patent for celluloid, presented it as an ivory substitute, and won the award.

With his winnings, Hyatt produced billiard balls and discovered other uses for the new material. In 1872 the celluloid name was trademarked and Hyatt started the Albany Dental Plate Company. Its first successful celluloid products were false teeth, piano keys, "wipe-clean" shirtfronts, cuffs, collars, and combs. Other uses that followed included dental plates and children's toys. In 1889 Kodak introduced celluloid photography film, and Thomas Edison used film strips to create motion pictures. The next significant advancement in plastics came from a Belgian-American scientist named Leo Hendrik Baekeland. In 1906 he created, trademarked, and promoted another plastic and rubber substitute called Bakelite. Other polymer-based products appeared in the following years, extending the types of plastics available. They included rayon, polyvinyl chloride (used in plastic pipes), plastic tableware, Plexiglas, and Teflon. During World War II, plastics provided a wealth of substitutes for materials in short supply. After the war, the research and development of new uses for plastics exploded into an industry that is still growing today.

Consider This: One invention can lead to the development of an entirely new industry. Keep your eye on the cutting edge.

A LITTLE SOMETHING EXTRA

And if anyone forces you to go one mile, go with him two miles.
JESUS CHRIST

Like the extra day that is tacked on to leap year, we all notice a little something extra we get for our money. Everyone is familiar with the prize in Cracker Jack. But would Cracker Jack be around today if the company had not thought of that innovative extra? Children will always pick out the cereal that has something extra inside. In service businesses, something extra might be a callback after a job is finished to see if the customer is satisfied. IBM's policy is to make a callback to customers within twenty-four hours. The little something extra may be a bonus or recognition to an employee for a helpful idea. Encouragement costs nothing, yet many managers hold on to it as if it were gold. In fact, it only becomes gold when it is given away. The same thing can be said of friendliness to a customer.

Many people use the phrase "go the extra mile." This concept comes from the Sermon on the Mount in the Bible. In it, Jesus tells his followers that if a soldier requires that they carry his equipment for one mile, they should carry it for two. People expect to get what they pay for, and they seldom notice when they get only that. When someone goes the extra mile to give the customer more than is required, the customer remembers that good feeling, develops loyalty, and tells others about their good experience. Doing business or serving others is no more complicated than treating people with respect, kindness, and concern for their satisfaction. Go the extra mile in everything you do.

Consider This: When someone receives something from you, do they feel that they got their money's worth—and more?

OTIS ELEVATORS

*With ordinary talent and extraordinary
perseverance, all things are attainable.*
THOMAS BUXTON

In the mid-1850s, elevators were too dangerous to be used for anything but freight. If the rope snapped, a rider would certainly risk life and limb. It was this problem that Elisha G. Otis solved in 1854. Otis had a knack for all things mechanical. By age fifteen he was already an engineer at a bedstead factory. In 1852 Otis was sent to Yonkers to supervise the construction of a new factory. He developed several new enhancements to the elevators designed for and installed in each building. Otis's elevators were equipped with a simple spring device that would trigger if the cable broke and prevent the elevator from falling. The invention was patented, and *Scientific American* called the device "excellent." Otis built a similar elevator at another factory. While he was installing that one, he received a request for another.

Otis was encouraged by the interest in his elevator and formed the E. G. Otis Company in 1853. But then orders virtually stopped. Companies were simply unwilling to build an elevator for public use. Otis decided to prove his safety device's usefulness and address this fear by building an elevator and demonstrating it to the crowds at a New York fair. Although he was successful, orders still came slowly. Not until 1857 did Otis finally build his first elevator specifically for passenger use. Although he died in 1861, Otis's sons took the company into prosperity. By the turn of the century, Otis elevators were a crucial element in the appearance of skyscrapers.

Consider This: Success may take time, even when you have the right idea. Keep trying. Prove your concept. Stick to your beliefs.

JOHN H. JOHNSON AND *EBONY*

Nothing beats a failure but a try.
JOHN JOHNSON'S MOTHER

John H. Johnson stands as an example to individuals of all races that people can overcome poverty if they refuse to buckle under failure. Born into poverty in Arkansas City, Arkansas, Johnson lost his father when he was only six years old. When he reached high school age, there was no school available for African Americans. His mother saved enough money during the Great Depression to send John to school in Chicago. Once there, he became editor of the institution's newspaper and yearbook. He later took a job at an insurance company. He was assigned to search newspapers and magazines for stories relevant to the African-American community. That experience convinced John of the need for an African-American publication. To help John raise funding, his mother allowed him to pawn her furniture. And with the money he started the *Negro Digest*. In 1945 John founded *Ebony* magazine, and although it sold well, virtually no one would advertise in the fledgling periodical.

His mother kept telling him, "Failure is not in your vocabulary!" John continued to diplomatically approach potential advertisers. Before talking to Eugene McDonald, the president of Zenith, John researched McDonald's life thoroughly and discovered that McDonald greatly admired African-American explorer Matthew Henson. McDonald was impressed with John's interest in him and how he handled himself. After Zenith agreed to advertise in *Ebony*, other companies followed suit. In addition to owning the Johnson Publishing Company, John E. Johnson sat on the boards of some of the most influential corporations in America until he died in 2005. Today his family keeps his legacy alive at Johnson Publishing.

Consider This: The best way to interest other people in you is to show a genuine interest in them.

COLONEL SANDERS

Genius, that power which dazzles humans,
is oft but perseverance in disguise.
H. W. AUSTIN

Before beginning his famous franchise, Colonel Harland Sanders worked as a streetcar conductor, a railroad fireman, a justice of the peace, an insurance salesman, and other occupations. In 1930, at the age of forty, he was operating a service station in Corbin, Kentucky, when he decided to offer food to his customers. At first Sanders served them right off the dining table in his living quarters. His food was popular, and he eventually opened a restaurant across the street from the station. Over the years Sanders developed the secret combination of eleven herbs and spices for his chicken recipe. But when a new interstate highway bypassed his town, Sanders sold his business and began collecting Social Security. That could have been the end of the story, but the colonel decided he was not ready for the retired life.

At sixty-six Sanders took to the road in an old station wagon. Every time he saw a restaurant, he stopped, knocked on the door, and prepared a batch of his special recipe chicken. Restaurant owners made handshake deals to use the recipe and pay Sanders a nickel for every chicken they sold. After introducing the Kentucky Fried Chicken recipe, most restaurants found that their customers couldn't get enough of the "finger-lickin' good" chicken. Success blossomed, and KFC restaurants were franchised throughout the United States and around the globe. In a poll taken in the late 1970s, Colonel Sanders was listed as one of the five most recognized individuals in the entire world.

Consider This: It's never too late to begin, but once you start, it takes enthusiasm, perseverance, and patience to realize success.

EARL TUPPER'S PARTY PLAN

The most successful men have used seeming
failures as stepping-stones to better things.
GRENVILLE KLEISER

While still in his teens, Earl Tupper began a small business selling fruits and
vegetables to his neighbors. He was good at it and learned quickly about the
finer points of salesmanship. This was a significant asset to Tupper when, years
later, he began a new business. That enterprise, started in 1945, was a line of
plastic containers that he dubbed "Tupperware." At first, Tupper used the conventional method of marketing his product through retail stores. But after five
years of mediocre sales, he began to envision a new plan of action. Recalling
his earlier days, when he sold produce directly to housewives, Tupper decided
to try this same direct approach in selling Tupperware.

It was 1950 when Tupper began selling his plastic containers directly to the
people who would use them most. He invited people into homes and demonstrated the product. Sales were good, better than they had been in retail stores,
and it was clear that this approach had considerable promise. But it was also
clear that Tupper could not sell enough products by himself, so he arranged for
housewives to become Tupperware dealers. They could hold parties at friends'
houses, and each hostess would receive a gift. As a result, the housewives would
have a part-time income while maintaining their freedom to take their children
to school and do household chores. By 1954 Tupperware had a network of
over nine thousand dealers across the United States. Sales eventually spread to
Europe, and today Tupperware is found in kitchen cabinets worldwide. And its
patented "burp" to seal in freshness remains an icon of its success.

*Consider This: A product alone is not enough. You must devise a plan to sell your
product, sometimes with a unique method, to your customers.*

BILL GATES

Only the paranoid survive.
ANDREW GROVE

Bill Gates was an Edison- and Ford-type entrepreneur for the twentieth century. He became a success not just by being in the right place at the right time but also by being prepared, intelligent, committed, and lucky. As a teenager, Bill was a voracious reader. He scored high enough on the SAT to get into Harvard, with a plan to become a lawyer. But he got sidetracked. He and Paul Allen, his future partner, began playing around with a clunky teletype terminal and got jobs finding bugs in computer programs. In addition, Bill helped write a scheduling program for his school and included instructions that put him into classes with the girls of his choice.

While still at Harvard, Bill became even more committed to computing and saw a technical revolution coming. He and Allen created a BASIC language interpreter for the first wave of microcomputers. But Bill's company was just one among thousands fighting for a share of the microcomputer market. He hired the brightest minds he could find. His Microsoft firm competed well and established itself as a "language" company. Microsoft's big break came when IBM searched for a company to help it write an operating system for the new IBM personal computer. IBM initially went to another company already marketing the leading micro-operating system, called CP/M. The other company was reluctant to sign a nondisclosure agreement, so IBM continued its search. When IBM approached Microsoft, Bill saw the potential and grabbed the deal. The resulting PC-DOS and MS-DOS operating systems established Microsoft's dominance in the software market and laid foundations for Windows and many other popular application programs.

Consider This: If you want to be lucky, be smart and be prepared. Hire the brightest people you can afford, and fight to take advantage of every opportunity.

PRACTICE IN THE MIND

Imagination is more important than knowledge.
ALBERT EINSTEIN

Concentration is one thing that Americans often seem to lack. We are frequently too busy to think about any single idea for too long. But research and practical examples have shown that concentration can significantly train our minds for success. For example, air force colonel George Hall endured five and a half years as a prisoner of war in North Vietnam. Many of those days were spent in solitary confinement, leaving him with plenty of time for concentration. Colonel Hall "played" a round of golf each day to pass the time. As he paced back and forth in his tiny cell, he remembered his best shots and how the ball had landed in just the right spot. Every detail of his imaginary game was real to him, from the Titleist balls to the blue tees he placed in the grass still wet from the morning dew. In those times, the smell of the fresh grass replaced the musty smell of the prison. For a while, the colonel was having the time of his life.

Day after day, Hall mentally played and replayed every golf course he had ever been on. He climbed up the hills, looked out onto the fairways, and studied the greens. In his imagination, he played a good game of golf. Colonel George Hall finally made it back to the United States at the war's end. One month after his arrival, he played in the New Orleans Open. He was paired with a professional golfer named Orville Moody. Hall shot a sizzling round of seventy-six. His years of "practice" had not been in vain.

Consider This: We become what we practice in our minds. If we imagine failure, it will come. If we imagine success, it will come. Are your thoughts leading you toward your goals?

HELEN KELLER

We can do anything we want to do if we stick with it long enough.
HELEN KELLER

When Helen Keller suffered an illness that made her blind and deaf, she gradually adopted animal instincts to survive. That is how teacher Anne Sullivan found Helen when she arrived in Tuscumbia, Alabama, to teach the child. What transpired next was a clear example of tough love, leadership, and discipline. Sullivan literally had to fight Helen and attempted to communicate with her through the sensation of touch, the only real sense the youngster still recognized. Week after week, Anne pressed her hand into Helen's, making symbols with the positions of her fingers against Helen's palm. She was spelling out words, but they made no sense to Helen. Then, all at once, Helen finally understood the relationship between the word "water" and the patterns pressed on her palm. She later recalled, "I was caught up in the first joy I had known since my illness."

Anne was tough on her pupil. "As soon as I knew right from wrong," Helen wrote, "she put me to bed whenever I committed a misdeed." The story of Anne and Helen has become an American wonder, as the physically challenged girl eventually grew up to be one of the brightest minds of her time. Helen became a communicator and a symbol of a person's power to rise above difficult circumstances. Still, she did not (could not) do it independently. Anne Sullivan demanded that her pupil learn beyond expectations and gave her love and fulfillment. Until her death at age seventy, Sullivan continued to be a traveling companion and supporter of Helen Keller.

Consider This: Whom are you teaching and encouraging? How are you making them stretch beyond their expectations? Who is waiting for you to encourage them into discovering their own genius?

VOIT BOUNCES BACK

Persistent people begin their success when others end in failure.
EDWARD EGGLESTON

In a discussion of successful businesspeople, it is rare to find someone who made it big the first time around. It is much more common for success to play hard to get and to come only after several attempts. Many achievers experience several failures and some small victories before attaining lasting success. William Voit is an example of that pattern. Voit worked as a salesman for several rubber companies during the 1910s and early 1920s. In 1924 he decided to start his own operation and began producing camelback, a material used in the tire recapping process. Voit expanded his business by introducing an inflatable multicolored rubber ball, popular on California beaches. In what could be called a preview of today's state of affairs, his ball was knocked out of the market by cheaper products manufactured in Japan. The stock market crash of 1929 also spelled trouble for Voit's business.

In 1932 Voit developed a plan for a comeback. At that time, athletic balls were primarily made of leather. Voit took advantage of a new rubber vulcanization process to create balls that were superior to the leather balls that dominated the market. He also developed icosahedron winding in which nylon threads were wound over the ball's bladder to add strength and consistency in shape. These innovations also improved machine-based mass production. His product line soon included basketballs, footballs, soccer balls, and volleyballs. When William Voit died in 1946, Voit athletic balls were standard equipment at many American high schools, colleges, and universities. Voit drew on his experience with failure to help him avoid past mistakes and create lasting success.

Consider This: Live your life like an excellent running back. When one lane is blocked, look for another and plow ahead.

CHARLES MICHAEL SCHWAB

I have yet to find a man, however exalted his station, who did not do better work and put forth greater effort under a spirit of approval than under a spirit of criticism.

CHARLES SCHWAB

Charles Michael Schwab was one of the first individuals to ever collect an annual salary of $1 million. How could anyone be worth that much money? The person who paid Schwab that unprecedented salary was industrialist Andrew Carnegie. Although Carnegie had made his fortune in steel manufacturing, he knew little about steelmaking. Carnegie possessed the business acumen, but for the daily operation of this plant, he had to rely on the abilities of Charles Schwab. Schwab first came to work for Carnegie as an engineer. He quickly rose through the ranks and became a general superintendent of one of Carnegie's mills in 1890. At only thirty-five years old, he took over as president of the Carnegie Steel Company in 1897.

Schwab possessed a talent that is as valuable today as it was many years ago. Anyone with the same skill as Schwab could deserve the same kind of compensation. Schwab revealed that his salary was earned because he could deal with people effectively. His secret was simple: first, he aroused enthusiasm in people; second, he developed the best in a person through genuine appreciation and encouragement; and third, Schwab never criticized anyone. He was aptly described as "anxious to praise but loath to find fault." After helping Carnegie sell his company, he took over as president of the new United States Steel Corporation in 1901. Carnegie appreciated Schwab's secret. On his tombstone, he continued to praise his associates with the inscription, "Here lies one who knew how to get around men who were cleverer than himself."

Consider This: No one works well under the spirit of criticism. But most people will rise to meet the task if they know their work is genuinely appreciated.

HARLEY-DAVIDSON IS HOG HEAVEN

It is teamwork that makes the dream work.

JAY ROCK

William Harley and Arthur Davidson grew up a few houses apart in Milwaukee, Wisconsin. They both loved their bicycles. So much, in fact, that William took a job at a bike factory at the age of fifteen. He started at a low-level job and worked his way up to the drafting department. That led to another job at the Barth Manufacturing Company, where he learned how to build an internal combustion engine. William used his machine and bike knowledge to create a prototype motorcycle with his friend Arthur. But they lacked the skills to make the company feasible. So, they brought in two other Davidson brothers, Walter and Bill. The four put their minds and skills to the task and, in 1904, created a workable bike. They entered their new creation in a race. It didn't win, but it gave them confidence. By 1909 they had created a solid product, set up a factory, and began churning out motorcycles.

Because William Harley had the original idea (and served as chief engineer and treasurer), they named their business Harley-Davidson. Arthur liked sales and sold the early versions to the post office, police, and military. He also started a Harley-Davidson mechanics school. Bill became the "Works Manager," setting up the factory with the machinery needed to churn out the product. Walter's talent was as the factory manager and the spokesperson to investors. With their innovative, efficient, and powerful two-cycle engine powering their bike, they produced 3,200 motorcycles in 1910. When their racing team "Wrecking Crew" winner took a victory lap with a pet pig on the gas tank, people started calling them "Harley Hogs," and the name stuck.

Consider This: Teamwork, where everyone contributes with their own skills, is a way to multiply each other's possibilities. So, get a team, and create magic.

HERMAN MILLER

*The deepest principle in human nature is
the craving to be appreciated.*
WILLIAM JAMES

Herman Miller produces fine office furniture and systems. Working for a company that makes desks and chairs could be just another job if it had not been for the death of an employee named Herman Rummelt in 1927. Company founder D. J. DePree visited the man's widow and discovered that Rummelt had excelled at handicrafts, with beautiful examples showcased throughout the house. He also was a World War I hero and had written poetry. "I walked away from that house that morning rather shaken up," DePree recalled. "God was dealing with me about this whole thing, the attitude toward working people . . . I had looked on him as a man who was good at fixing machinery and motors." That day, DePree decided that his company would make an effort to consider each employee as a person. He believed that there was a relationship between the way employees were treated and the quality of their work.

As a result of DePree's experience, his company's management direction changed. Innovations were instituted, including the Scanlon Information Meeting, which brought together employees once a month to discuss performance. Today, more than 40 percent of Herman Miller employees own stock in the company. In addition, the firm contributes to a childcare referral service, adoption aid, and productivity bonuses. One of its manufacturing plants is described in the *AIA Journal* as "a splendid workplace." Even the bottom line has benefited, and Herman Miller today is a highly profitable enterprise that maintains its commitment to its owners and its employees.

Consider This: Sincerely care about your workers, and they will care about you.

ADOLPH'S MEAT TENDERIZER

*Observation is more than seeing; it is knowing what
you see and comprehending its significance.*

CHARLES GOW

Like Ray Kroc with McDonald's and Colonel Harland Sanders with his family chicken recipe, many good ideas are waiting in the wings. You simply have to discover them. The next major business success story may well be about that person who keeps their eyes (and taste buds) open to the right idea. An example is the story of Adolph's Meat Tenderizer. During and after World War II, Adolph Rempp owned steak houses in Los Angeles and Santa Barbara, California. They were popular not only for their delicious steak but also for their low prices. Rempp had a secret. He'd discovered a way to use extract of papaya as a meat tenderizer. Using the concoction, he could transform inexpensive cuts of meat into tender steaks that could pass for much higher-priced selections. One evening after the war, two hungry veterans named Larry Deutsch and Lloyd Rigler visited Rempp's steak house.

Deutsch and Rigler liked the steaks a lot. But they were curious how such an inexpensive cut of meat could taste so good. So they did a little research and found out about the secret papaya tenderization process used by Rempp. After some persuasion, Deutsch and Rigler contracted with Rempp to market the extract to local grocery outlets. The product, named Adolph's Meat Tenderizer, was introduced in 1949. It quickly became popular in the Los Angeles market and was soon introduced throughout the United States. The product was eventually sold to Unilever. The transaction made Deutsh and Rigler wealthy enough to fund the Lloyd E. Rigler-Lawrence E. Deutsch Foundation. One of its projects is the Classic Arts Showcase, a free noncommercial cable channel promoting the arts.

Consider This: If you find something you like, other people will probably like it as well.

WILLIAM HOY SIGNALS GREATNESS

However difficult life may seem, there is always
something you can do and succeed at.
STEPHEN HAWKING

William Hoy grew up in Ohio when baseball was becoming a national pastime. He embraced the game, even though he was deaf and mute. Because of his disability, people gave him the nickname "Dummy Hoy." It sounds cruel today, but "Dummy" was a common nickname in his era, and he embraced the name. But he was no dummy. He graduated valedictorian from the School for the Deaf in Columbus, Ohio, and after graduation joined the family's shoe business. Still, he spent his free time playing baseball. One summer a man passed by and saw him playing. Even after learning William was deaf and mute, he invited him to join the Kenton team to play against their bitter rival, Urbana. William outplayed everyone. This convinced him that he could play professional ball.

William left his shoe shop and looked for a team. Many said no, but Oshkosh said yes. After that start, he moved to the Washington team in the National League. Hoy played with many teams during his fourteen-year professional career. He appeared in 1,797 games and had 2,048 hits, 1,429 runs, 40 homers, and 725 RBIs. His batting average was .288. But that's not the end of his story. Since William couldn't hear the umpire's calls, he helped develop umpire hand signals. Although he's not the only one to introduce such signals, he helped standardize them into the ones used today. Hoy has received many honors for his groundbreaking career (but not yet the Hall of Fame). Shortly before his death, at ninety-nine years old, Hoy threw out the first pitch for a World Series game between the Reds and the Yankees.

Consider This: Never be defined by what you can't do. Instead, embrace your skills and reach for the stars.

LEO BURNETT'S ADS

Give the world the best you have, and the
best will come back to you.
MADELEINE BRIDGES

Leo Burnett graduated from the University of Michigan in 1914. He got a job as a reporter at the *Peoria Journal Star* in Illinois. As part of his job, he wrote advertising copy. He liked it so much he started his own firm in 1935. Until his death in 1971, Leo Burnett inspired his company with his personal motto, "Reach for the Stars." Minimizing the value of advertising awards, Leo concentrated on selling products. After all, what good was advertising if it didn't sell the product? Thus, the Burnett Agency's primary criterion for superior advertising was not awards but sales. The firm tried to become an adjunct marketing department for its clients to achieve that goal. They "held the hands" of their clients and met with them regularly, essentially becoming another member of the client's family. After the Burnett Agency got to know its client well, it devised an advertising campaign to sell products. As a result, his company became one of the world's best-known advertising concerns.

Leo was known for being hardheaded, argumentative, and difficult to get along with when he thought a client's ideas were terrible. But he generally won those arguments, and his clients were the winners at the bank. Leo's results speak for themselves. For example, when United Airlines suffered from a big, uncaring company image, Leo brought out the "friendly skies" campaign. When Maytag wanted its washing machines to be seen as reliable products, the lonely Maytag repairman was the answer. Other creative strategies included the McDonald's "American slice of life" campaign, the Jolly Green Giant, Charlie the Tuna, and the Pillsbury Doughboy. Campaigns like these resulted from a thorough knowledge of the client's needs.

Consider This: It is not always the awards from peers that make a business great. What really counts is the reason you got into the business to begin with.

GATORADE MAKES A SPLASH

*Every problem has a solution. You just have
to be creative enough to find it.*
TRAVIS KALANICK

Are you thirsty? Chances are if you've been running around on a hot and humid football field for two hours, you are. In fact, playing a football game in hot weather can make players lose up to eighteen pounds of water weight. And that's not good. In 1965 the Florida Gators faced such a problem. In fact, in one August weekend of that year, team physician Dr. Robert Cade treated more than two dozen players for dehydration and heatstroke. After mulling over the situation, Cade realized the players were sweating away too much fluid. So he started studying sweat. He tried giving the players more water, salt, and sugar. But it gave them cramps and made them sick. There had to be a solution.

Cade consulted with his doctor friends. They experimented with several concoctions to replenish lost body fluids caused by excessive sweating. One mixture consisted of water, sugar, salt, and phosphate. Cade took a drink. It made him throw up. His wife, Mary, suggested adding lemon juice. That was the ticket! They named the drink Cade's Cola but soon changed it to Gatorade. Now for the test on the field. It worked! Gator teams that used it during games didn't get as tired during the second half and outplayed their opponents. The new drink made headlines in 1966, and by 1967 it began appearing in stores. After Cade tweaked the formula a little, Gatorade began flying off the shelves. It also made Cade a handsome piece of cash. In 1983, after the New York Giants won a critical game, the team poured a bucket of Gatorade over the coach. Gatorade had become a sports icon.

Consider This: Don't ignore a problem. It may be an opportunity to find a solution that will not only benefit your game but also change the game worldwide and forever.

WYNTON MARSALIS

Invest yourself in everything you do. There's fun in being serious.
WYNTON MARSALIS

Most people have talent, but few are serious enough to develop their talent into excellence. For those who do build their talent, it is often because someone prepared them and pushed them toward making a commitment. Ellis and Dolores Marsalis were parents determined to prepare their children for success. Since Ellis was a jazz pianist, his children were exposed to music at an early age. As a result, four of the six Marsalis sons pursued professional musical careers. All were raised to take education seriously, go to church on Sunday, and join the Boy Scouts.

Although Wynton, the second eldest, learned to play the trumpet, he liked to play Little League baseball better. Then one day, as he was listening to his father's albums, he came across the song "Cousin Mary" played by John Coltrane. The music consumed Wynton with wonder, and he felt a warm sensation throughout his body. He tried to play the melody himself but couldn't come close. He went to his mother and told her that he "couldn't fool around with baseball anymore." Wynton had found the love of his life and dedicated himself to becoming the best trumpet player his talent would allow. He studied under the best musicians, played in jazz bands, and attended prestigious music schools. His first album sold 100,000 copies, and in 1983 Wynton won Grammy Awards for both a jazz and a classical album. Today Wynton has produced over one hundred albums and (at last count) has chalked up an impressive nine Grammy Awards and received honorary doctorates at over thirty universities.

Consider This: Talent alone will not give you success. Instead, you must dedicate yourself to excellence, work hard, study the best in the field, and set your sights high.

HALLMARK CARDS

*Every day is a new day, with new possibilities
and unlimited opportunity.*
ERNEST REEVES

Ask people in and around Kansas City, Missouri, "What's so special about your community?" One thing they will probably mention is Hallmark Cards. Few companies have such warmth associated with them. Greeting cards as we know them began to appear some 150 years ago when the Penny Postage Act of 1840 put the cost of mailing letters within reach of almost everyone. The Hallmark company started when eighteen-year-old Joyce Clyde Hall came to Kansas City in 1910. He and his brothers had owned a small gift store in Nebraska, and Hall came to Kansas City seeking a better market. His brother Rollie soon joined him. They opened a store known as Hall Brothers, Inc.

Joyce carried postcards in his store and noticed that they were big sellers. He recognized this trend as the beginning of a greeting card industry. Hall Brothers, which became Hallmark in 1954, now has one of the most prominent art departments in the world. Its creative staff of over six hundred people produces more than ten million greeting cards each year. Joyce led the company until 1966, when his son Donald became president. Under their leadership Hallmark has carefully manufactured high-quality greeting cards designed and produced by some of America's top artists, writers, and printers. It has also ventured into entertainment on its Hallmark and Movies & Mysteries cable channels. The Hall family has created a company proud to be known as one of the best one hundred companies in America and one of the top places for women to work.

Consider This: Do you see the beginning of an infant industry in your midst? If not, look. If so, how are you going to take advantage of it?

THE INTERNET

Getting information off the Internet is like
taking a drink from a fire hydrant.
MITCH KAPOR

When the internet goes down, work is thrown into chaos. Stores can't make sales. Gasoline stations can't pump gas. Entire businesses grind to a halt. It even makes it impossible to binge-watch a favorite online series. So how did this pervasive infrastructure become so indispensable? The original concept was to create a robust network to make communications between computers possible. The incentive was the fear of nuclear war. In 1957 the reality of the Soviet's advanced technology was evidenced by the launch of the Sputnik satellite. With that expertise, they could rain down atom bombs all over America. Thus, connecting important military computers became a high priority. Vinton Cerf and Bob Kahn came up with the idea to create the ARPANET (Advanced Research Project Agency Network.) In 1969 it sent its first message from one computer to another (from UCLA to Stanford). After that, the number of military computers on the network grew.

Within a few years, the concept of email was born. Soon many diverse and independent computers worldwide joined the network, and it became known as the internet. When the dot-com (.com) address was introduced to the internet in 1985, commercial activity took off like wildfire. Further enhanced by a graphical interface called the World Wide Web, the world had a new way to communicate, educate, entertain, and buy online. (And, unfortunately, participate in nefarious activities.) As a result, the internet led to the most profound change in human life on this planet since the industrial revolution. It provided jobs for millions of workers around the globe. It gave entrepreneurs significant ways to start businesses and create new products. And its continued growth influences what happens in our everyday lives.

Consider This: Necessity is a powerful motivation for innovation. Find where a need exists, and create a solution.

DOING THE RIGHT THING

The truth of the matter is that you always know the
right thing to do. The hard part is doing it.
NORMAN SCHWARZKOPF

No team, cause, or organization succeeds at excellence by luck or chance. It is the person or group willing to do the hard things that accomplishes the most extraordinary things. For example, in 1955, Chapter 6, Section 11 of the Montgomery City Code said bus drivers had the authority to demand that Black passengers give up their seats. Rosa Parks had worked all day as a seamstress and was bone-tired when she got on the bus on December 1, 1955. She sat in a row designated for Black people. But as the bus filled, the driver told colored people to move farther back in the bus. Three people complied. Rosa didn't. Her arrest led to a bus boycott that lasted 381 days. It ended not because the Montgomery County government recognized the wrongness of the law but because the Supreme Court recognized Rosa's rights.

In 1939 Howard University proposed a concert in Constitution Hall in Washington, DC, featuring a famous Black singer, Marian Anderson. The petition was refused because Black people were not allowed to perform there. After much unsuccessful negotiation, including pressure from First Lady Eleanor Roosevelt and others, an alternate concert was planned at the Lincoln Memorial. Instead of the few thousand that would have attended at the Hall, seventy-five thousand people of all races heard her performance. The concert became a watershed moment in the advancement of racial equality.

After World War II, Colonel Oveta Hobby, the woman who'd created the Women's Army Corps, stood against the City of Houston's decision to include only white men in an Armed Services Day parade. She demanded that all people who had served be invited to march regardless of race or gender. She won, and the parade went forward.

Consider This: Take a stand for what is just. Then, even if your position is controversial or challenging, dare to hold it anyway.

MARC RANDOLPH AND NETFLIX

What new technology does is create new opportunities
to do a job that customers want done.
TIM O'REILLY

Marc Randolph grew up in Chappaqua, New York, in a family that knew something about technology. (His father was a nuclear scientist.) At his first postcollege job at Cherry Lane Music, Marc headed up the mail-order department. After a few years he moved to Borland International, where he experienced direct-to-consumer marketing by selling software. Marc participated in the heady days of tech startups in California's Silicon Valley, serving in critical roles in several of them. At the same time, Amazon began its rise to power as a book retailer. Impressed by Amazon, Marc decided to replicate that success with a different product. He noticed that a new format for movies called a DVD was emerging. So he decided to sell (and/or rent) movies.

Since DVDs were so new, and he couldn't get his hands on one of them, Marc bought a music CD, put it inside a greeting card, and mailed it to his friend and partner Reed Hastings. This test would prove if the CD could survive being sent by mail. It arrived at Reed's house and worked flawlessly. At that moment they knew they'd stumbled on a workable direct-to-consumer movie business model. Putting together a handful of investors, they started Netflix. After creating an online ordering system, their plan to rent DVDs by mail went into action. Soon they'd grown to millions of subscribers worldwide. Marc left Netflix in 2002, but the behemoth kept expanding. In 2007 it introduced on-demand streaming of movies just in time to meet user demand and technological capabilities. By 2021 Netflix had more than 200 million subscribers.

Consider This: New technologies are being invented daily. And that means opportunity. Do you already have some expertise that can be remolded to take advantage of emerging tech?

CHRYSLER'S DECISION

Be true to your highest conviction.
WILLIAM ELLERY CHANNING

Walter Percy Chrysler was born in 1875 in Wamego, Kansas. His father was an engineer with the Union Pacific Railroad, and young Walter became interested in big machines. As an apprentice machinist, he traveled the railroads and built a reputation as an extraordinary mechanic. Walter was also an auto enthusiast. At the Chicago Auto Show in 1908, he fell in love with a sleek new car called a Locomobile. He bought one for $5,000, even though he only made $4,200 a year (and didn't know how to drive it). His love for this automobile and his mechanical genius led him to take it apart and put it back together to understand how it worked. And although he was later making $12,000 a year with the railroad, he went to work for half that amount as manager of a Buick factory to get in on the automobile craze.

At Buick, Chrysler introduced a series of innovations and was made president of the division within a few years. Soon, however, his ideas clashed with those of General Motors (GM) president W. C. Durant, and Chrysler resigned. Then, in 1921, he was offered the position of president at the ailing Willys-Overland Company and the Maxwell Motor Company. While Chrysler got those companies on their feet, he designed a new automobile with innovations the industry had never seen. In 1924 he introduced the Chrysler, and it wasn't long before even the company bore the name of Walter Chrysler. Chrysler soon acquired Dodge Brothers and began the Plymouth and DeSoto lines. By the time he retired in 1935, Walter Chrysler's company was the second-largest producer of automobiles in America.

Consider This: Salary should not be the only factor to consider when looking for a job. Instead, choose work that provides the best long-term advantage for your desired career.

WALTER WHEELER AT PITNEY-BOWES

Six essential qualities that are the key to success: sincerity,
personal integrity, humility, courtesy, wisdom, charity.
DR. WILLIAM MENNINGER

Many historians find Walter Wheeler a study in contrasts. He admittedly was a hard-nosed executive determined to promote company profit. Yet at the same time he instituted some of the most farsighted employee benefit programs known to any company during his era. Wheeler was educated at Harvard and came to work at Pitney-Bowes when that company made a stamp-canceling machine. By age twenty-seven he had taken a leadership role in the company. In 1920 he spearheaded the project to convince the government that a postage meter was a good idea. When the machine was approved, seven other manufacturers were also allowed to produce devices. But Pitney-Bowes's innovations and efficient workforce gave it an advantage as it produced goods at the lowest cost and claimed the majority of the market.

One of the reasons the company's workforce was so productive was its annual jobholder meetings. These gatherings brought some 250 workers face-to-face with the president and top executives to discuss labor and management issues. This strong emphasis on worker-management communication provided Pitney-Bowes's employees with some of the best working conditions and benefits packages in the nation. In addition, it created a highly motivated workforce. Walter Wheeler devoted fifty-five years of his life to Pitney-Bowes and served as CEO for three decades. His firm belief in making the company responsive to human needs made it one of the most profitable businesses in its industry. Plus, his determination to make his company the best means that today Pitney-Bowes products are the standard machines used by businesses and the United States Postal Service.

Consider This: Human needs count. In the long run, a company can't generate exceptional profits without the enthusiastic support of its workers.

NIK WALLENDA—KEEP YOUR EYES ON THE GOAL

I've trained all my life not to be distracted by distractions.

NIK WALLENDA

We're a product of our past and our vision of the future. Nik Wallenda's career is no exception. Nik was born a year after his famous grandfather, Karl ("the Great Wallenda"), lost his life doing an "easy" tightrope walk in Puerto Rico between two buildings without a safety net. Nik grew up knowing the dangers of his family's business. Nevertheless, he stepped onto a rope at age two and performed before a crowd at age thirteen. After graduating from college, he worried that the tightrope walking entertainment industry was old and outdated.

To make a living with his passion, he couldn't just look at the past. He couldn't focus on past tragedies. So Nik and his wife, Erendira, remade and rebranded the family business with new ideas and challenges. Remembering his famous grandfather's adage, "Fear is a liar," they embraced a respect for the sport's danger. At the same time, they invented new stunts devised to break old world records. Millions watched Nik become the first person to walk over Niagara Falls. They watched him step across a blustery Grand Canyon. He entered the *Guinness Book of World Records* by walking between two skyscrapers (blindfolded!). He also (successfully) repeated the walk that had taken his grandfather's life. Time and again, Nik, Erendira, and his entire family revitalized his family's death-defying sport and made it entertaining for today's world.

Consider This: Respect your past, but don't get stuck in its failures. Begin your own new journey. Put all of your concentration, passion, and creative energies into the task at hand.

JASMINE CROWE—EVERYONE SHOULD EAT

*I heard "no" so many times, but I didn't get defeated
because what I was fighting for was worth it.*
JASMINE CROWE

When Jasmine Crowe volunteered at a food bank in Atlanta, Georgia, she was excited to provide meals for the homeless and needy of her community. But as she helped hand out boxes of food, she became concerned that what they were providing was mainly packaged snacks. She wondered if they could do better. After some research, she found out that a considerable amount of food from grocery stores and restaurants was simply thrown away. This led to her founding Goodr, a company with a goal to reduce food waste by leveraging technology. Her plan was to convince more stores and restaurants that their leftover food should go to nonprofit organizations. After all, the companies could earn tax deductions in the process: a win-win for everyone. It would benefit hungry people, donor businesses, and the environment. Her motto was, "Feed more, waste less."

In 2017 Goodr developed an app that allowed donors to specify what items were available. It then located drivers and arranged to deliver the donated food directly to nonprofits and needy individuals. This resulted in more efficient distribution and less spoilage. As of 2019, Goodr's donors included over two hundred businesses, who diverted over two million pounds of edible foods from landfills and into the hands of needy people. Goodr also worked to open food stores in "food deserts" to give the disadvantaged access to convenient, fresh, and affordable groceries. One of Jasmine's long-term initiatives is to change laws to require grocery stores to donate viable leftover food rather than throw it away.

Consider This: Even when a plan is already in place to address a problem (like hunger), consider if it can be improved. Maybe it's time to reconsider your good and acceptable way of addressing an issue. Reimagine and rethink. Turn something good into something extraordinary.

NAPOLEON HILL

If we abide by the principles taught by the Bible,
our country will go on prospering.
DANIEL WEBSTER

Virtually every salesman has read (and probably reread) Napoleon Hill's classic motivational book *Think and Grow Rich*, first published in 1937. Although it's decades old, it's often considered the grandfather of most other self-help and motivational books. Hill began writing the book at the suggestion of Andrew Carnegie, who wanted him to document strategies for success. Its message is simple, and people who follow it will see results. Hill's primary emphasis was on your personal belief in who you are and what you can accomplish. The messages are uncomplicated but profound: Don't quit too soon. Follow your dreams. If other people think it is impossible, it must be worth doing. There is no such thing as bad luck. The beliefs you choose can make you poor or rich—take your choice.

These simple messages provide a strong foundation for individuals to anchor their lives. Many of the people profiled in the book you are now reading adopted the principles found in Hill's book. (The only other inspirational book mentioned more often is the Bible.) Other leaders have found inspiration by studying character-leaders such as Lincoln, Washington, and Emerson. In contrast, a person with a weak character foundation will find it difficult, if not impossible, to build one under himself while the rest of his world is falling down. Whatever the source, character-building stories can provide a needed lift when circumstances are challenging and success seems improbable. Like the pig who built his house of bricks, those who build their beliefs on something solid will survive the "big bad wolves" of defeat, failure, and rejection.

Consider This: What is your foundation? When things go wrong, where will you turn? What will you do? Where will you go? Make sure you are preparing now for tough times to come.

BEING A MILLIONAIRE

It isn't about how much you make. It's about how much you keep.
SHAQUILLE O'NEAL

Amazingly, there are over twenty million millionaires in the United States. The wide-eyed dream of children, and the more serious dream of college graduates, is to be a member of that elite club (although a million dollars isn't what it used to be). Surveys and opinion polls of young Americans today show that becoming well-off is often a significant life goal. Even with its high-sounding mystique, millionaire status no longer requires a person to be a corporate magnate or a Hollywood idol. Instead, today's millionaires made their money "the old-fashioned way"—with a long-term strategy to live below their income, consistently save, and intelligently invest. Almost anyone with a job can do it (over the long run). In fact, a recent survey found that the top three occupations of millionaires are engineers, accountants, and teachers.

According to Professor Thomas Stanley of Georgia State University, 80 percent of all millionaires (or multimillionaires) are self-made (not inherited). The average millionaire has an ordinary job or owns an ordinary business. For example, Dave Drum took advantage of the camping craze and began Kampgrounds of America. Valerie Freeman, a former business administration teacher, founded the Wordtemps temporary personnel service. These people took ordinary ideas, worked long and hard at making them successful, and turned their hard work into hard-earned dollars. In contrast, many people (but not all) who make extreme salaries (sports stars, entertainers, etc.) often spend their money as soon as they earn it. They invest in get-rich-quick schemes and have little or no savings in later life.

Consider This: Prosperity is based on how hard and long you're willing to work and how consistent and intelligent you are in saving and investing

RITA MORENO

A smooth sea never made a good sailor.
OREN ARNOLD

Rita Moreno was born Rosa Alverio in a small town in Puerto Rico. After her parents divorced she moved with her mother to New York, where they lived in a tenement in the Washington Heights section of Manhattan. Rosa took dancing lessons and was soon able to supplement the family's income by performing. She often imitated popular entertainer Carmen Miranda at parties, bar mitzvahs, and weddings. Rosa seemed to be a natural at performing and landed parts in various children's plays and then in the Broadway production of *Skydrift*, which lasted only seven performances. By the mid-1940s, Rosa had changed her name to Rita Moreno, taking the last name of her stepfather. One of her first big opportunities was dubbing the voices of Elizabeth Taylor and other stars for films being prepared for distribution in Spanish-speaking countries.

Rita broke into the movies at MGM with *So Young, So Bad*. Other films followed, but she was stereotyped as the sultry Latin temptress. Seeing her career going nowhere drove Rita into depression. Finally a story in *Life* magazine brought her back into the public spotlight, and she was given fresh roles. Her revitalized career propelled her to new heights. During her career Rita captured the four most impressive entertainment awards in America. These include an Oscar (*West Side Story*), a Tony, a Grammy, and two Emmys. This feat landed her in the *Guinness Book of World Records*. In 2004 Moreno received the Presidential Medal of Freedom from President George W. Bush, and in 2009 she received the National Medal of Arts from President Barack Obama.

Consider This: Sometimes the awards go to those who can stick it out through the bad times and who can do their best when the good times come along.

ARMSTRONG WORLD INDUSTRIES

*I attribute my success to always requiring myself to
do my level best if only driving a tack straight.*
RUSSELL CONWELL

In 1860 Thomas Armstrong worked for a Pittsburgh glass company, but he ran a small business on the side that made cork stoppers for bottles. Armstrong's slogan for that company was a twist on the motto "Let the buyer beware." His more positive slogan was, "Let the buyer have faith." Plus, unlike other cork manufacturers, he put his name on every bag to make sure people knew his company. He also included a guarantee. Customers soon realized the quality of his corks, and by 1890 his company was the largest cork supplier in the world. Using cork remnants as an ingredient, he expanded his business by manufacturing linoleum. At the time linoleum was a commodity with virtually no known brand names. Armstrong changed that. He knew he produced a superior product, and he wanted customers to know his name.

In 1917 Armstrong began a campaign of informative ads in the *Saturday Evening Post* that offered the reader helpful ideas and information about his product. Although some of his associates thought the ads were too noncommercial, they proved effective and popular with readers. The ads created a strong sense of quality and helped build strong product loyalty. The Armstrong name soon became one of the most well-respected names in floor coverings. In fact, when a 1960 survey about carpeting was conducted, Armstrong ranked fourth in consumer preference—even though the company had never produced carpets. Today Armstrong offers a wide variety of floor coverings, building products, furniture, and specialty items, and its products can be found in buildings worldwide.

Consider This: The company name and its association with quality are an essential part of developing sales and product loyalty.

KELLOGG'S CEREALS

Advertising is to business what steam is to machinery, the great propelling power.

THOMAS MACAULAY

Every morning millions of Americans scoop up spoonfuls of cereal as a part of their breakfast. But several generations ago, no one had ever heard of breakfast cereals. Will Kellogg, born in Battle Creek, Michigan, never finished high school. Instead, in 1879 he sought his fortune in Dallas, Texas, as a broom salesman. He was pretty good and helped the owner turn the ailing business around. He later returned to Battle Creek and worked with his brother John at the family-owned health sanitarium. There, he and John developed a wheat flakes breakfast cereal. The idea was sound, and the Battle Creek entrepreneurs produced forty-two brands of the flakes. But John refused to allow Will to spend much money on the project. When the breakfast cereal market became dominated by rival Charles Post, William looked for a way to bring his own cereals to the market. In 1905 Charles Balin, a patient, offered Will the financing to begin his own company to produce a new idea—corn flakes.

Production began modestly at about thirty-three cases of cereal a day. Then Will started to advertise. He placed an ad that encouraged people to convince their grocer to buy a case of corn flakes, offering cereal boxes to the person who secured such a sale. The plan worked, and by 1909 the company was selling over a million cases of corn flakes a year. Kellogg sensed the value of advertising and spent over $2 million in 1911 to promote his products. During the Great Depression, Kellogg doubled his advertising budget, and sales continued to grow. Today Kellogg's is one of the leading breakfast-cereal brands in the world.

Consider This: When others are afraid to advertise, that is a prime time for you to gain market share through new advertising.

MARSHALL FIELD

Follow the river, and you will get to the sea.

UNKNOWN

Marshall Field was born in 1834 in Conway, Massachusetts. As a teenager, Marshall became a clerk in a dry goods store in Pittsfield, but he left at the age of twenty-two to go west. Landing in Chicago in 1856, Marshall found a job as a clerk and saved his money by sleeping in the store. His first year's salary amounted to $400, of which he saved $200. Within five years he was general manager of Cooley, Farwell & Company and later became a partner. By 1867 Marshall was the principal partner and head of the business. In 1881, with the other partners in retirement, the company became Marshall Field and Company. The firm sustained severe losses in the Chicago fire of 1871, the Panic of 1873, and another fire in 1877. Somehow it continued making a profit.

Field adopted the successful merchandising methods of Stewart in New York and Wanamaker in Philadelphia. Prices were clearly marked for each item. Field sold quality goods and built a reputation on honesty and the Golden Rule. He was also adept at finding and hiring managers with excellent capabilities. Field bought goods worldwide and often paid cash to underbid other stores. Until his death in 1907, Marshall Field used considerable sums of his money to fund buildings for schools. Although his namesake store is now gone, his legacy continues. It includes the Columbian Museum at the Chicago World's Fair (now the Field Museum), a library in his hometown, and significant funding to begin the University of Chicago.

Consider This: Find out what works for others and use the same idea, perhaps improving on it with your own touch and hard work.

KNOX GELATIN

Let us endeavor to live so that when we die,
even the undertaker will be sorry.
MARK TWAIN

Rose Markward married Charles Knox in 1893, and the couple bought a small gelatin business in Johnstown, New York. Rose tested gelatin recipes in her kitchen at home. The ambitious couple also acquired several other companies, including a newspaper, a hardware store, and even a power company. But Rose sold all the companies except her favorite, the gelatin business, when Charles died. Because of her interest in finding new ways of using gelatin, she set up an experimental kitchen to conduct research. Rose's enthusiasm to make something from gelatin showed as the company's profit line tripled from 1908 to 1925, with sales topping the $1 million mark.

Besides being involved in the business operation, Rose became active in the Johnstown community. She founded the Federation of Women's Clubs for Civic Improvement. In 1949 she was named America's Foremost Woman Industrialist by *Collier's* magazine. Rose continued as president of the company until she was ninety years old. She died in 1950 at age ninety-three. Rose Knox was a determined soul who took the business she loved and devoted all her energy to making it a success. In a 1937 interview in *Time*, she stated, "I just used common sense—a man would call it horse sense—in running my business. But from the first, I determined to run it in what I called a woman's way."

Consider This: Your business, career, or job is an extension of your personality. To achieve success, your personality and occupation must meld together like a team.

EDDIE BAUER

*Ideas must work through the brains and arms of good
and brave men, or they are no better than dreams.*
RALPH WALDO EMERSON

Eddie Bauer was an experienced hunter and fisherman, but one fishing trip almost cost him his life. It was in 1928, and his partner had gone to the car while Eddie stayed to pack one hundred pounds of fish. A sudden cold front came through, and Eddie found himself becoming sleepy and disoriented. His partner saved him, but the experience gave Eddie an idea. His family had emigrated from Russia, and he remembered stories of Russian soldiers who wore down-filled jackets to survive the freezing temperatures of Manchuria during the Russo-Japanese war of 1904. Eddie decided to design a down jacket for himself. He showed it to friends, who liked the idea, so he made a few. Eddie's friends told their friends, which resulted in more and more outdoorsmen wanting down jackets. Eddie saw an opportunity, so he patented his design.

When World War II arrived, the United States Army needed cold-weather supplies. Eddie applied for and received a contract to make goose-down-insulated sleeping bags, flight suits, and high-altitude bags. But Eddie did something other manufacturers didn't do. He made sure his name was on each item he made. After the war, his products were instantly recognized by thousands of former servicemen. The end of the war brought an end to Eddie's war contracts and almost meant the end of his business. But Eddie survived by developing mail-order sales. Offering a "100 percent, unconditional, money-back, lifetime satisfaction guarantee," Eddie Bauer created a business that became a friend to nearly every outdoor sportsman who used his quality products.

Consider This: Opportunity may get you started, but you will have to keep finding new opportunities to replace the old ones that pass.

SUCCESS IS MORE THAN TALENT

A dream does not become a reality through magic;
it takes sweat, determination, and hard work.
COLIN POWELL

What makes one person successful while another can make only modest gains? Often we see only the successful person's innate talents as the answer. We often think that if someone is not blessed with talent, no hard work can make a difference. But studies have shown that this is not correct; there is more to success than talent. In fact, the reason for most success is often good old-fashioned hard work. In his book *Developing Talent in Young People*, Benjamin Bloom reported the results of a five-year study undertaken to discover what made some people extraordinarily successful. The study consisted of detailed research into the lives of 120 of the nation's top artists, athletes, and scholars.

Bloom was surprised to find that natural abilities played only a small part in the development of those individuals. The children were often mediocre musicians, baseball players, or math students. Still, Bloom found that they possessed a powerful drive to succeed. They practiced the piano hours every day, rose at five thirty every morning to swim, or spent hours alone working on science projects. Parental support was also a key factor. Parents of successful individuals exposed their children to great ideas and influential individuals. Many made sacrifices to ensure that their offspring received the necessary coaching or training. In his book *Talent Is Overrated*, Geoff Colvin came to a similar conclusion about musicians. He said, "One factor, and only one factor, predicted how musically accomplished the students were, and that was how much they practiced."

Consider This: Opportunity for success often comes from hard work. Are you preparing yourself for opportunity?

MARIANO MARTINEZ INVENTS YUMMY FROZEN GOODNESS

It's an excuse for a fiesta.
MARIANO MARTINEZ

When Mariano Martinez stepped inside a 7-Eleven store one summer's day, something caught his attention. There against the wall was a Slurpee machine. Customers were happily doling out frozen globs into cups. As a restaurant owner, he began to imagine something a little different. What did his customers crave with their enchiladas and tacos? Margaritas! So, what if you married a frozen lime slushie with a bit of tequila? Of course! An adult Slurpee, better known as a frozen margarita. Now, margaritas had been around since the 1930s, made one at a time using blenders. The problem was that this hand-made concoction was never consistent, was sometimes too watery, and took a lot of the bartender's time. But if you could pull a lever and, voilà, out came a glass of yummy, always consistent goodness, it would be a game-changer. Mariano looked for such a machine on the market, but none were available. So he decided to create something on his own.

Since 7-Eleven wouldn't sell him a Slurpee device, he bought a secondhand soft-serve ice cream machine. Then he began experimenting at his restaurant. With just the right amount of this and the right amount of that, he created a perfect margarita mix. His new concoction became an instant hit with his customers. Soon other restaurants wanted his new invention. It didn't take long before Mariano's frozen margarita machine populated bars and restaurants worldwide. Then in 2005, the Smithsonian Museum of American History came knocking—and Mariano loaned them the first frozen margarita machine for their collection.

Consider This: Is there a way to automate a labor-intensive process and improve it? One thing about machines (when they work right) is their consistency. Of course, not everything can (or should) be automated. But the modern world continues to look for devices that will take the drudgery out of everyday chores.

ROLE MODELS

Show me a successful individual, and I'll show you someone
who had real positive influences in his or her life. I don't care
what you do for a living—if you do it well, I'm sure there was
someone cheering you on or showing the way. A mentor.

DENZEL WASHINGTON

Whether we are aware of it or not, the character and personality we develop in our own lives are influenced by observing other people's lives. Your mother probably said something like, "Watch out. You'll become like the friends you hang around with." That proverb is thousands of years old and is as accurate now as it was then. Of course, each person is unique and has their own will. Still we learn about life by watching the actions of others. If we don't consciously select our role models, we'll have less control over who we become. During childhood we rarely have the opportunity to choose. Our initial role models are parents, siblings, or neighbors. Many people simply let happenstance rule who will be their models as they get older. But if we choose wisely, we can hang around people associated with our desired profession or who have the life skills we want to emulate.

In *The Scientific Study of Political Leadership*, Glenn D. Paige examines how many of the most-noted leaders of our time modeled themselves after other great leaders. For example, Oprah Winfrey called Maya Angelou "my mother, my sister, and my friend, from the first day we met." Director J. J. Abrams studied Steven Spielberg's filming techniques until he knew them backward and forward. Then he developed his own ideas. Woodrow Wilson wrote a biography of Washington. John F. Kennedy wrote of those he admired in *Profiles in Courage*. Napoleon read and reread *Plutarch's Parallel Lives*, and Winston Churchill researched the life of his ancestor Marlborough.

Consider This: Purposefully select your role models. Read biographies of people you admire. Make friends with those you want to learn from. Become the master of your own destiny.

SMALL WINS AND BIG SUCCESSES

For every disciplined effort there is a multiple reward.

JIM POHN

Sometimes we expect our American Dream to come true in the form of a million-dollar lottery win or an unexpected inheritance. But if we wait for that big event to occur, we'll likely never see our ship come in. Gambling with your future is a poor substitute for planning. Success is generally the result of a series of small steps, or "wins," said Tom Peters in the journal *Organizational Dynamics*. Only on rare occasions does success come suddenly and unexpectedly. Usually the process is slow. Some steps can be so small that they may not be readily evident. Or you may take a proverbial step forward and two steps back. For example, NASA's goal to put a man on the moon by 1969 did not happen due to a single space shot. It took thousands of small advances in space technology. In fact, the process consisted of both heart-wrenching failures and a few heady successes.

Advancements come from spending a lot of time working toward a goal and persisting when others give up. Participation by other people is often necessary, and you must reward those individuals with appreciation and recognition. Success often comes only after a tremendous number of attempts, so you must try many options. When an idea doesn't work, learn from the error and try another idea or another path. Finally, you must be an optimistic spokesperson for the task, explaining progress to those participating so they'll know something significant is being accomplished. Each advancement may be small, but small wins gain momentum and add up to a big finish.

Consider This: Expect good things to take time and perseverance. Many people give up too soon. Keep going and make those little steps of progress toward your goals.

STEVEN SPIELBERG

*I don't dream at night, I dream at day, I dream
all day; I'm dreaming for a living.*
STEVEN SPIELBERG

How we think has a lot to do with how much we can accomplish. If we believe we will succeed, our chances of success are great. On the other hand, if we cannot see ourselves as successful, we will likely never experience our dreams. William James was a noted American psychologist. He wanted to discover the human factors that led to success. One of the principles that James uncovered was the "as if" technique. Using "as if" means acting as if what you desire is already in hand.

By the time he was thirteen years old, Steven Spielberg knew he wanted to be a movie director. When he was sixteen, his dad helped him get onto the Universal Studios lot and meet with an assistant to an editorial supervisor, Chuck Silvers. They spent the day at the studios, walking and talking about moviemaking. Spielberg corresponded with Silvers during the school year and returned as an unpaid clerical assistant the following summer. Silvers gave him a one-day pass to get past security on his first day. After that Spielberg used his teenage prowess to sneak past the entrance any time he pleased. He shared an office with a purchasing agent, "worked" on the lot doing gofer tasks, and managed to become involved working on some scripts. Spielberg continued to apprentice in the studios for several summers, gradually learning more and more and making friends with the production staff. He became a studio regular, produced a short film, and was eventually offered a seven-year contract. Today Steven Spielberg is one of the world's most renowned film directors.

Consider This: Know what you want to be. Dream your goals. Learn everything you can about what you want to become. Associate with those who can take you where you want to go. Step out with confidence and begin working.

SAM MOORE, AN AMERICAN BY CHOICE

Be honest, work hard, and don't be afraid to take a chance.
SAM MOORE

America has long benefited from the energy and ideas brought by immigrant dreamers with pioneering spirits and can-do attitudes. One such dreamer was Sam Ziady from Beirut, Lebanon. In 1950, when he was nineteen, Sam's father gave him enough money to begin studies at South Carolina's Columbia Bible College. Sam sold Bibles and dictionaries door-to-door during the summer to continue his studies. As he worked his way through undergraduate college and then a master's program at the University of South Carolina, he expanded his business by hiring other students. When Chase Manhattan offered Sam an executive position, he was on the verge of realizing his dream of a banking career.

"Why do you want to work for Chase Manhattan Bank for $7,200?" asked his father when Sam returned to Beirut for a visit. "Security," said Sam. "How much did you make last summer with your door-to-door business?" asked his father. "Seventeen thousand dollars," said Sam. "Why do you need security? You have a master's degree, you are young, and you speak three languages," said his father. He encouraged Sam to expand his success in bookselling. Sam took his father's advice, returned to America, and started the National Book Company. When he became a US citizen, he changed his name to Sam Moore. His book business grew, and in 1968 Sam bought the American division of Thomas Nelson Publishers, one of the world's oldest publishing companies. His biography is called *American by Choice* because, as he said, "Only in America would a Lebanese immigrant have the opportunity to become one of the nation's leading publishers."

Consider This: You are what you are by choice. To achieve success, you must choose your dreams carefully and work smart and hard to bring them to fruition.

WILLIAM DANFORTH AT PURINA

When we do the best that we can, we never know what miracle is wrought in our life, or in the life of another.
HELEN KELLER

William H. Danforth was such a sickly child that a teacher once dared him to become "the healthiest boy in the class." Danforth responded by daring himself to become physically fit and excel in all areas of his life. "I dare you" (to become a better person) became his motto. He graduated from Washington University in 1892 and got a seasonal job in the brick business. Observing that "animals must eat year-round," he and a partner began selling formula feeds for animals. Instead of packaging his feeds in plain bags like his competitors, Danforth recognized the value of a distinctive trademark. He based his company's unique red-and-white checkerboard pattern on the clothing a family in his neighborhood always wore. That hometown, down-to-earth look soon became synonymous with Ralston Purina.

Danforth devoted much of his life to the development of young people. He organized the American Youth Foundation in 1924 to train young people in Christian leadership principles. His book, *I Dare You!*, has gone through countless printings and inspired youngsters and business executives to lead balanced physical, mental, social, and religious lives. In fact, he used his famous checkerboard design to explain his theory of success. Each of the four squares in the checkerboard pattern stood for a character trait. "Physical" life was on the left, "Mental" health on top, "Social" life on right, and "Spiritual" health on the bottom. A balance of all four characteristics was needed to have a successful life. Danforth and his wife established the Danforth Foundation in 1927 as a national educational philanthropy. Although he died in 1955, his philosophy remains relevant today: "Aspire nobly, adventure daringly, serve humbly."

Consider This: What we get from life has everything to do with how we respond to the call to be the best we can be while helping others become the best they can be.

ALEXANDRA CLARK'S SWEET SUCCESS

*There is nothing better than a friend unless
it is a friend with chocolate.*
LINDA GRAYSON

The *Forbes* 30 Under 30 list recognizes entrepreneurs under age thirty who have created something unique, invented something fantastic, or developed something world-changing. And what could be more fantastic than scrumptious chocolate candies? In fact, *Vanity Fair* called Alexandra Clark's Bon Bon Bon chocolate business "crazy unique packaging and flavors only a really stoned Willy Wonka could dream up." A lifelong Detroit native, Alexandra wanted to keep things real, and keep them local. She started her company using a $32,000 insurance payment from an auto accident. She traveled to sixteen countries to learn as much as possible about chocolate manufacturing. With ideas swimming in her head, she looked for funding from the money-people in Detroit. Rejected, but not dejected, she decided to bootstrap the startup herself. She began as a wholesaler but soon opened her door to the public as people clamored for her delicious confections.

What Alexandra has created is not your grandmother's bonbon. Instead, it's a new, fun, and unique re-creation of chocolate candy. Her approach was simple and direct. First, label all the chocolate so that, unlike Forrest Gump, you know what you're getting. Second, use the best chocolate in the world—from Ecuador, Peru, and other cocoa capitals of the world. Finally, add to the yummy fun by adding local (and sometimes extraordinary) ingredients. Her plan and product have taken the culinary world by storm. Now, firmly established as a community icon, the world is beating a path to her creations.

Consider This: Dreams take flight only when you are brave enough to jump away from the everyday sameness and soar into the unknown.

ELLA FITZGERALD

It isn't where you came from; it's where you're going that counts.
ELLA FITZGERALD

Ella Fitzgerald was born in 1918 in Newport News, Virginia. When she was very young, her parents died, and she had to attend school in an orphanage in Yonkers, New York. Ella loved to sing and dance and thought she was pretty good at it. So at fifteen she decided to put her talent to the test and entered an amateur contest at Harlem's Apollo Theater. At first Ella wanted to enter both the singing and dancing contests. But dancing made her too nervous, so she hoped singing would be enough. That proved to be the case as jazz drummer Chick Webb heard Ella perform and hired her on the spot.

Ella's natural talent was polished as she spent time as a vocalist with Webb's band. Together they wrote the hit song "A-Tisket, A-Tasket," based on the old nursery rhyme. Ella's melodious rendition of the song vaulted her to stardom. When Chick Webb died the following year, Ella took over the dance orchestra and became its soloist. Her initial hit recording was followed by many others, among them such classics as "Into Each Life Some Rain Must Fall" and "He's My Guy." Ella's friendly demeanor and upbeat style won the hearts of millions, and she became known as America's "First Lady of Song." The little orphan who decided to take a chance won thirteen Grammy Awards and received the Grammy Lifetime Achievement Award.

Consider This: Many people have talent but are too nervous or self-conscious to let that talent come to the forefront. Step out boldly. Let your talent shine. Give that gift to the world.

UEBERROTH RESPONDS TO THE CAUSE

*The person who says it cannot be done should
get out of the way of the person doing it.*
CHINESE PROVERB

The Olympic games are the greatest spectacle of human athleticism in the world. Held every four years, they shine an enormous light on the host country and the competitors alike. As a result, Peter Ueberroth wanted the 1984 games to come off without a hitch. But he had a massive challenge ahead of him. The XXIII Olympic Games were held during an era of terrorism, skyrocketing budgets, and boycotts. But to Ueberroth, it was precisely those problems that made the plan for the Los Angeles Games even more exciting. In a *Time* magazine article, Robert Ajemian wrote that Ueberroth "has a way of turning whatever he touches into a cause. To be involved in difficult problems with difficult goals lifts him up." To sell his Olympic cause, Ueberroth inspired his workers again and again with stories of climbing up "a majestic mountain."

When one employee asked for a raise, Ueberroth (a volunteer himself) responded, "You shouldn't be working here if you don't understand what we are trying to do." He was saying, "Either buy into this great idea or get out." Great causes have no place for slackers. By motivating and inspiring the entire team of Olympic workers, Ueberroth managed to pull off the Los Angeles Games with little disruption and in the unheard-of financial position with money left over. People responded to the impossible. Ueberroth motivated them with encouragement, helping them visualize in their minds the great thing they were about to accomplish. Everyone wants to be a part of the team that wins, and Ueberroth inspired his team all the way to the gold medal.

Consider This: It is no secret: people from the beginning of time have given themselves, even their lives, for a cause when the leader could articulate a great purpose and inspire the soul.

ELMER ANDERSEN OF H. B. FULLER

All of us encounter, at least once in our life, some individual who utters words that make us think forever.
BENJAMIN DISRAELI

When Elmer Andersen took over the H. B. Fuller company, it was on the verge of selling out to its competitor. Although it had survived for fifty years in the adhesives business, it had only a tiny portion of the market, and its leadership was getting old and tired. Andersen was a thirty-three-year-old sales manager when he took the helm at H. B. Fuller. Nevertheless, he had a dream that the company one day would be great. Toward that end, Andersen instituted comprehensive incentive plans for salesmen, executives, and employees, providing good incentives and benefits. Fifty years later, H. B. Fuller was a Fortune 500 company with over $425 million in sales.

One visionary leader had pulled the company from smallness to greatness. On the occasion of H. B. Fuller's one hundredth anniversary, Andersen reflected on the influences in his life. He recalled his Christian parents, who had died when he was just fourteen years old but had instilled in him the joy of work. He also recalled a grade school teacher who taught him to keep his mind open because "someday an even greater truth may come." Andersen also cited another instructor who had introduced him to the Robert Browning quotation, "A man's reach should exceed his grasp or what is heaven for." These and other influences led Andersen to develop H. B. Fuller into a business whose goals were "to do as well as it could in providing services to its customers and to share the fruits of its rewards with its employees."

Consider This: A leader must care about people, have a vision, and desire to share with others the gifts of his insight.

I LOVE LUCY

*I'd rather regret the things I've done than
regret the things I haven't done.*
LUCILLE BALL

Lucille Ball made TV history—several times. One of the most dramatic was on January 19, 1953. The *I Love Lucy* sitcom featured the birth of her Little Ricky. It was historical because it was the first time pregnancy had been portrayed on a show, plus a whopping 75 percent of homes with TVs tuned in. *I Love Lucy* remains one of the most-watched TV shows in history. But the show almost didn't appear. Although CBS wanted Lucy to do a show, they didn't want Desi Arnez to appear. They were afraid there'd be backlash for portraying a mixed-race couple on television. So Lucy and Desi took to the road and did stage shows all over the country. Their shows were a hit everywhere, so CBS relented. But Lucy and Desi had other stipulations. First, they wanted to perform the show in Hollywood with a live audience. They also required a three-camera setup using actual film (rather than a kinescope). These were all unheard-of conditions at the time. But all of these stipulations were genius.

The *I Love Lucy* show was an instant hit. When they advertised a product, stores were inundated the next day. The three-camera setup gave the studio a fresh, innovative, creative way to film the show. And capturing it on film meant it could be shown in high-quality reruns forever (which it has). The original show ran from 1951 to 1957. It's influenced every sitcom (and other television shows) since. In fact, Desilu Productions created other memorable shows, including *Our Miss Brooks*, *The Untouchables*, *Star Trek*, *Mission Impossible*, and others. Today, *I Love Lucy* appears in reruns (in more than ten different languages) and is watched by an estimated 40 million Americans each year and many more worldwide.

Consider This: Don't take no for an answer. If you really believe in your idea, prove its viability. Renegotiate. Create something brand new.

MAYA ANGELOU

> Without courage, we cannot practice any other virtue with consistency. We can't be kind, true, merciful, generous, or honest.
> **MAYA ANGELOU**

In 1969 Maya Angelou shot into the consciousness of the American people because of her memoir, *I Know Why the Caged Bird Sings*. It quickly became the first nonfiction bestseller by an African-American woman. Maya was sexually molested by her mother's boyfriend as a young girl. In retaliation, her uncle killed the perpetrator. Maya was so stricken by the horror of the incidents that she stopped talking for almost six years. During World War II she moved with her mother to California. There Maya learned to dance and act at the California Labor School, and she showed talent. In the mid-1950s she joined a touring production of *Porgy and Bess*. In 1957 she appeared in an off-Broadway production of *Calypso Heat Wave* and released her first album, *Miss Calypso*.

Angelou joined the Harlem Writers Guild, became a civil rights activist, and served as the Southern Christian Leadership Conference's northern coordinator. She also spent time in Egypt and Ghana, working as an editor and a freelance writer. Continuing her acting career, she garnered a Tony nomination for *Look Away* in 1973 and an Emmy nomination for the *Roots* miniseries in 1977. Her star as a poet began to shine with the release of her book *Just Give Me a Cool Drink of Water 'Fore I Diiie*, which was nominated for the Pulitzer Prize. At Bill Clinton's 1993 inauguration, she recited her poem "On the Pulse of Morning." Until her death in 2014, she served as Reynolds Professor of American Studies at Wake Forest University. She faced many challenges in her life and career, yet she summed up her resilience by saying, "But still, like air, I'll rise."

Consider This: Life can beat you down. Discrimination, hardship, poverty, lack of education, and terror can destroy you. Or you can choose resilience, and you can rise beyond your adversities.

SILLY PUTTY

He that waits upon fortune is never sure of a dinner.

BENJAMIN FRANKLIN

Japan's invasion of rubber-producing countries at the beginning of World War II cut off the world's supply of natural rubber. America responded with research as several companies worked to create synthetic rubber. One promising idea involved the "rubberization" of silicon. Since silicon is derived from sand, many believed rubber made from silicon would be cheap and abundant. Researchers experimented with several compounds in their quest to produce synthetic rubber. One of those experiments involved combining mineral oil with boric oxide. The result was a bouncing putty. It wasn't suitable for what they intended, but it bounced. In fact, the fame of this curious substance circled the globe as researchers tried in vain to find a good use for the strange material. It did, however, become an unusual conversation piece at cocktail parties.

In 1949 the bouncing putty appeared at a party attended by catalog toy retailer Ruth Fallgatter. She showed the new plaything to her catalog designer, Peter Hodgson, who put it in Fallgatter's next catalog on the same page as a spaghetti-making machine. The bouncing putty outsold everything in the catalog except Crayola crayons. When Fallgatter decided not to include the new toy in her next catalog, Hodgson took it as his own product. He named it Silly Putty, copyrighted the name, packed it in colorful plastic eggs, and slowly convinced retailers to carry it. When an article about Silly Putty appeared in a New York magazine, it became an overnight sensation. Within three days of the article's appearance, Hodgson received orders for over 750,000 Silly Putty eggs.

Consider This: Keep your eyes open. Find a popular new product, and make it your own. Market it with enthusiasm until it catches on. Then be prepared for success.

OPRAH WINFREY

I have been driven many times to my knees by the overwhelming conviction that I had nowhere else to go.
ABRAHAM LINCOLN

Oprah Winfrey's childhood experiences may account for her compassion for those in need and for her keen understanding of life's struggles. Born in a small Mississippi town in 1954, Oprah found little stability in her early home life. She moved back and forth between her separated parents and grandmother and eventually rebelled. But Oprah found strength in faith, education, and the performing arts even amid life's uncertainty. While still in high school, she was hired by a local radio station to read the news. Then, as a sophomore at Tennessee State University, she was hired as a reporter for a local television station. From there Oprah became coanchor of a news program in Baltimore and, in 1984, was given a chance to revive a dying half-hour talk show called *A.M. Chicago.*

Her emotional and honest style soon made the show a hit. When its ratings surpassed the popular *Donahue Show*, it was renamed *The Oprah Winfrey Show* and expanded to one hour. Her namesake show ran on 120 channels and grossed $125 million its first year. She soon gained control of her show and, under the auspices of Harpo Productions, eventually reached an audience of forty million viewers a week in 150 countries.

In 1985 Oprah appeared in the movie *The Color Purple* and was nominated for an Academy Award. Always an entrepreneur, she launched her own magazine, *Oprah*, in 2000. Then in 2008, she created the Oprah Winfrey Network (OWN) in a joint agreement with Discovery Communications. Her ever-expanding influence and popularity culminated in being awarded the Presidential Medal of Freedom in 2013.

Consider This: Your beginnings may be rough. But don't let that stop you. Instead, look to the future and leave the troubles of the past behind.

FREDERICK WEYERHAEUSER

Necessity is the mother of invention.

PLATO

The life of Frederick Weyerhaeuser is an example of how American Dreams can come true. Immigrants from Germany, Weyerhaeuser's family had heard of the opportunities in America and had left the village that had been their ancestral home for three hundred years. Arriving in Pennsylvania at age eighteen, Frederick found work as a brewer's assistant, a farmhand, and then as a laborer at a sawmill. He was a good worker and was rewarded. "My wages were raised from time to time," he recalled later. "The secret of this lay simply in my readiness to work. I never counted the hours or knocked off until I had finished what I had in hand." Within a few years Frederick joined his brother-in-law to run his own sawmill in Rock Island, Illinois.

Economic times were rough. Weyerhaeuser had to trade lumber for eggs, meat, and grain. He then traded the food to men to bring logs down the river. At that time, northern Wisconsin and Minnesota were covered with forests. The trees were being discarded as people cleared the land. Weyerhaeuser had the foresight to see that the timber was not worthless and that other parts of the country would soon need it for their growing cities. He bought all of the timberlands he could afford, taking on lumbermen as partners. Weyerhaeuser gained the confidence and respect of many in the lumber trade. He spoke the language of the lumberjacks, was known for his honesty, and made business decisions with intelligent courage. His company grew as the country grew, and Weyerhaeuser became the wealthiest American of his time.

Consider This: What resource are people overlooking that will someday be worth much more than it is worth today?

KEN COOPER'S AEROBICS

*Exercise is a journey, not a destination. It must be continued
for the rest of your life. We do not stop exercising because
we grow old—we grow old because we stop exercising.*

KEN COOPER

Joggers fill parks and streets every day. In fact, thousands of miles of special jogging lanes have been built around the country in the past few decades. Although running has been around forever, it only became an everyday activity for millions a few decades ago. Its popularization can be traced to one person, Dr. Kenneth Cooper. During his thirteen years of service in the United States Air Force, Cooper developed a method for keeping score of aerobic exercise and published the book *Aerobics* in 1968. Cooper's book and his evangelistic promotion of aerobics were significant contributors to the emergence of the jogging boom. As a result of the increased emphasis on exercise throughout the country, Americans experienced a 14 percent reduction in heart disease during the 1970s. In addition, Cooper's message has been carried around the world. "Have you done your Cooper today?" is a frequently asked question in Brazil, and around the globe in Japan, a new 750-acre Cooper's Aerobic Center has been constructed.

Aerobics has caught on because it saves lives and helps people manage stress. With the cost of health care soaring, wellness programs save businesses money and save employees' lives. While the drudgery of work has vanished for many people, the mental stresses of modern life can exact a heavy toll on the body. Exercise relieves stress, helps to eliminate depression, and builds stamina. By now it should be apparent to everyone that jogging and exercise are not simply fads. They have become a regular part of many people's daily routines, particularly those who want to make the best of their lives.

Consider This: What good is it to become wealthy, successful, or famous when you cannot enjoy life because of depression or if you die early because of poor health? Good health must be a high priority in your life.

APRIL 19

JOHN F. QUEENY AT MONSANTO

Determination and gumption will carry a man far.
E. F. GIRARD

John F. Queeny worked hard to see his dreams pay off. After the Chicago fire of 1871, Queeny dropped out of the sixth grade to earn money for his family. He got a job as an office boy in a pharmaceutical firm and slowly worked his way up to buyer. In 1896 he married Olga Mendez Monsanto and moved to St. Louis to become a buyer for Meyer Brothers Drug Company. Queeny saved his money and, in 1899, opened a sulfur refinery on the side. It promptly burned down, costing him $6,000. It took Queeny two more years to save $1,500 in hopes of beginning a chemical shop. As a drug buyer, he was aware of the growing popularity of saccharin, which was purchased from Germany. He needed $5,000 to launch his enterprise. Queeny convinced a saccharin buyer to loan him $3,500 and give him a contract to buy a five-year supply.

In 1901 Queeny opened his new company, naming it Monsanto. Since chemists were hard to come by, especially those who knew how to make saccharin, Queeny imported three PhD chemists from Switzerland. Due to a tight budget, most of the factory was outfitted with used equipment. It was a month before the first small batch of saccharin was made, and when Queeny tasted it, it was not sweet. Something was wrong! But he had promised a victory dinner, and when he arrived at the restaurant, their waiter tasted the substance. "This is so sweet!" he exclaimed. Queeny and his chemists realized their taste buds had been deadened by constant exposure to the saccharin dust. They suddenly leaped to their feet and did a victory dance around the table.

Consider This: What you want may not come out right the first time. Those who find triumph are those who keep trying.

MACK TRUCKS

You don't have to focus on everything to be successful.
But you do have to focus on something.

AL RIES

While other mechanics were busily inventing passenger automobiles, Jack and Augustus Mack had different ideas. At the dawning of the horseless carriage age, the brothers reasoned that there would also be a need for large trucks and passenger wagons. The Macks began experimenting with vehicle construction as early as 1892. First they tried constructing steam-driven and electric-powered wagons but were dissatisfied with the results. So in 1900 the brothers built an unusually rugged vehicle, christened "No. 1," which began its life as a bus that carried passengers around Brooklyn's Prospect Park. No. 1 was later converted into a truck and used for seventeen years in all—not bad for a first-of-a-kind vehicle. In the 1930s Mack trucks were used during an era of rapid American construction, including at the Hoover Dam, the Empire State Building, and the New York City subways.

The Macks produced several buses and trucks known for their durability in the following decade. Vehicle No. 9 became a sightseeing bus, and it remained in use until the 1950s, recording more than a million miles. Of course, other automobile manufacturers were also building trucks and buses. For most of those companies, larger vehicles were a sideline business. Mack Trucks, Inc. retained its focus. In 1910 it created another unique vehicle, America's first motor-propelled hook-and-ladder fire truck. The firm's 1918 AC model was popular during World War I. Its distinctive blunt-nosed design reminded British troops of a bulldog. The truck's tenacious character made the analogy stick and inspired the bulldog logo used by Mack Trucks today.

Consider This: Find your niche in the marketplace and become the best there is. Focus on what you do best.

BETTE NESMITH'S LIQUID PAPER

A person who never made a mistake never tried anything new.
ALBERT EINSTEIN

Bette Nesmith, like many other secretaries in 1951, had a problem. It was difficult to erase when she made a mistake at the typewriter. She had been a freelance artist, and it occurred to her that artists never erase. They simply paint over any errors. With that in mind, Bette tested a variety of concoctions in her kitchen until she devised a paint-like substance that she initially called Mistake Out. Bette convinced the secretaries around her to begin using it. An office supply dealer encouraged her to manufacture the paint. She was willing to try, so she looked for someone to provide financing. Everyone turned the idea down. Finally Bette decided she would have to produce the paint independently.

At first she hired a college student to help sell the product, but the first year's sales amounted to only $1,142.71, and Bette's expenses were $1,217.35. As a single parent, Bette found it hard to juggle her new enterprise and a full-time secretarial position at the same time. So she took a part-time job to spend more time promoting her paint. Next, she hired a chemist to develop a faster-drying formula. She soon took the improved product on the road, demonstrating it to office supply dealers throughout the United States. After giving her sales presentation, Bette would leave behind twelve sample bottles. Eventually, her hard work paid off, and orders began to increase. Liquid Paper Corporation continued to grow and was sold in 1979 for $47.5 million. Although Liquid Paper is much less needed in the computer age, Bette's legacy funds services for unwed mothers and battered women and provides college scholarships for mature women.

Consider This: Even if an idea is good, it still may take the evangelism of a fanatic and the patience of Job before it will finally catch on.

LEADERS AS LEARNERS

The more that you read, the more things you will know.
The more that you learn, the more places you'll go.
DR. SEUSS

Authors Warren Bennis and Burt Nanus reported on a comprehensive study of ninety American leaders in their 2007 book *Leaders: Strategies for Taking Charge.* Well-established leaders in several areas were asked to identify leadership qualities. They never mentioned charisma, time management, or how a person dressed. Instead, they cited character traits. These included persistence, continual learning, taking risks, and being consistent, committed, and challenged. Many leaders (maybe most) were avid book readers. They learned from the people around them. This included the people who worked for them and their customers or clients. And they purposefully studied new strategies and remained open to new ideas and new areas of thought.

Of course, a big concern is what you choose to learn and where you learn it. Not all knowledge is beneficial or valuable. With such a vast amount of information available in the world today, acquiring knowledge, in the words of one leader, is much like "taking a sip of water from a fire hose." Leaders need to be choosy in the knowledge they acquire. They must filter out useless information while paying attention to what really matters. For example, they deliberately seek out information valuable to their specific organization or the market segment they serve. Leaders seek information (from books, speakers, seminars, and other resources) that will answer their own uncertainty about specific topics. They examine failures to learn from them. They look at the future to see how it will affect them. Most importantly, they nurture their interpersonal skills to be good listeners, for without listening, they would never learn.

Consider This: What new areas of thought are you exploring? What is your source of learning? Are your interpersonal skills such that you can learn from those around you?

STANLEY MARCUS'S BUSINESS SENSE

There is never a good sale for Neiman Marcus
unless it's a good buy for the customer.
STANLEY MARCUS

Years ago, Stanley Marcus did a radio ad for a car dealership. Wasn't he the CEO of the prestigious Neiman Marcus department store? Yes. But why did he do it? He was out to show that the same message used to promote high fashion was relevant to car customers. In fact, nothing is more important to a customer than quality and service, no matter the business. Stanley Marcus should know. He learned about customer service from over fifty years of managing one of the most celebrated retail stores in the world. His concern and message to all who would listen was that it was too easy for American businesses to give lip service rather than genuine service. His claim made decades ago is as relevant today as it was then. There are two problems with retailing: standardization and public ownership.

Standardization comes when all buyers hook into the same networks. The result is clear. Everyone carries the same merchandise. Restaurants serve the same canned green beans and french fries. The buyer pays more attention to the price per pound than to the customer's wants and needs. As a result, the customer gets bored and frustrated, and looks elsewhere. The second problem is public ownership. Companies led by families (e.g., In-N-Out Burger, Chick-fil-A), or who have a clear mission (e.g., Disney), are more likely (although not always) to put service and quality before short-term profits. Which businesses break away from the pack? Do they have a secret? Yes. They customize products to meet customers' needs, whether their product is fancy chocolates, haircuts, retirement plans, or high-end electronics. These companies typically have plenty of customers and rack up healthy profits.

Consider This: Give your customers more than they expect, then they will become loyal customers and walking advertisements for your business.

DESKTOP PUBLISHING

What is required is sight and insight. Then
you might add one more: excite.
ROBERT FROST

We live in an era when new technologies emerge in the blink of an eye. There are plenty of ways these technologies could be used to start a new business for the shrewd and inventive mind. Often the best strategy is to find a need and fill it. That means finding an industry doing a task an old, inefficient way and creating a more efficient process using new technology. Such was the case with the computing industry in the late 1970s and early 1980s. Apple Computers grew from a small garage workshop to compete with industry giant IBM. At the same time, fledgling companies such as Microsoft provided innovative software that drove the new industry. One potentially lucrative new market made possible by advances in personal computing was desktop publishing, a term coined by Aldus Corporation's Paul Brainerd. Desktop publishing enables a desktop computer operator, using special software, to create sophisticated layouts that formerly could be produced only by expensive publishing equipment.

Aldus convinced Apple Computers that desktop publishing would be viable in order to form an alliance with them. Thus, when Apple introduced its Macintosh personal computer, a capability that set it apart from other computers was its ability to run Aldus's PageMaker. Since almost every business needed brochures, newsletters, pamphlets, and reports, the market was ripe. Aldus sold more than fifty thousand copies of PageMaker in its first eighteen months of production. Unfortunately, although it had opened the door to desktop publishing, technology never remains static, and those who don't innovate are left behind. Such was PageMaker's fate. Over the years, QuarkXPress became the industry standard. But Aldus (now Adobe) reinvented itself with Adobe InDesign and retook the lead.

Consider This: What innovations in technology are opening up possibilities for new products? How can you capitalize on these product possibilities?

DISNEYLAND

*The idea of Disneyland is a simple one. It will be a
place for people to find happiness and fun.*
WALT DISNEY

Walt Disney began thinking of creating his own park when he took his young daughters to local amusement parks. He would sit on a bench and watch his girls ride the carousel round and round. Other parents and grandparents did the same, but they didn't seem to be enjoying themselves. The parks were dirty and run by workers with cigarettes hanging out of their mouths. So, Disney thought, what if a park were clean and fun for children, parents, and grandparents alike? What if workers (or cast members) were trained to help visitors have a happy time? What if it was the happiest place on Earth?

Initially Disney considered opening a small Mickey Mouse Park at the Disney Studios. The more he thought about it, the more his dream grew. But he lacked financing. Then, when ABC provided Disney with the opportunity to create his own television show, it gave him a brilliant idea. "That's how we'll finance the park!" he declared. Disney convinced ABC to become a key investor in his park and used the TV show to promote it. Every Sunday, America watched Disney's dream grow. Known as Disneyland, the park started as an orange grove and became a wonderland. It was clear that Disneyland would be different from all other parks. Buildings were planned with exquisite detail. Rides were unique, imaginative, and entertaining. Disney carefully orchestrated every aspect of the visitor's experience, from hand-clapping music to patriotic shows and flower-filled gardens. Disney's dream continues today, and his parks are some of the most profitable ventures worldwide.

Consider This: Even an idea that has been around for hundreds of years can be improved. Develop your dream to its fullest potential, and you will stand alone at the top.

JOHN WOODEN

*If you don't have time to do it right, when
will you have time to do it over?*
JOHN WOODEN

John Wooden was the basketball coach at UCLA for twenty-seven years. He never had a losing season. Wooden's teams won seven consecutive national championships, and UCLA posted an eighty-eight-game winning streak that spanned four seasons. Surprisingly, he never talked to his players about winning. Wooden's formula for success was to emphasize constant improvement and performance. He avoided getting his teams "up" because he knew they would eventually end up in a valley. Instead, he concentrated on improving the team's performance. Past games were over, and they could be used to discover problems. These problem areas could always be improved, which meant rigorous preparation toward new goals. "I believe that failure to prepare is preparing to fail," Wooden told his players. But the coach never prepared his teams to play a particular opponent; he prepared his teams to play anyone, at any time.

Wooden preached that success was not outscoring the opponent. It was holding your chin up after the game and knowing that you've given your best effort. Of course, if you've done your best, the score will usually be to your liking when you are deserving. Wooden was also more concerned about a player's character than their ability. A person with good character will respond to adversity by learning and overcoming it. Wooden believed that good players will be honest, consistent, and work together. If those players also have natural ability, they will become true champions. After his death at age ninety-nine, one of his favorite sayings summed up the strategy that guided his life: "Make each day a masterpiece."

Consider This: Should winning or profits be an ultimate goal? Or are those expected by-products of doing something better than anyone else? Which concept will produce the most long-term success?

PROCTER & GAMBLE'S IVORY SOAP

Opportunities are seldom labeled.

JOHN SHEDD

Procter & Gamble's founders thought their original products—candles and twenty-four kinds of soap—were good enough. Harley Procter, son of one of the founders and head of marketing, was anxious to promote a white soap to counter European castile soaps. James Gamble, son of the other founder, had developed such a soap, but it was designated only as White Soap. One Sunday, Harley listened as the minister read from the forty-fifth Psalm: "All thy garments smell of myrrh, and aloes, and cassia, out of ivory palaces, whereby they have made me glad." The next day, he designated the soap "Ivory." Unfortunately, Harley could not get approval for advertising funds. Still, he gathered materials that could be used to promote the soap.

Chemical analyses compared the European soap to Ivory. While some soaps contained fillers, Ivory was 99.44 percent pure. Also, Harley received a letter from a retailer who asked for more of the "soap that floats." After checking, it was found that an error in a stirring machine had caused the white soap to have an additional mixture of air. Since the customer liked the idea, Procter & Gamble adjusted the production of Ivory so it would float. When the company finally approved advertising funds, Harley included those two features in promoting Ivory soap. In the end, Ivory's 99.44 percent purity claim gave it a compelling advantage that rang true with customers and set it apart from its competitors. Advertising for Ivory has kept this original image for more than one hundred years.

Consider This: If your product has some unique or memorable feature, point it out. Play up every discernible advantage, and your customers will remember it.

BANK OF AMERICA

*Life constantly presents the greatest opportunity
brilliantly disguised as the biggest disaster.*

DAVID ICKE

During a disaster, we often find out who can be trusted and who really cares. Such was the case in the days following the massive San Francisco earthquake of April 28, 1906. At 5:12 a.m. the city was rocked by a temblor. Although much of the financial district survived the quake intact, numerous blazes were kindled as ruptured gas lines ignited and the city's water systems failed. Nevertheless, Amadeo Peter Giannini, the founder of the small Bank of Italy on Montgomery Street, traveled seventeen miles from his home in time to reach the bank before the fire did. Since the bank had no vault, Giannini had to hide $80,000 in cash under orange crates in a wagon, which he then drove to his home so that he could hide the money in his fireplace.

Many banks expected to remain closed for months. Giannini reopened his bank on a wharf, loaning money for reconstruction and spearheading an effort to buy shiploads of lumber. Loans were made on a handshake basis. Soon the bank began to get deposits, which before long outnumbered the loans. Giannini had an abiding faith in the people and ran his bank that way. It was his customers' bank, a place where they could feel appreciated. Giannini thought banking should be simple and that transactions should be done quickly. So he introduced branch banking throughout California and eventually offered various services worldwide. Giannini was proud of his achievements in making banks more user-friendly. The tiny makeshift bank on a San Francisco wharf eventually became the Bank of America, one of the largest financial institutions in the world.

Consider This: When you open a business, make it simple and convenient for people to get the services they need.

SERVICE ORGANIZATIONS

There, but for the grace of God, go I.
JOHN BRADFORD

You won't find the Tyler Street Community Service Outreach (CSO) described in Wikipedia. It's too small and obscure. Instead, we envision the Salvation Army, the Red Cross, or Doctors Without Borders when we think of service organizations. Perhaps you support one of them. You should. They help millions each year. But local organizations also help millions. They are small and serve only a specific locality, but they are also important. Often sponsored by churches, synagogues, businesses, universities, or civic organizations, they provide specialized services such as legal help, job training, shelters, food, clothing, or protective care.

Helping others has always been a part of the American DNA. The Tyler Street CSO is typical. It originated as a ministry of Tyler Street Church. Its area of Dallas had its share of people in need. Perhaps by providence, a young man who'd had a tough life came to the church one Sunday. He'd experimented with drugs such as LSD. Because of tormenting flashbacks, he'd committed himself to a mental institution. Then he had an encounter with Christ, and his life turned around. Ray Truesdell was the perfect choice to work with the homeless and down-and-outs. He spoke their language. He sympathized with their plight. He saw through their cons and lies and loved them anyway. God's love changed him, and he extended that love to others in the form of food, clothing, spiritual counseling, and support to help them come back to a productive life. He devoted his life to helping thousands upon thousands of other lives for forty years. The ongoing mission of that CSO, compounded by thousands across America, continues to help those in need.

Consider This: If you have resources, you have the opportunity to help others. Thankfulness is most evident when shared with others who are not as blessed.

JANTZEN SWIMWEAR

The world is starving for new ideas and great leaders who will champion those ideas.

LISA SU

John and Roy Zehntbauer started a small knitting company in Portland, Oregon, in 1910. They soon invited their friend Carl Jantzen to join them. While tinkering with the knitting machinery, Jantzen developed a rib-stitching idea that produced a fabric with excellent stretching qualities. Initially considered for use in sweaters, he used it to make a pair of trunks for a friend who was a member of the Portland Rowing Club. The rower returned to report that the trunks were the best-fitting he had ever worn, and he ordered a full suit for swimming. The swimming suit was also well received, but it was too heavy when wet. Zehntbauer and Jantzen experimented and developed a fabric that provided the proper comfort and lightness.

In 1916 the company introduced its bathing suit made from this stretchable fabric. To promote the item in the firm's 1920 catalog, they included a drawing of a diving girl in a red swimsuit. To their surprise, young men came asking for the picture and put it on their car windows. So Zehntbauer and Jantzen decided to capitalize on the new famous symbol. Renaming their company Jantzen Knitting Mills, they promoted the diving girl in their advertising. As their bathing suits became more popular, they abandoned their other knit lines. By 1922 they stopped using the term "bathing suits," and in 1924 promoted the slogan, "The suit that changed bathing to swimming." From these beginnings, the founders built Jantzen into one of the nation's most innovative and successful swimwear companies.

Consider This: Great logos are gold. Even a good product needs a promotional idea that will catch the public's eye and become a "spokesperson" for the product.

LONGTIME ROCK AND ROLL

What's so fascinating and frustrating and great about life is that you're constantly starting over, all the time, and I love that.

BILLY CRYSTAL

Rock-Ola started in 1927 building record-playing jukeboxes and is still in business today, selling nostalgic jukeboxes and foosball tables. Many people think the Rock-Ola name is a combination of "rock and roll." In fact, the name comes from David C. Rockola. He made mechanical scales when he moved into a more modern growth industry. With the record industry booming and jukeboxes appearing in every café across America, Rockola believed the coin-operated music business was here to stay. And for a while, its sales rose like a rocket. But times changed. Its original place in ordinary cafés across America morphed into a market for jukebox collectors and nostalgic restaurant locations. By adapting his machines to keep pace with changing consumer tastes and advances in electronic wizardry, Rockola kept his business viable while others failed. The company remained in the family past his ninetieth birthday.

Antique Apparatus acquired the Rock-Ola Corporation and name in 1992. They continued updating the machine to keep pace with the home entertainment and commercial markets. In 2019 Games Room Company bought Rock-Ola and refocused the brand toward the luxury entertainment market. Even though the brand has been passed down from the original family and its original intent, Rock-Ola maintains its longtime reputation. It gives its customers what they want, from futuristic machines with bubble tops and light shows to nostalgic 1950s models that allow customers to select records using a telephone dial. The tenacity of this brand illustrates that even when the original era of rapid growth levels off, companies can adapt their product to a changing modern market to survive.

Consider This: Once you find something you do very well, stick with it. And if the market changes, refocus and retool your product to meet the wants and needs of a new generation.

STEPHEN CANNELL OVERCOMES DYSLEXIA

You have set yourselves a difficult task, but you will succeed if you persevere; and you will find a joy in overcoming obstacles.
HELEN KELLER

We often see the final product of someone's work and immediately decide, "The person who created this has it all together." Not necessarily so. Many (maybe most) achievers have to overcome challenges to arrive at their destination. Stephen J. Cannell was convinced that he was a loser as a kid. He attended private schools but flunked classes almost every year and repeated three grades. Although there was little known about it at the time, Stephen had dyslexia. He often saw words and numbers transposed. "Dog" was "God," and "123" was "321." And many words were just scrambled lines and dots. Because of this, he had trouble reading, writing, and doing math. Many thought it impossible that Stephen would perform anything but the most rudimentary jobs.

But Stephen didn't give up on himself. What he lacked in academic talent he made up for with grit. He persevered through college and went to work for his father and then at Universal Studios. Even though he had trouble putting ideas on paper, he thought in stories. Although he admits he was "scared to death," he finally wrote and sold his first television script for the series *It Takes a Thief* for Universal in 1968. He kept writing scripts for existing shows and finally created his own series. That began a string of successful shows, including *The Rockford Files*, *Baretta*, *The A-Team*, *Baa Baa Black Sheep*, and others. Cannell became an internationally known producer-writer and produced dozens of successful TV series. He summed up his career by observing, "Failure in school does not mean failure in life."

Consider This: When we overcome a weakness (education, handicap, personal issues), we often end up with more extraordinary skills in that area than those who never had to struggle.

TRUETT CATHY IS CLOSED ON SUNDAY

How do you identify someone who needs
encouragement? That person is breathing.
TRUETT S. CATHY

When Truett Cathy left military service after World War II, he started the Dwarf Grill restaurant in Atlanta, Georgia. Since he lived next door to the restaurant, he worked all day, every day. But he didn't work on Sunday. Having become a Christian at the age of twelve, Truett felt that he could not be robbed of his day of rest. "If it takes seven days to make a living," he often said, "I ought to be doing something else."

Renamed the Dwarf House, business was successful, and Truett enjoyed experimenting with new dishes to serve his patrons. Some concoctions were well received, and some were not. But in 1961, one of his new ideas stood out above all the rest—a pressure-cooked chicken breast served on a sandwich. He called it a Chick-fil-A. Since it was so popular, Truett decided to try his sandwich in a fast-food location at Greenbriar Mall in Atlanta. Customers loved his sandwich, and his little site outsold every other food place in the mall (even though he was closed on Sundays). Truett was a stickler for quality. He kept his restaurants private, rather than creating a public franchise, to maintain consistency and quality in all stores. He insisted on superior customer service ("How may I serve you?"), giving his employees opportunities for growth, and his closed-on-Sunday philosophy. Teenage employees of Chick-fil-A stores have a chance to receive college scholarships. Many of them have also become Chick-fil-A store owners/managers. Even without Wall Street's money (and stockholder pressures), Chick-fil-A has become one of the largest restaurant chains in the world.

Consider This: Stick to principles that make your ideas work, even if they go counter to popular wisdom.

CAROL CHANNING'S BIG BREAK

Laughter is much more important than applause.
Applause is almost a duty. Laughter is a reward.
CAROL CHANNING

Young people hear it all the time: "Without experience, I can't hire you." But how does one acquire the needed experience? Perhaps you have to convince an employer that you're worth a reasonable risk. Carol Channing was a drama major at Bennington College, and her ambition was to be on Broadway. During her college winter break, each student was encouraged to go out into the "real" world to seek a job in their major. Carol hoofed it to New York and went straight to the William Morris Agency, one of the most prestigious talent agencies in the world. With a client list that represented the biggest superstars of the day, they had no use for a college student. They wouldn't even give Carol a chance.

But Carol refused to give up. She camped out in the waiting room with other actors, pretending to be just like them. Suddenly, a door opened. Someone official stepped into the room. They pointed a finger (at another actor) and said, "You!" Carol jumped to her feet. This was her chance. She marched into the president's office like she knew what she was doing. She sang one tune but drew no response. She tried again, putting her whole heart into the song. No response. The agent got up to escort her out. Fearlessly (she had nothing to lose), Carol launched into another song. "Wait, my grandmother used to sing me that song," the agent said. Carol was hired. In her career she created the star character in *Hello, Dolly*, won a Tony award, and appeared in countless other shows and movies.

Consider This: Don't be afraid to step forward and be counted. When an opportunity knocks, be the first to jump up and say you'll do it. You never know where it might lead.

LANDING ROCKETS

*Space exploration is a force of nature unto itself
that no other force in society can rival.*
NEIL DEGRASSE TYSON

Beginning in the 1950s, one of the most expensive problems of going into space was the cost of each launch. Millions of dollars were burned up in a matter of seconds as a payload was hurled into space. Beginning in 1981, the space shuttle program introduced a partial solution—a vehicle that could be launched, landed, and launched again. But there were still two problems. First, it took months to get a shuttle ready for a relaunch. Plus, the launch vehicles (rockets) were lost after each trip. So the next step in space travel was reusable launch systems. The idea that a rocket could be reused quickly (not after months of expensive refurbishment) would make each launch much less costly. It would also open up space to a wider variety of projects, including expanded human space travel. But getting reusable rockets to work was not easy.

Because NASA's budget wouldn't sustain research, the idea waited for independent entrepreneurs. One new enterprise was Elon Musk's SpaceX. His first rocket launch (Falcon 1, 2006) was a disaster. It took four tries to achieve success. SpaceX tried to recapture the rockets in these early flights using a parachute system. It didn't work. In 2011 SpaceX started experimenting with a powered landing system for its Falcon 9 rockets. It took many test flights with prototypes before a rocket (Orbcomm OG2-M2) successfully landed in December 2015. In the meantime, Blue Origin, headed by Jeff Bezos, also had a successful vertical landing with its New Shepard (suborbital) booster in November 2015. From those moments onward, space travel became less expensive. With many other advances in the offing, the sky's the limit.

Consider This: The impossible becomes possible with imagination, creative thinking, and unrelenting experimentation.

HARRY S. TRUMAN

The buck stops here.

HARRY S. TRUMAN

At the outbreak of World War I, young Harry Truman wanted to stand up and be counted. But since he was virtually blind in one eye, he had to memorize the eye chart to pass the physical exam. Once in the US Army, he excelled and rose quickly to the rank of captain. His most challenging assignment was commanding an unruly artillery battery in France. Harry shook in his boots as he faced the men for the first time. The soldiers made bets between each other about how long their new captain would last.

Soon after taking command, Truman's battery was sent into battle. The troops pounded a German position with the intention of quickly moving back to safety before fire could be returned. Things started to go awry. The horses needed to move the artillery pieces arrived late. The weather was stormy, and the gun carriages became stuck in the mud. Before Truman's unit could retreat, the Germans opened fire. With shells falling all about, the Americans began to scatter. Truman stood his ground and yelled at the top of his lungs, calling them back to their posts. They listened. When the men were gathered back in, he reorganized them and marched them to safety. None of his troops were lost in action. As a result, Truman won their allegiance for the duration of the war. This critical event in his life helped Truman define himself and his leadership capabilities. After the war and after failing in business, Truman entered politics. He rose from a local commissioner to US senator to vice president of the United States. Upon the death of Franklin D. Roosevelt in 1945, Truman became our nation's thirty-third president.

Consider This: If you want people to follow and respect you, take a stand for integrity when others seek the easy way out.

JOHN D. ROCKEFELLER

If you want to succeed you should strike out on new paths,
rather than travel the worn paths of accepted success.
JOHN D. ROCKEFELLER

The direct approach is often best when trying to resolve strife. Working through third parties can take the personality out of any negotiation. Listening to individuals who have problems, talking directly to those who are hurting, and seeing for oneself what is really happening can quell the storms of mistrust and anger. John D. Rockefeller knew he had a fight on his hands. But he also knew how to communicate. And he was willing to step forward. For two years, Colorado miners had staged a bitter and violent strike. Rockefeller decided to approach the miners directly because there was no resolution to the conflict in sight. After doing his homework about the reasons for the strike, Rockefeller was prepared to make the best of a bad situation and went to Colorado to see, talk to—and listen to—the disgruntled workers.

At a meeting with a group of miners that could quickly have become a lynch mob, Rockefeller began by saying, "This is a red-letter day in my life . . . I am proud to be here, and I shall remember this gathering as long as I live." He mentioned that he had visited all of the mining camps. He'd visited the miners' homes and met their wives and children. He felt that he and the miners were meeting in a "spirit of friendship." Making friends with the "enemy" enabled the opposing sides to begin to see eye to eye, and they soon moved toward a solution to their problems.

Consider This: People who have ill feelings about each other will seldom agree on anything. On the other hand, friends will make a valiant effort to reconcile differences.

FRED ROGERS' NEIGHBORHOOD

Those of us in broadcasting have a special calling to give
whatever we feel is the most nourishing that we can for our
audience. We are servants of those who watch and listen.

FRED ROGERS

Perhaps no television personality affected so many lives as did Fred Rogers. From 1968 to 2001, he welcomed viewers to his neighborhood, where it was always a "beautiful day." Fred was an unlikely TV star, not boisterous or over-the-top, but unassuming, gentle, and quiet. What made him appealing was his realness. His genuine love and care for his audience. His ability to take complicated subjects and boil them down to something even kids could grasp.

Fred's first college degree was in music. Then, fascinated with the emergence of television, he took a job at WQED in Pittsburgh. He worked first as a floor manager for music programs and then became a puppeteer for *The Children's Corner*. He continued his education and received a divinity degree in 1962. The church encouraged him to use his knowledge and skills in children's entertainment. Although he had a brief stint in Canada on a program called *Misterogers*, he soon returned to Pittsburgh to create his signature show, *Mister Rogers' Neighborhood*. He wrote the scripts and songs and (of course) appeared in all the shows as a friendly neighbor. The show's contents were often related to behavioral and social problems. A particularly famous episode dealt with overcoming racism when many public swimming pools were segregated. He invited a Black policeman to share a kid-size swimming pool, where they washed their feet together. Rogers received four Emmys and many other accolades. One of his red cardigans was retired to the Smithsonian's collection of Americana.

Consider This: Servants can also be leaders. Leaders produce changes in the people they encounter. When your life sets a standard for fairness, decency, and honesty, it has a lasting effect on all those you meet.

THE MOTHER OF MOTHER'S DAY

A mother's arms are made of tenderness,
and children sleep soundly in them.
VICTOR HUGO

Anna Jarvis was never a mother herself. The daughter of a Methodist minister, she became a schoolteacher, worked as an advertising executive with an insurance agency in Philadelphia, and spent fifteen years caring for her ailing mother. Anna never married. After her mother died in 1905, Anna wanted to find a way to honor her mother's memory. She remembered a Sunday school lesson her mother had taught. In it, she'd said, "I hope and pray that someone, sometime, will found a memorial mothers day commemorating her for the matchless service she renders to humanity in every field of life. She is entitled to it." Anna found a connection between her mother's wish and a yearly commemoration held in Virginia. This event, called Mother's Friendship Day, was created to help heal the emotional wounds of those who had lost sons during the Civil War. Anna thought it ought to be expanded to honor all mothers.

Obtaining a patent copyright for the phrase "Mother's Day," Anna explained her idea to state and federal government officials. She even approached President Woodrow Wilson with a persuasive argument for making the day a national celebration. Finally, Anna's years of persistence paid off when Wilson signed a proclamation in 1914 declaring Mother's Day a national observance. Once the celebration was deemed official, Anna worked to keep Mother's Day from becoming too commercialized and ensured that honoring mothers remained the prime emphasis of the day. Her efforts spread throughout the world. When Anna died in 1948, forty-three carnations were placed on her grave to signify the forty-three nations that had adopted "her" day.

Consider This: Who is it that you should honor? Do you feel strongly enough about a cause to give your time and energy to make it happen?

BLACK AND DECKER

No idea is worth anything unless you have the guts to back it up.
AL DECKER

S. Duncan Black and Alonzo Decker joined together in 1910 to start the Black & Decker Company. Black sold his prized Maxwell car for $600, and Decker borrowed $600 to launch the enterprise. At first they built a milk bottle–capping machine, a candy-dipping machine, and other devices. In 1916 their most successful machine for the industrial market was introduced—an innovative handheld portable drill with a pistol-grip trigger. Black and Decker built a showroom on wheels and traveled throughout the country to promote their drill and other tools. In 1929 they equipped a Travel Air monoplane as an airborne showroom. Unfortunately, in 1930, when they attempted to enter the consumer market with a washing machine, they priced it too high for the economically depressed era, and the venture was abandoned.

During World War II the company built a wide range of portable industrial tools. After the war the two noticed a small newspaper article describing how workers stole electric tools from their companies to use personally. Black and Decker felt the time was right to tap the consumer market. They redesigned their portable drill as a smaller and simpler device, this time with a lower price and aimed at the home market. Their production expertise enabled them to market their electric drill for only $16.95. This price was as low or lower than that offered by most competitors. It sold like gangbusters. Building on that success, Black and Decker designed many successful, low-priced, high-quality, do-it-yourself tools. Over the years, they acquired other brands. By 2017 their portfolio included consumer and professional tools by brands such as Black+Decker, DeWalt, Stanley, Craftsman, Irwin, Bostitch, Porter-Cable, and more.

Consider This: Often, the key to expansion is to do what you do best, but perhaps expand the same idea to a fresh market.

BILL VEECK'S HOME RUNS

The most beautiful thing in the world is a ballpark filled with people.

BILL VEECK

Bill Veeck left a lasting impression on baseball. As the owner of several clubs, he was a master of hype. He introduced the exploding scoreboard, placing players' names on uniforms, after-game fireworks, bat night, fan appreciation night, and a host of other special ballpark promotions. No doubt about it, Veeck knew how to draw a crowd. In 1948 his Cleveland Indians attracted 2.6 million fans, an attendance mark that stood for more than a dozen years. Who could forget the night in 1951 when the inventive Veeck sent three-foot seven-inch Eddie Gaedel to the plate to bat for the St. Louis Browns? Eddie wore the number 1/8 on his uniform and drew a walk.

Veeck constantly learned from the people around him: the players and fans, and the business types. Veeck read five or six books every week of his adult life. Baseball was not his only interest; Veeck was an expert on tropical fish and cultivated rare strains of flowers. He knew virtually everything there was to know about dogs and horses. People remember Veeck as a "people person." He never used obscenities; he had the door to his office removed so that anyone could see him anytime. Veeck would often take off his shirt and sit in the bleachers with the fans during games. He always wanted to know what they thought and what ideas they had. Bill Veeck paid attention to what the fans wanted, and then he figured out ways to make it happen. Veeck was inducted into Baseball's Hall of Fame in 1991.

Consider This: Do you stay in touch with the "fans," your customers? Do you really know what they want? Isn't it time you found out?

DRESS YOUR BUSINESS FOR SUCCESS

The clothes make the man.
LATIN PROVERB

Much has been said about the concept of individuals "dressing for success." But what a business "wears" also makes a difference to customers and employees. For instance, when people enter the national headquarters of Frito-Lay, they see a large bowl of hand-selected chips. They're all carefully chosen to represent the best snacks the company produces. A customer walking into Sewell Cadillac of Dallas finds a showroom filled with beautiful antiques. Trammell Crow, one of the largest real-estate developers in the United States, made a fortune constructing warehouses. But his were different. They offered attractive buildings, first-class offices, and manicured lawns with fresh flowers and shrubs. Part of the continued success of the Disney theme parks is their constant attention to authenticity and cleanliness. Likewise, Chick-fil-A restaurants are strict in the upkeep and cleanliness of their stores. A famous admonition to restaurant workers is, "If you have time to lean, you have time to clean."

It should not be surprising that these companies are among the top producers in their fields. Their concern about public perception carries over to their attention to the other details of the business. There are probably small mom-and-pop stores you are familiar with that have a reputation for always being attractive and pleasant. Clear signs that a retail store is in trouble include sloppily arranged items on the shelves, a parking lot that is not swept, and clerks that can never be found. A company that pays attention to its public image dresses the entire organization for success.

Consider This: How is your organization presented to the public, customer, and employee? Are you concentrating on getting the details right?

THE CHIP THAT CHANGED THE WORLD

We expected to reduce the cost of electronics, but I don't think anybody was thinking in terms of factors of a million.
JACK KILBY

That phone in your pocket is there today because of Jack Kilby. It is said that his invention of the integrated circuit (IC) was the most important innovation since the electric light bulb. An IC can hold millions of circuits on a chip smaller than the head of a pin. It's the heart of your personal computer, smartwatch, cell phone, television, and so much more. In your car, it determines your engine's correct fuel mixture and senses if you're getting out of your traffic lane. Only a few decades ago, any of these tasks would have required a house-size computer. But with a tiny IC, the billions of calculations needed to control these devices are performed in nanoseconds.

At Texas Instruments, the young engineer Jack Kilby didn't have enough seniority to take days off for a vacation. So instead, he stayed in the lab and decided to fool around with the problem. He understood that complicated circuits required the interconnection of transistors, diodes, rectifiers, and capacitors, each made from a different substance. Jack reasoned that if all of those components could be fashioned from the same material, the resulting circuitry would be smaller, cheaper to manufacture, and more reliable. In September 1958, Jack put his idea to the test. He demonstrated a strange contraption made of semiconductor material and wires glued to a slide. The invention was the first integrated circuit, and this grandfather of the chips provided the foundation for today's enormous computing and electronics industry. Jack Kilby and Robert Noyce (who independently made a similar discovery a few months later) are credited as coinventors of the integrated circuit.

Consider This: Sometimes fooling around with a problem is the best advice. Consider possibilities. Search for a new way to approach a problem. Your idea may change the world.

CHANG APANA—A MODEL FOR GREATNESS

My heroes are those who risk their lives every day to
protect our world and make it a better place—police,
firefighters, and members of the armed forces.

SIDNEY SHELDON

In 1904 the soft steps of policeman Chang Apana approached a building in a dangerous part of Honolulu's Chinatown. Apana knew that a group of men operated a gambling den in a hidden upstairs room. He slipped by guards stationed around the building. At the top of the stairs, he reached for the coiled bullwhip that hung on his belt. Standing barely five feet tall, he threw open the door to the gambling hall and stepped into the smoke-filled room. Forty rough and hardened men turned their eyes toward Apana. They gasped. All of them knew Chang's reputation as a tough but fair cop. To escape the kiss of his leather whip, all forty surrendered without incident. Although many states had Jim Crow–type laws preventing Chinese citizens from holding significant jobs, Chang Apana bucked the trend. When historians looked back on the twentieth century, they named Chang Apana one of the hundred most influential people in Hawaiian history.

That's not his entire story. When novelist Earl Derr Biggers wrote his first mystery novel in 1925, he set it in Honolulu. Named *The House Without a Key*, the book introduced Charlie Chan, a Chinese-Hawaiian policeman modeled after Apana. (Today one of Honolulu's most popular restaurants is named House Without a Key.) Chan appeared in many other novels and movies. Apana loved the Charlie Chan movies and was proud to be honored by them. Another author, George Lucas, vacationed in Honolulu in the early 1970s and heard stories about the whip-wielding policeman. Many believe Indiana Jones was inspired by Apana's legend.

Consider This: It doesn't matter if you're five feet tall or seven feet tall. What matters is your professionalism, honesty, integrity, and enthusiasm for doing what's right.

FLIGHTSAFETY INTERNATIONAL

The best safety device on any aircraft is a well-trained pilot. That's our motto, and I believe it.
ALBERT UELTSCHI

Al Ueltschi (pronounced *Yule*-chee) was a military pilot trainer before World War II. Ueltschi particularly remembers when he fell out of the plane as he was demonstrating a snap roll. He managed to struggle out of his seat and pull the parachute's rip cord just in the nick of time. Inspired by the likes of Charles Lindbergh in the 1930s, Ueltschi began flying as a teenager. After World War II, as he piloted Pan American World Airways chairman Juan Trippe around the globe, he noticed a swell of interest in business travel. Ueltschi also noticed that, except for the military, there were few places where pilots could acquire training. So with $10,000 he obtained by taking out a second mortgage on his house, Ueltschi opened his first training facility in a leased space at New York's LaGuardia Airport.

Ueltschi was also aware that small plane manufacturers wanted to get out of the pilot-training business, so he contracted with the manufacturers to provide that service. Several corporations that employed pilots became his first backers. Ueltschi sold them five years' worth of training to get the capital he needed to purchase his first flight simulator. Al Ueltschi continued to work as a pilot for Pan Am until 1968 when his FlightSafety International went public. Aircraft manufacturers increasingly became convinced that Ueltschi's company could provide better training. As a result, FlightSafety grew to include dozens of simulators. The company also broadened its curriculum to include simulation training for nautical shipping firms and power company employees. At age ninety-five Al sold his business to Berkshire Hathaway for $1.5 billion.

Consider This: Can you offer a service for a company superior to its own in-house service?

HOLIDAY INNS

*My own success was attended by quite a few failures
along the way. But I refused to make the biggest mistake
of all: worrying too much about making mistakes.*
KEMMONS WILSON

Before World War II a large portion of the hotel-motel industry catered to the business traveler. After the war, families began to take vacations across America. The nation's new interstate highway system was expanding, automobile production had resumed, and postwar affluence put travel within reach of millions of American families. In 1952 Memphis businessman Kemmons Wilson took his family on vacation. Unfortunately, he repeatedly found uncomfortable, inconsistent, and overpriced lodgings. As a result, Wilson believed that the hotel-motel market was "the greatest untouched industry in the country." He opened his first Holiday Inn motel on the outskirts of his hometown of Memphis, Tennessee. It featured 120 rooms, each offering a private bath, air-conditioning, and a telephone (amenities not found in many roadside lodgings of the day). Other features were a swimming pool, free ice, free parking, and a kennel. Children under the age of twelve stayed free. His brand, which became known as "The Nation's Innkeeper," set new motel standards and forced competitors to develop better and more traveler-centric inns.

This first Holiday Inn offered a wide range of amenities that were revolutionary for the hotel-motel industry of the mid-1950s. Kemmons Wilson's idea proved to be a major success, and his hotels began appearing across the country. The company went public in 1957, and its entire offering was sold on the first day. The first international Holiday Inn was built in Montreal in 1960, and in 1968 the company opened its one thousandth hotel. Wilson retired in 1979, but his grand idea changed how all travel motels and hotels operate today.

Consider This: If something bothers you, it probably bothers many others. Is this a business opportunity?

FROM FAILURE TO SUCCESS

> I no longer worry about being a brilliant conversationalist.
> I simply try to be a good listener. I notice that people
> who do that are usually welcome wherever they go.
>
> **FRANK BETTGER**

Success usually has less to do with one's innate talent than it does with one's attitude. Some people's lives are guided by negative attitudes, and they handicap themselves and never recognize their potential. Other people learn that by changing their perspective, they can improve their chance of realizing their dreams. The power that attitude can exert is illustrated by Frank Bettger in his autobiography, *How I Raised Myself from Failure to Success in Selling*. Frank started out as a baseball player in the minor leagues. He had ability but was traded from team to team, often at a lower salary. Then someone told him why he wasn't getting anywhere: He had no hustle and no enthusiasm for the game. Frank agreed and determined that he would improve his attitude. He turned his career around and was soon signed by the St. Louis Cardinals.

When Frank left baseball and embarked on a career selling insurance, he found himself in the same boring mold that had plagued him in the minors. Frank was getting nowhere fast. His sales were mediocre, and he wasn't enjoying what he was doing. The answer proved to be the same one that saved his baseball career. Frank deliberately cultivated enthusiasm for his work. His improved attitude helped him move to the top of the sales force. Although Frank's solution may sound simplistic, it contains a key ingredient to the recipe for success. His daily mantra was, "If you don't *feel* enthusiastic, *act* enthusiastic. Soon, you'll *be* enthusiastic. Double your enthusiasm and you'll probably double your income."

*Consider This: Are you enthusiastic about your work? Are you **deliberately** cultivating enthusiasm?*

ANDY GRIFFITH

*I was being laughed at. I hated it, so I made an adjustment
to control the situation. All comics learn that.*

ANDY GRIFFITH

Actor and comedian Andy Griffith was born in Mount Airy, North Carolina. He attended the University of North Carolina at Chapel Hill. He considered becoming a minister at one time but soon decided on an entertainment career. For seven years, he appeared as Sir Walter Raleigh in the Carolina Playmakers' production of *The Lost Colony*. He also taught music in Goldsboro and performed at various functions. He was once scheduled to appear before the same group a second time and was forced to develop a different act. The result was a monologue based on a joke called "What It Was, Was Football." Orville Campbell, head of a small recording company, heard Andy's act and asked him to make the comedy routine into a record. A Capitol Records executive listened to the recording on the radio and signed Andy to a contract.

Griffith made his first nationwide appearance in January 1954 on *The Ed Sullivan Show*. "I was not an overwhelming success," he admits. Continuing to perform his act in the South, Griffith read the Mac Hyman novel *No Time for Sergeants*. He believed he could play the part of Will Stockdale better than anyone else. He was persuasive with the show's producer and got the part for the TV production, played 354 performances on Broadway, and starred in the movie version. In 1960 the William Morris Agency got Andy together with Sheldon Leonard. He created the pilot for *The Andy Griffith Show*, which was a spin-off from the popular *Danny Thomas Show*. *The Andy Griffith Show* lasted eight years on television, often commanding the number one position in the national Nielsen ratings.

Consider This: Sometimes you just have to keep trudging along, looking for the breaks that will move you one step further down the road toward success.

WHAT THE CUSTOMER REALLY WANTS

To earn the respect (and eventually love) of your customers,
you first have to respect those customers. That is why Golden
Rule behavior is embraced by most winning companies.
COLLEEN BARRETT

Some of the most successful American companies have a reputation for aggressively seeking out what their customers really want. For example, Sam Walton visited each of his Walmart stores every year. He made a point to talk to the salespeople on the floor and the customers. He worked in his corporate office only a half day each week. He spent the rest of the week wandering around his various stores. Similarly, a former chief operating officer at PepsiCo spent as much as 40 percent of his time on the road to find out how business was faring on the front line. At Hewlett-Packard, computer engineers often leave their work on display so that coworkers passing by can play with it and offer their comments. At 3M all of the corporation's research and development people take part in sales calls to see what the customer wants and thinks. Former Apple chairman Steve Jobs often answered service calls to see what his customers liked and hated about his products.

Take a look at the tactics of successful companies. Many of them regularly expose employees to the sales floor, the customer service department, or online comments. No matter their job, be they accountants, assembly-line workers, or executives, finding out what people really think of the company's products is golden. There is simply no substitute for direct knowledge. Statistics, reports, computer printouts, and seminars cannot accurately tell what is happening in the marketplace. To gain an accurate understanding of what people feel and what they want, you have to get out of your daily rut and find out for yourself.

Consider This: Are you sitting in a corporate ivory tower, believing that you really know what's going on in the sales trenches? Wake up, and get out there and find out for yourself!

PEPPERIDGE FARM

An enterprise when fairly once begun should
not be left till all that ought is won.
WILLIAM SHAKESPEARE

Life throws you curveballs. You may set out wanting to do X and do Y instead. And in the long run, Y may be much more enjoyable and profitable. Margaret Rudkin had that experience. She'd never baked a loaf of bread in her life. But her young son had asthma, and the doctor suggested that she bake whole wheat bread from only natural ingredients as part of her son's treatment. As her son remembers, the first loaf came out like a brick. But gradually, as Margaret experimented with the recipe, the bread became quite tasty. It was soon the only bread served at the Rudkin house, and visitors often would ask where they could purchase it. Finally, to see how marketable her bread really was, Margaret baked twelve loaves, took them to the local grocer, and had him taste it. The grocer immediately ordered more bread. Margaret remembers, "Although I knew nothing of manufacturing, of marketing, of pricing or of making bread in quantities, with that phone call, Pepperidge Farm bread was born."

The bread was first baked in the family kitchen. Soon, as its popularity grew, the enterprise was moved to the family barns, which had to be converted into kitchens. Margaret Rudkin was very picky about the quality of her product. If a loaf wasn't wrapped neatly or if anything about the bread looked wrong, she would not let it be sold. As a result, Pepperidge Farm became well known for its tasty, high-quality products that consumers perceived to be a cut above other baked goods. Today the company's products, including freshly baked products, biscuits, and frozen foods, are sold nationwide. And although Margaret sold her business in 1961, her heritage continues to be evident in every product.

Consider This: You can become good at almost anything if you put your mind and energy into it. Furthermore, you can become a master with diligent and deliberate practice.

MICHAEL JORDAN

If you work hard, you will get the things you want.

JAMES JORDAN

As a youngster, Michael Jordan took sports seriously. He always wanted to win, and he hated to lose. Standing only five feet ten inches tall as a sophomore, he made his high school's junior varsity basketball team. Still, he was passed over in favor of another athlete when the coach needed a taller player for a state championship tournament. Michael never forgot that moment.

When he returned to school the following fall, Michael startled everyone. He'd grown five inches during the summer. "It was almost as if Michael willed himself taller," said his father. Michael took advantage of his new-found height. To gain as much practice time as possible, he began skipping classes. His deeds led to suspension from school. With the help of his father, he learned to strike a balance between academics and sports. And although Michael took his father's advice, he never lost any of his passion for winning. He worked harder than any of his teammates and demanded more of himself. After high school he entered the University of North Carolina. Michael Jordan helped the Tar Heels win a national championship as a freshman. He was the leading scorer during his sophomore year. And in his final season he was selected as college basketball's 1984 Player of the Year. Drafted that spring by the Chicago Bulls of the National Basketball Association, Michael Jordan became an instant sensation with his easygoing smile and slashing style of play. His formidable skills and dogged determination helped the Bulls win six NBA championships (1991–93, 1996–98).

Consider This: Obstacles, even physical ones, may block your dreams. But don't give up. If you keep trying, and keep working hard, there's no telling what might end up giving you an advantage.

DALE CARNEGIE TEACHES BUSINESS LEADERS

In my office, you will not see the degree I have from
the University of Nebraska, or the master's degree
I have from Columbia University, but you'll see the
certificate I got from the Dale Carnegie course.
WARREN BUFFETT

Emotional Intelligence (EQ) gained popularity from a book titled *Emotional Intelligence: Why It Can Matter More than IQ,* written by Daniel Goleman in 1995. In it, he claims EQ is more important than IQ in predicting a person's success. Boiled down to its basics, EQ helps you connect your experiences with others. Characteristically, people with high EQ bounce back after rejection and come up with alternative ways to succeed. One famous author, Dale Carnegie, taught EQ techniques for decades, although he'd never heard of the term. Graduates of his course (which started in 1912) include billionaire Warren Buffet; popcorn magnate Orville Redenbacher; CNN correspondent Dr. Sanjay Gupta; and former First Lady Rosalynn Carter. His courses are characterized as lessons in treating other people the way you want to be treated and developing a genuine interest in other people's needs and desires. Its core values of integrity and character are as relevant today as when his courses began a hundred years ago.

But Dale had a hard start. His local YMCA didn't allow him to conduct his public speaking courses there, because they didn't believe anyone would take his class. So Dale used the lessons from his own course to find a solution to this problem. First, he didn't accept no as a final answer. Next, he considered possible win-win solutions that would address their concerns. Finally he convinced them to offer his course on a commission basis. Soon, Dale's course was making him fifteen times more in commissions than he would have made from their standard salary. And it has now been a success for more than one hundred years.

Consider This: Treating other people with courtesy and understanding their side of a disagreement is the first step in gaining other people's respect.

CRACKER BARREL

*There never was a day that couldn't be improved
by some good country cookin'.*
CRACKER BARREL MENU

Dan Evins operated a small filling station business in Lebanon, Tennessee, in 1969, about the time the interstate highway system was beginning to open up many rural areas. Wondering how he could take advantage of the traffic, Dan realized that travelers would be hungry and in need of gasoline, so he considered selling food at his stations. At first, he thought about adding fast food, which seemed to be the trend. But, ultimately, he determined that many people would rather have "real food" instead.

Dan decided to create a highway restaurant that would buck the trend. Move over McDonald's, Burger King, and KFC. Dan decided to be more than a drive-through fast-food place. Cracker Barrel would be comfortable and reflect the nostalgia of rural America. It would be like a country store, with big jars of candies and homemade jellies, potbellied stoves, handmade quilts, and other quality items. With the help of some investor friends, Dan opened the original Cracker Barrel Old Country Store as a combination family restaurant, gift shop, and service station. Travelers liked the idea, and soon people were standing in line to eat his country cooking. Dan obtained more investors and built more stores, eventually omitting the service station. By 2020, more than six hundred Cracker Barrels dotted the interstate landscape. Dan believed that authentic country cooking, American values, and an honest-to-goodness rural lifestyle could be preserved, and he intended to do his part in his stores. As a result, Cracker Barrel serves more than eleven million plates of chicken and dumplings each year. And those rocking chairs out front? They sell more than two hundred thousand of them every year.

Consider This: When everyone is following one trend, look for a part of the market that's forgotten. Someone will find it. Will it be you?

HAROLD ROSS AND THE *NEW YORKER*

If you can't be funny, be interesting.
HAROLD ROSS

It seems ink was in the veins of Harold Wallace Ross from the day he was born in 1892. Starting with his high school newspaper, Ross flitted from one newspaper to another during his early years. He chalked up seven newspaper jobs from the *San Francisco Call* to the *Atlanta Journal* and many in between. During World War I, he worked on the *Stars and Stripes* in France, returning to New York to work at several other magazines. Then, in 1925, Ross (with his wife, Jane Grant, whom he met in France during the war) started his own weekly, the *New Yorker*. Grant had her own literary career. She began at *Collier's* and soon became the city room's first woman reporter for the *New York Times*.

Ross was a member of a group of writers called "The Vicious Circle" that met for lunch at the Algonquin Hotel every day. He took advantage of these contacts to recruit the talents of New York's most flamboyant and exciting writers. These included Dorothy Parker, James Thurber, E. B. White, J. D. Salinger, and others. Ross defined the *New Yorker* as "not edited for the old lady in Dubuque." Thurber described the magazine's intention as having "an offhand, chatty, informal quality. Nothing was to be labored or studied, arty, literary, or intellectual." A perfectionist, Ross edited every copy of the magazine until he died in 1951. His anti-intellectualism, drive, and obsession with detail guided the writers in the magazine's early stages and remain today as a testament to his vision. Over the years the *New Yorker* gained a reputation for humor pieces (and cartoons) living comfortably with serious, precise, and fact-checked journalism.

Consider This: Know your talents and ambitions. Then recruit others to help you maximize your reach.

EXAMPLING

Integrity is as integrity does.
PHILIP B. CROSBY

In his book *Running Things: The Art of Making Things Happen*, author Phillip B. Crosby pointed out problems associated with decaying morality in business. He said that company management is responsible for and can correct many of those problems. Crosby explained that most people have high integrity and do not usually do things they consider wrong. The problem lies in the fact that what is considered wrong often changes from time to time and from place to place. For example, people don't worry about crime in many small towns. They know everyone in the area, and everyone generally lives up to the community's expectations. In a company, employees' perceptions of appropriate office behavior are shaped by managers and the examples they set. His own experience came from running the US Army Pershing Missile program. Using a Zero Defects program and exampling a "get it right the first time" management strategy, he reduced the missile rejection rate by 25 percent.

Managers are sadly mistaken if they think commandments or inspirational posters on the wall will convince their employees to behave professionally. Like children taking after their parents, employees imitate those above them who set the example. Workers will mimic the behavior if supervisors come in late, take extra time for lunch, and run personal errands on company time. They will feel justified in surfing the internet, making personal calls, and playing the latest online game while on the job. In most companies (or at least in most departments), everyone knows nearly everything that goes on. There are few secrets. The examples set by managers are seen by everyone, and they will affect the level of integrity of the company's workforce.

Consider This: If you are a manager, a supervisor, or an executive, workers will follow your example, whether it is good or bad. If you want your employees to meet specific standards of behavior and performance, you must meet those standards yourself.

KLEENEX TISSUES

Don't put a cold in your pocket.
KLEENEX ADVERTISEMENT

During World War I the Kimberly-Clark company developed a super-absorbent material that could be used as a surgical dressing and a gas-mask filter. After the war the same material was used in Kleenex brand tissues, originally intended to be used as a cold-cream remover. For years the product was promoted only to help remove cold cream. But marketers kept receiving letters from customers. They asked, "Why don't you say it's good for blowing your nose?" At first, no one paid much attention to the suggestion. Still, the letters came in so frequently that the marketing department decided the concept was worth some research. Then, one Kleenex employee suffering from hay fever started using the tissue instead of his handkerchief. That convinced the company to try a new approach.

A novel advertising campaign was devised. Half of the newspapers in Peoria, Illinois, carried an ad urging people to use Kleenex for removing cold cream plus a coupon good for a free box of the tissues. The remaining newspapers also included a coupon but touted Kleenex as a handkerchief substitute. The handkerchief version drew the most response, accounting for 61 percent of the coupons redeemed. The experiment showed that Kleenex could be more popular if used as a disposable handkerchief rather than for its original purpose. With that evidence, a new ad campaign was devised to promote both uses of Kleenex, with its role as a handkerchief getting most of the coverage. Eventually, Kimberly-Clark composed a list of forty-eight "typical" uses for Kleenex.

Consider This: Be alert for new or different uses of a product or service. This can be a natural avenue for expansion.

MALCOM P. MCLEAN'S SHIPPING CONTAINERS

Every once in a while, a new technology, an old problem, and a big idea turn into an innovation.

DEAN KAMEN

There was a problem in the shipping industry. Goods were loaded onto ships in Europe in boxes or barrels, but some of the cargo would be gone when they reached the United States. Such losses are called "shrinkage," costing American consumers millions of dollars. Malcom McLean recognized this problem and believed he had an answer. McLean had started a trucking company during the Great Depression with a single used truck, and he had sold the company in 1955 for $6 million. He used the proceeds from that sale to purchase the Pan-Atlantic Steamship Corporation, which McLean renamed Sea-Land Services (SLS). Investors purchased additional ships for SLS from the US Navy, who then leased them to McLean. The investors were attracted by a highly favorable tax advantage. The navy vessels were fully depreciated since they were more than forty years old. Still, the reconstituted containers were given a short seven-year depreciation life.

McLean's answer to the shrinkage problem came from his experience in the trucking industry. Instead of shipping goods in small containers, McLean utilized large sealed containers, the same type that fit onto the backs of trucks. He called them intermodal shipping containers. The trucks pulled up to the dock with his new system, and the containers were hoisted aboard the ship. At the end of the voyage, the procedure was reversed. In addition to reducing loading and unloading time, the sealed containers made it difficult for thieves to get to the cargo. Other shippers soon adopted the idea and have saved untold millions of dollars in shipping costs and reduced shrinkage.

Consider This: A large deal takes more than a good idea. It also requires an innovative financial plan.

JOSEPHINE COCHRANE AND KITCHENAID

If nobody else is going to invent a dishwasher, I'll do it myself.
JOSEPHINE GARIS COCHRANE

The automatic dishwasher took a long time to reach American homes after its invention in 1886. It all started when Josephine Garis Cochrane, the wife of an Illinois political leader, got mad at the servants who kept breaking her china. After one terrible evening, Josephine exploded at the kitchen staff. She declared that she would invent a dishwasher. Unfortunately, she had no mechanical experience and rarely washed dishes herself. Nevertheless, she dove into the task. Working in a backyard woodshed, Josephine devised a dishwashing contraption. Then, with the help of mechanic George Butters, she built a prototype and dubbed it the Garis-Cochrane machine. Her invention worked so well that it was patented and won an award at the 1893 Columbian Exposition. Friends and business associates helped her establish a company. The heavy-duty dishwashers it produced were sold to hotels and restaurants. Josephine directed the firm until she died in 1913.

In 1926 another company came into the picture. The Hobart Corporation, founded in 1897, produced equipment for grocers and institutional kitchens. Hobart acquired the Garis-Cochrane but continued to concentrate on heavy-duty dishwashers. It was not until 1949 that the company finally introduced a home model called the KitchenAid. But its marketing research found that many women of the period actually enjoyed washing dishes. So they had to find a compelling reason for women to buy the dishwasher. Researchers also discovered that women felt guilty about leaving dirty dishes in the sink after late-night snacks. That information, plus the added benefit of sterilization, gave dishwashers the boost they needed, and they soon became a permanent fixture in many American homes.

Consider This: A good idea may be so innovative that people won't even know it's needed. You'll have to convince your customers of its benefits before they'll give it a try.

VICTOR KIAM BOUGHT THE COMPANY

Entrepreneurs don't sit on their haunches, waiting for
something to happen. They make things happen.
VICTOR KIAM

In his autobiography *Going For It!*, Victor Kiam was the first to admit that
he was no entrepreneurial genius. He simply learned what it took to operate
and build a company by watching it happen. After graduating from Harvard
Business School in 1951, Kiam spent the next few decades climbing the corporate ladder at Lever Brothers and Playtex. After a merger, Kiam became
disenchanted with the company's direction and left. As many executives do,
he went to a corporate headhunter to begin the process of finding a new position. When that didn't work out, George Haley of Haley Associates steered
him in a different direction. "You should go out on your own," he told Kiam.
"Find a company you're interested in, buy it, and run it yourself. Or start a
new company."

Haley's advice surprised Kiam, but he let the idea settle. He attended the
worldwide seminar of the Young Presidents' Organization. After the conference, Kiam looked for a company to purchase. He bought the Benrus Watch
Company and in 1979 acquired Remington. Both companies were having
problems, but Kiam turned them around. He became a celebrity of sorts by
appearing in television commercials and telling viewers about his purchase of
Remington. Attired in a bathrobe, Kiam declared that he liked Remington's
electric shaver so much, "I bought the company." When Kian died at the age
of seventy-four, a close business associate, Jonathon Lyons, remembered him as
"a truly remarkable entrepreneur of the old kind—the kind they simply don't
make anymore."

*Consider This: Is there some project you've been mulling over, thinking about
doing, but haven't dared to attempt? Now may be the time to jump in and do it.*

L. FRANK BAUM AND *THE WIZARD OF OZ*

Never give up. No one knows what's going to happen next.
L. FRANK BAUM

Our own American Dreams are frequently fashioned by the ideas we hear about in stories, particularly those stories we encounter in our youth. *The Wonderful Wizard of Oz* is one of those stories. Its author, Lyman Frank Baum, began his career as a journalist. He frequently entertained neighborhood children by telling stories, often making up the tales on the spot. In 1899 Baum penned his first children's book, *Father Goose*, which was commercially successful and encouraged him to write more.

One of the stories he told the neighborhood children seemed to stand out among the others. It was about a girl named Dorothy who was swept from her Kansas home by a twister and stranded in a magical land. When one of the neighborhood youngsters asked Baum the name of the land, he was stumped at first. Then, so legend has it, he looked over to his file cabinets and the drawers labeled A–G, H–N, and O–Z. Baum quickly dubbed the magical land "Oz," and the children liked the name. When he originally titled this story, he called it *The Emerald City*, a title over which he and his publisher disagreed. They considered *From Kansas to Fairyland* and *The City of the Great Oz* before finally deciding on *The Wonderful Wizard of Oz*. Baum went on to pen more than sixty children's books, many about the wonderful land of Oz. Even after he died in 1919, more than twenty additional Oz books were published, penned by other authors. Baum's stories have inspired movies, Broadway productions (including *Wicked* and *The Wiz*), toys, artwork, and (since 1957) The International Wizard of Oz Club.

Consider This: Like a stand-up comedian trying out material, if possible try your product on potential consumers. Observe their reactions. Keep what works. Get rid of what doesn't. And soon you'll have something just right.

CALVIN KLEIN'S FASHIONABLE SUCCESS

The soul of this man is his clothes.

WILLIAM SHAKESPEARE

At almost any department store, you'll find racks filled with designer fashions—polo shirts with logos, jeans with designer names embroidered on back pockets. In fact, designer labels can be found on virtually every kind of apparel. This was not always the case; before the 1970s designer fashions were found only in the most exclusive stores. But Calvin Klein changed all that.

Calvin seemed to have a knack for fashion even as a child. Sometimes he would help his friends buy clothes. It was natural for Calvin to consider fashion as a career. So he studied at Manhattan's Fashion Institute of Technology to become a designer. After graduation Calvin struggled, working low-paying jobs around New York's fashion district for six long years. Eventually he believed he was in the wrong industry and considered joining a family friend in the grocery business. Instead, that friend was so convinced of Calvin's talent that he provided $10,000 in seed money to enable the fledgling designer to start Calvin Klein, Ltd.

In 1968 Calvin began by designing women's coats. They were classy, simple, elegant, and fit right into the changing lifestyles of the era. Calvin seemed to have a knack for the tastes of the post-hippie generation. His comfortable, stylish, and relatively inexpensive clothes introduced the concept of designer fashion to an entire generation. By 1975 Klein had won three consecutive Coty awards and was inducted into the Coty Hall of Fame. Although the Calvin Klein brand was sold to Phillips-Van Heusen in 2003, it remains an iconic part of fashion history.

Consider This: What are you good at doing? What do you enjoy doing? Is there any way you can do it for a living? Can you use that talent in the work you are doing today?

CRACKER JACK

I know you're looking for a ruby in a mountain of rocks, but there ain't no Coupe de Ville hiding at the bottom of a Cracker Jack Box.
MEATLOAF

In 1871 F. W. Rueckheim came to Chicago to help clean up after the Great Chicago Fire had destroyed much of the city. Rueckheim was a German immigrant who had saved $200 working as a farmhand and wanted to carve out his own piece of the American Dream. Once in Chicago, he decided to use his money to go into the popcorn business, and he and a partner set up a small stand at 113 Federal Street. Rueckheim eventually bought out his partner, and his brother Louis joined him in 1873. Together the brothers purchased candy-making equipment to expand their product line. They added marshmallows and other confections to their growing business. Then, in 1893, at the first Chicago World's Fair, they began selling their wares. One of the Rueckheims' products was a tasty blend of popcorn, caramel-coated peanuts, and molasses.

The popularity of this new treat exceeded their expectations. As they retooled and reordered, the demand outgrew their production capacity more than once. But it didn't have a name. That changed when Louis gave a sample of the popcorn-peanut treat to a salesman. After crunching a few bites, he exclaimed, "That's a Cracker Jack!" "So it is," replied Rueckheim. He promptly trademarked the name. Another customer provided the slogan, "The more you eat, the more you want." In 1910 Cracker Jack boxes began carrying coupons redeemable for prizes. And in 1912 they included toy surprises in every box. The popularity of this promotion turned into the company's hallmark "prize in every package" campaign.

Consider This: Give the customers what they want, then give them a little extra. Without satisfied customers, there is no business.

JENI'S SPLENDID ICE CREAM

Mistakes are part of the game. It's how well you recover
from them that's the mark of a great player.
ALICE COOPER

Can you blend art with ice cream? Jeni Britton Bauer did. It started one day when her grandmother told her she could become anything—a doctor, a lawyer, or even an astronaut. Jeni remembers going outside and thinking, "I'll be an ice cream maker." That idea ruminated in her mind for years. Then, while studying art in college, she had a eureka moment. Ice cream was a culinary canvas. So in 1996 she blended her art and ice cream interests into an ice cream shop in a public marketplace full of chocolate, wines, fruit, and flavors' merchants. In 2002, she reopened her store as Jeni's Splendid Ice Cream. Her company steadily grew to more than thirty stores. It became known worldwide as the artisan of ice creams, featuring freshly sourced ingredients and unique flavors.

Then disaster struck. Bacteria called listeria were found in a pint of ice cream. Jeni had been proud of going beyond food safety standards. Now she was devastated. She recalled 262 tons of ice cream and closed their stores. All ideas were on the table. With their small kitchen, it would take too many months to recover. The company had to rethink its business processes. What did they do best? Could anything be outsourced without compromising quality? Of course, they created the ice cream recipes. They personally acquired ingredients directly from farmers and spice merchants. But once ingredients were in a machine, the process was standard. So they kept the creative side of the business intact and farmed out the machine work to industrial kitchens. Using this method, they recovered while keeping their quality intact. Today, they sell more than two million pints of ice cream every year.

Consider This: Even great beginnings can get sidetracked. Sometimes you have to rethink, retool, and restart to recover from life's twists and turns.

SELLING YOURSELF

A man's success in handling people is the very yardstick by which the outcome of his whole life's work is measured.
DR. PAUL PARKER

There is a difference between being an "order taker" and a salesperson. High school students can be hired to take orders at McDonald's or Burger King. Becoming a professional salesperson requires more expertise, thought, and training. Most sales relationships are more than just a single chance encounter, such as at a grocery store checkout or fast-food restaurant. In fact, the salesperson-customer relationship is much like a marriage. There is a courtship, a wedding, and mutual support after the sale is made. The quality of the "marriage" depends on how well the seller manages the relationship. If the marriage is good, the seller's reputation is enhanced. Both partners are happy. This results in continuing opportunities for sales. If the salesperson slacks off or does something that sours the relationship, their reputation is tarnished. Sales dry up, and the relationship may dissolve.

What if you're not selling any kind of product? The sales relationship can still be significant. For example, in life's usual course of events, our talents and service become the product. We sell our skills to our employer, project mate, or business associates. Just like someone selling insurance, medical implants, or baby furniture, our job is not a one-off event. Success in life or business requires genuine relationships. We must recognize that competitors (maybe someone in line for the same promotion) are lurking around every corner. Creating solid relationships and nurturing our business contacts with productive work, steady support, and loyalty, creating long-term growth and success. Hard work builds appreciation. Honesty builds trust. Being there when troubles surface builds loyalty.

Consider This: Relationships don't just happen. Like a marriage, they require time, commitment, and energy. Give of yourself to others, and you will see friendships develop.

AMELIA EARHART

As soon as we left the ground, I knew I myself had to fly.
AMELIA EARHART ON HER FIRST FLIGHT

When Orville and Wilbur Wright made their famous first flight at Kitty Hawk, North Carolina, Amelia Earhart was barely five years old. She may not have known it at the time, but it was a turning point in her life. As a bright student, Amelia dreamed big dreams. She read the newspaper and cut out clippings of famous first events. She was particularly impressed when a woman achieved a remarkable feat or landed an impressive job. But Amelia had trouble finding a field where she could make her own mark on history. Then, one day in 1920, her father took her to an air show.

Inspired by what she had seen, Amelia took her first plane ride a few days after the show. She was exhilarated! She found a woman pilot, began taking lessons (which cost $1 a minute), and became an accomplished pilot. She set a women's altitude record while still a student pilot, climbing to fourteen thousand feet above sea level without bottled oxygen. In 1928, accompanied by two male aviators, she became the first woman to fly across the Atlantic. In 1932 she became the first woman to fly solo across the Atlantic. She took off from Canada and experienced trouble only four hours into that journey. A severe storm rattled and tossed her airplane, and she lost her fuel gauge and two navigational instruments. Nevertheless, she held on to her course and doggedly continued flying east until she spotted Ireland. Amelia Earhart continued to set aviation records, but she was lost over the Pacific in 1937 while attempting to circumnavigate the globe.

Consider This: If you dare to be great, set high goals for yourself. Then go where no one has dared go before, and enjoy the ride while it lasts.

THE PET ROCK

Some Pet Rock owners have found that the ticking of an alarm clock placed near the box has a soothing effect, especially at night.
FROM THE PET ROCK MANUAL

In 1975 Gary Dahl introduced the most unusual fad of all time, the Pet Rock. The craze lasted only one Christmas season, then it was gone. Some called the Pet Rock stupid, but the concept made Gary a millionaire. The idea came to Gary while some friends were relaxing at a local pub. After listening to everyone else talk about the woes of owning a pet, Gary said, "My pet is no trouble at all. I have a Pet Rock." Making up the tale as he went, he told his friends about the care and feeding of his imaginary companion. Everyone had a good laugh and then swapped jokes for another hour. Gary left the pub feeling that the Pet Rock was an idea worth thinking about.

A former copywriter, Gary first wrote a book about owning a Pet Rock, patterning it after a popular dog owners' manual. He soon revised his idea, marketed an actual rock in a box, and included a small instruction manual. Luck, coupled with persistence, resulted in publicity about Gary's novel idea in major newspapers and magazines. As word of the novelty spread, Pet Rocks began to sell like gold nuggets, and Gary had to work virtually twenty-four hours a day to keep up with the orders. But he sensed that the craze would remain popular for only one Christmas season. Gary was correct. Sales fell off as quickly as they had soared. Although its popularity was short-lived, few products have approached the success of the Pet Rock. Of course, great ideas have a way of coming back around. The Pet Rock came back to life in 2012 and can be purchased on several gift retail websites.

Consider This: Fads have short lifespans. If you can't get in and make a profit quickly, you may lose your shirt.

MAYTAG'S WASHERS

All will come out in the washing.
CERVANTES, *DON QUIXOTE*

At the turn of the nineteenth century in Newton, Iowa, Fred Maytag and several of his friends were busy running a small business that made farm machinery. They were reasonably successful, but sales were seasonal. To stabilize sales, the partners decided to diversify and make other products. Fred's company tried designing types of machine-oriented products. As with almost every other manufacturer in America at the time, that included a crack at the burgeoning automobile market. But the Maytag automobile failed. They tried another idea. In 1907 they created the Pastime Washer for clothing. The device consisted of a cypress wood tub that was fitted with hand-operated washing blades and had grooves in the interior that imitated the function of a traditional washboard. Finally they had a viable product. In 1911 they added an electric motor, and continued adding more improvements each year.

With the success of the clothes washer, the company discontinued the production of its farm implements. Fred turned the company over to his son, L. B. Maytag, in 1920. By then Maytag washers were the dominant clothes washer in the American marketplace. The company continued to concentrate on making its washers more innovative. It introduced such features as an all-aluminum tub and gentle blades that worked better than competing brands. In 1923 Maytag dropped its other product lines, and its sales rose from the 1921 level of $1.25 million to $28.7 million in 1925. In 1927 the number of Maytag washers sold hit the one-million-units mark. The company held a leadership position in the washer industry until it was overtaken by Whirlpool in 1950.

Consider This: Once you know what you do best, focus your attention on that one occupation and eliminate those tasks that distract you from your primary business.

DONUTS: THE HOLE STORY

As you ramble on through life, brother, whatever be your goal,
keep your eye upon the doughnut, and not upon the hole.
"THE OPTIMIST'S CREED"

There is nothing more American than the sweetness of a warm donut. But where did that hole come from? The history of this pastry begins, like a lot of American history, in Europe. Early Dutch settlers brought a pastry fried in lard or fat, called an "oily ball" or "fried dough cakes"—a glob of sweet bread, fried in fat, made a small, sweet, crunchy cake. These Dutch treats became popular in New York (New Amsterdam, then). That's where a fellow named Hanson Crockett Gregory comes into the story. Born in 1821 in Rockport, Maine, as a teenager he served on ships as a baker's assistant. The cook fried up some oily cakes for breakfast, and the sailors munched them down. Their other name for the cakes was "sinkers" because the middle of the dough was uncooked, and they sunk in the belly like a cannonball. That's when the idea popped out of nowhere. Taking a pepper can, Hanson poked holes in the blobs of dough. Now, when the cakes cooked, they were crispy all over. The crew ate them up.

These "holey cakes" quickly grew in popularity. Like many food innovations, other people claim to have invented it, but Gregory's story seems to have substantial validity. The name "doughnut" (now often "donut") is traced back to 1808. It was first mentioned by Washington Irving to describe pastries served at a fancy dinner. Wherever it came from, it quickly grew in popularity. Another advancement in their popularity came in World War I when Salvation Army women made them for soldiers in France as a "taste of home." These "donut girls" inspired a "National Donut Day," now celebrated on the first Friday of June.

Consider This: A good thing is just one idea away from becoming a great thing. So let your imagination run wild. How can you poke a hole in something ordinary to make it extraordinary?

POST-IT NOTES

*What we have here isn't just a bookmark. It's
a whole new way to communicate.*

ART FRY

On Wednesday nights Art Fry, a scientist at 3M, practiced in the choir of North Presbyterian Church in St. Paul, Minnesota. He marked pages in his hymnal with small pieces of paper. Then, when he opened the hymnal on Sunday morning, the slips fell out. Suddenly he had a "eureka moment." *What if there were a little adhesive on the paper to keep it in place?* Art thought. He remembered a novel adhesive invented some years earlier by another 3M scientist, Dr. Spencer Silver. For more than a year Fry and Spencer conducted experiments to bring his adhesive bookmark to fruition. The work was not officially sanctioned, but 3M's corporate culture allowed people to spend some of their work time developing new ideas.

The optimal formula for the adhesive was a challenge to determine. The glue had to be strong enough to hold the paper in place but not so strong that it damaged the surface to which it adhered. When Art had samples of the slips to test, he began using them for more than bookmarks. He wrote notes on them and then stuck them on things as reminders. He called the invention Post-It Notes. Sensing success, Art passed around the notes at meetings. Soon people at 3M took notice, although there were still those who failed to see the product's value. In fact, the company's first attempt at selling Post-It Notes was a disaster. No one understood it. But when the marketing department finally began passing out samples, the product took off like wildfire. Today Post-It Notes are considered possibly the most important invention at 3M since Scotch brand transparent tape.

Consider This: It often takes a champion, someone who really believes in a product, to push it past the corporate doubters to success in the marketplace. Does your organization encourage such champions?

ROY, THE FORGOTTEN DISNEY

*I've been made the skinflint, but I really wasn't. . . . All I've
been trying to do is help Walt do what he was trying to do.*
ROY O. DISNEY

Walt Disney's movies and parks are some of the most well recognized and
profitable enterprises worldwide. But without his brother Roy, Walt might be
an unknown today. Roy was seven years older than Walt, and they grew up
together, first in Chicago, then in Marceline, Missouri. Walt developed his
artistic talents early, and Roy was the business brother. Soon after high school
Roy became a bank clerk. After a brief stint in the navy during World War I,
Roy contracted tuberculosis and was hospitalized in Los Angeles. In 1923
Walt went to Hollywood to be near Roy. Together they began Disney Brothers
Studios. Walt married Lillian. Roy married Edna, and they built houses next
to each other. Walt, of course, was the creative genius while Roy managed the
business. In fact, Roy served as CEO of the Disney partnership until 1968.

In the early years the company faced bankruptcy, lost rights to prized
cartoon characters (such as Oswald the Rabbit), and had creative setbacks. But
Roy was the glue that held the company together. When Walt decided to do a
full-length animated movie (*Snow White and the Seven Dwarfs*), Roy secured
the financing. When Walt had the idea for Disneyland, Roy worked with
ABC to secure funding. Walt often exasperated Roy with his harebrained (and
expensive) ideas. Somehow Roy found resources for Walt to follow his dreams.
Often seen as a tightwad, Roy's heart was as big as Walt's. When buying land
that would eventually house Disney World, he encountered an older woman
who wanted $5,000 for her property. Roy gave her $12,000, saying, "It really
meant something to her." After Walt died in 1966, Roy completed and opened
Disney World in 1971, shortly before his own death.

*Consider This: Great partnerships are gold. A finance person is rarely creative. A
creative genius is rarely a business leader. But talented teams with multiple skills
can often produce spectacular results.*

GRACE HOPPER ON LEADERSHIP

If everyone is thinking alike, then no one is thinking.
GENERAL GEORGE S. PATTON

Many people in the computer industry consider Grace Hopper the mother of computer programming. In an industry usually dominated by men, she stands as a pioneer. When Hopper worked on IBM's first computer during World War II, the Mark I, it consisted of a series of delicate electromechanical switches. Hopper recalled that the computer wouldn't work one day and that a painstaking search of the equipment revealed a dead moth in one of the switches. The moth was removed and taped in the day's journal. Hopper, an ensign in the navy, noted that she had "debugged" the computer—thus becoming the first person to use that phrase. In addition, Hopper played a pivotal role in developing programming languages for computers. In fact, she created the computer compiler, codeveloped the COBOL language, and taught computing to countless early programmers. She remained in the navy until 1986 when she retired as a rear admiral.

In a CBS interview, Hopper related her thoughts on leadership: "Somewhere along the line we lost our leadership. Quality of leadership is a two-way street. It is loyalty up and loyalty down. Respect your superior; keep him informed of what you're up to, and take care of your crew. When the going gets rough, you cannot manage a man into battle. You must lead him. You manage things. You lead people." Then she revealed a secret: "[Leaders], when in doubt, don't ask, just do; many times it is easier to apologize than to get permission. The big rewards go to the people who take the big risks. A ship in port is safe, but that's not what a ship is built for."

Consider This: Do you believe in something enough to be a leader? Will you take the risk involved? Are you prepared to take responsibility for the failure and success?

BUSTER BROWN STARTED SOMETHING

*I've lived all my life in this weird wonderland; I keep buying things
that I don't understand, 'Cause they promise me miracles, magic,
and hope, But, somehow, it always turns out to be soap.*

"CHIM CHIM CHER-EE," FROM *MARY POPPINS*

For decades the Buster Brown Shoes mascot dotted the advertising landscape all across the United States. It was one of the most widely known icons in American marketing for many years, which is why it's important today. The Brown Shoe Company was founded in 1878 and produced a line of shoes for boys and girls. In 1902 cartoonist Richard Outcault introduced a comic strip based on Buster Brown, his sister Mary Jane, and their dog Tige. John Bush, a sales executive for the Brown Shoe Company, recognized the sales potential that a tie-in with the cartoon character would create. He purchased the rights to use Buster Brown to promote Brown Shoes.

Bush hired actors to tour the country and portray the mascot to make the Buster Brown persona well known to the public. Actor Ed Ansley (one of the smallest men in the world at only fifty inches high) devoted twenty-seven years to performing in a Buster Brown outfit and wore out five "Tige" dogs in the process. Today it's not essential that you remember the Buster Brown character (but look him up on the internet). Its fundamental importance is how it inspired an entire industry in using famous (often cartoon or action hero) characters to promote another product. Today these tie-ins are seen every day at places like McDonald's, Burger King, Taco Bell, and in numerous product placement opportunities. So next time you notice a Disney character featured on a soft drink cup, give Buster a shout-out for his role in initiating a new way to sell products.

Consider This: People see a familiar and likable character on a brand. The association creates goodwill—and a purchase.

JUNE 12

W. EDWARDS DEMING

I told them Japanese quality could be the best
in the world instead of the worst.

W. EDWARDS DEMING

When your car starts the first time on a cold morning, thank W. Edwards Deming. The problem of poor-quality automobiles started after World War II. At that time American companies didn't worry about quality. They sold everything they made. When Deming approached them with information about how to improve their products using quality-control techniques, they weren't interested. So in 1949, at the request of General Douglas MacArthur, Deming offered to help get Japanese industry back on its feet.

At that time "Made in Japan" was synonymous with cheap and poorly constructed products. Deming described to the Japanese how they could stop making terrible products by adopting the management principles of statistical quality control. Rather than placing responsibility for product quality on inspectors at the end of the manufacturing process, quality control should begin at the design stage. Throughout, production workers should test quality and suggest improvements.

Many Japanese industrialists adopted Deming's methods. This launched the world's most influential quality revolution. Unfortunately, US industry still didn't take notice. As Deming's quality measures slowly took hold in Japan, their cars and electronics surpassed American products in reliability. When these products took a chunk out of American industry's bottom line, US companies finally considered Deming's message. As a result, the world has seen vast improvements in product quality in almost every manufactured product, including your car.

Consider This: A memo doesn't implement quality. Instead, quality begins with a passionate commitment throughout the entire concept, design, and production phases of a product.

CRAYOLA'S COLORFUL HISTORY

Artists are just children who refuse to put down their crayons.

AL HIRSCHFELD

A typical activity for young children is drawing pictures with crayons. These colorful drawing sticks are in every school, every house with kids, every day-care, and even on tables at restaurants. So who came up with this pervasive coloring stick? In 1900, Edwin Binney and C. Harold Smith began the Binney & Smith Company. They initially produced a black paint pigment called lamp-black and a red pigment used for painting barns. Then, in 1902, they used their pigments to develop a black wax marking pencil called Staonal. Its purpose was for marking items in industrial or business settings. But educators saw the product's potential. So Binney's wife, Alice, who was a schoolteacher (wouldn't you know it), came up with a name. She must have been a wordsmith because she combined the French words for "chalk," *craie* (anglicized to "crayon"), and "oily," *oleaginous*, to come up with "Crayola." The company quickly turned its efforts to making Crayola crayons.

Crayons were initially marketed to parents and educators. The original Crayola set (the No. 8 box) had eight colors: red, orange, yellow, green, blue, violet, brown, and black. Although kids were the prominent consumer of Crayola products, crayons have been used for everything from protest signs to fine art. Many other companies have produced other brands of crayons over the years, but only one is the original Crayola. Truth is, Binney and Smith's idea for the coloring stick isn't exactly original. Methods for combining pigments with wax existed thousands of years ago. Their contribution was to reimagine the concept and turn it into a modern and marketable product.

Consider This: Take an old idea and turn it into a modern product. If people used something hundreds (maybe thousands) of years ago, there is undoubtedly a market for a reimagined product today.

BOOKER T. WASHINGTON

*You must understand the troubles of that man
farthest down before you can help him.*
BOOKER T. WASHINGTON

America has long been a country of opportunity. Still, there have been significant problems for African Americans in the South to overcome. One person who provided a model for the education and advancement of African Americans was Booker T. Washington. Born into slavery in 1856, his family walked to West Virginia when he was nine, and he began attending school at night after working in a mine during the day. Adopting the name Washington, he left home at sixteen to attend school in Hampton, Virginia. When he graduated he was given a position on the faculty.

Some time later, in Tuskegee, Alabama, George Campbell, a former slave owner, and Lewis Adams, a former slave, joined together to establish a "Negro Normal School in Tuskegee" (now Tuskegee University). After securing $2,000 in funding from the state legislature, they invited Washington to become the school's principal. When he arrived, Washington asked to be shown the school. "There isn't any—yet," he was told. Although the legislature had authorized the school, there were no buildings, land, or faculty. Nevertheless, the school opened in a borrowed church as Washington searched for money. People from both races contributed to the school. Many white Southerners were greatly impressed by Washington's sincerity, intelligence, and commitment. He called on people to "invest in the Negro race" and was an able spokesman for the cause. When he approached railway magnate Collis Huntington for a donation, he was offered just $2. Washington persisted. As a result, Huntington gave $50,000 to the school and later donated the money for a new building named Huntington Hall.

Consider This: Gentle and persistent persuasion is often the best method for bringing a person to your way of thinking.

INVENTORS VERSUS ENTREPRENEURS

Being an entrepreneur is not for the faint of heart.
It is a high-risk, high-reward proposition.
JOHN C. BOGLE

Many people tend to lump inventors and entrepreneurs together. While this may be correct in some instances, inventing is much different from creating a company and bringing a product to the market. An inventor creates a solution to a particular problem; the entrepreneur organizes, manages, and assumes the risks of making the solution commercially viable. Although Christopher Latham Sholes invented and marketed the first practical typewriter, it took the Remington company to make it a commercial success. Ole Evinrude developed the outboard motor. Yet without the business acumen of his wife, Bess, the boat engine would have likely faded into obscurity. James Murray Spangler invented the vacuum cleaner, but William Hoover made the invention a household word. Apple computers didn't invent the computer mouse (it was developed by Douglas Engelbart). Still, Steve Jobs had the insight to adapt it to the growing computer market and make it an essential part of the personal computing experience.

Inventors may have enough business sense to start a small company and carve out a niche for the product. But if the enterprise becomes large, it often becomes unmanageable. The company either folds, is acquired by another enterprise, or finds the proper management to help. Entrepreneurs may or may not actually invent anything. They may find an inventor and develop a team that can bring the idea to fruition, as with the Hoover vacuum cleaner (and many other examples.) A few individuals can invent a product and operate a successful business, such as Thomas Edison, Henry Ford, or Bill Gates. But a good invention does not in itself create a viable business.

Consider This: Ideas don't mean a thing unless they can be successfully sold in the marketplace.

IBM'S SECRET OF SUCCESS

*It's a funny thing about life; if you refuse to accept
anything but the best, you very often get it.*
W. SOMERSET MAUGHAM

Throughout much of the twentieth century, IBM has been one of the most respected corporations in America. Among the reasons is its dogged determination to stick with its stated corporate beliefs. These beliefs have been a part of the company from its beginning. The father-son team of Tom Watson and Tom Watson Jr. persistently promoted a three-part mission for the corporation that became ingrained in every aspect of IBM's operation. The principles are:

1. Respect for the individual
2. Unparalleled customer service
3. Excellence and superior performance

What's the big deal? Nearly every company has similar principles in some document, somewhere. Words alone don't mean anything unless the upper management clings to them, believes them, and promotes them. Tom Watson drilled these ideas into the very fabric of IBM. Employees were rewarded when they exhibited outstanding support of these values. One example is the IBM representative who needed to deliver a part for a broken computer across town. Lousy weather had closed most of the city's bridges, and traffic was backed up for miles. Not to be deterred, the quick-thinking IBMer put on a pair of skates, wove his way through the gridlock, and got the part to the customer in time. Stories like this are repeated again and again within the company to illustrate how to support the company's values. Take the initiative. Be creative. Help the customer. Get the job done.

Consider This: We all pay lip service to our principles. Do you believe in yours enough to make them an everyday part of your life? Expect the best of yourself, and very often you will get it.

BILL PICKETT INVENTS BULLDOGGING

Like many men in the old-time West, on any job he did his best, he
left a blank that's hard to fill, for there will never be another Bill.

COLONEL ZACK MILLER

The son of former slaves, young Bill Pickett watched from his porch as cowboys drove cattle herds across the dusty prairie. He waved at them, and they
tipped their hats at him. At twelve, he took a job at a local ranch and earned a
reputation as an expert cowpoke. Then one day changed his life. He watched
as the cattle-herding dogs (bulldogs) bit the lip of steers to get their attention.
Curious. Then one day when an errant steer got loose, Bill rode up beside it
and, remembering the bulldog's trick, grabbed the steer by the horns and bit
its bottom lip. The beast yielded and was wrestled to the ground. Word got
around, and people wanted to see this impressive feat. Sometimes they'd throw
loose change in a hat to pay Bill for the exhibition. He called his new sport
"bulldogging." Sure enough, the sport became popular among other cattlemen.
Nowadays at rodeos a good bulldogger can wrestle a steer to the ground in five
to eight seconds (without biting the bull's lip!).

Bill was the best. He performed all over the Western states and even at
Madison Square Garden in New York City. That night Will Rogers rode as his
hazer (second rider and assistant). When a steer ran into the stands, Bill and
Rogers caught the beast and returned it to the arena. Although Bill's performances were mostly limited to African-American rodeo events, his fame spread
across the country. He was inducted into the National Rodeo Hall of Fame
in 1972 and the Pro Rodeo Hall of Fame in 1989. In addition, the US Postal
Service honored him with a postage stamp in 1994, and a bronze statue of Bill
was unveiled at the Fort Worth Stockyards in 1987.

*Consider This: Talented and diligent people will become stars before the crowd.
They will not languish in obscurity.*

GERBER BABY FOODS

If you want to emerge as a market leader in your industry, you should start preparing early. The sooner you decide to start, the bigger advantage you will gain over your competitors.

POOJA AGNIHOTRI

Like many dads over the centuries, Daniel Frank Gerber took his turn feeding hand-strained foods to his six-month-old baby. Since his family business, the Fremont Canning Company, was involved in food processing, Dan wondered if there might be a market for canned baby foods. But the baby-food industry had a high risk. Suppose a mistake was made in the canning process, and the mistake harmed a baby. The incident could destroy the reputation of the entire company. Baby food also costs more to produce than conventional canned goods. At that time, a 4.5-ounce can of baby food sold for fifteen cents, while a 10.5-ounce can of regular vegetables sold for a dime. The company studied the problems and the market and weighed their options. A survey of mothers and pediatricians indicated a significant need for baby-food products.

In 1928 Fremont came out with five canned baby foods. Although the country began to slide into the Great Depression, the company continued promoting its baby food, and sales increased. Competitors soon began to enter the market. To garner a competitive edge, the firm sought to gain the trust of parents by becoming experts in baby care. Part of the approach included providing informational pamphlets to pediatricians' offices. Dorothy Gerber, Dan's wife, answered more than twenty thousand letters from parents seeking help with problems ranging from how to get babies to sleep to the best way to remove stains from bibs. In 1941 the enterprise changed its name to Gerber Products Company. Today they continue to dominate the baby-food market with commitments to food quality and parental support.

Consider This: Carefully weigh the problems and opportunities of emerging markets. Don't be stifled by challenges. Instead, do your homework, make a decision, and, if you choose, enter new markets with commitment and enthusiasm.

OPAL LEE, "GRANDMOTHER OF JUNETEENTH"

All men are created equal, that they are endowed by their Creator with certain unalienable Rights, that among these are Life, Liberty and the pursuit of Happiness.

THE DECLARATION OF INDEPENDENCE

The founders of the United States promised freedom for all people. But it took a while for this to become a reality (and in some cases, freedom is still not complete). Such was the case during the Civil War. On January 1, 1863, President Abraham Lincoln issued a proclamation freeing the enslaved people in all states that had seceded. As a result, formerly enslaved people were recognized as American citizens. But in reality, enslaved people were not really freed until Union forces took over an area. Such was the case in Texas.

Two and a half years after Lincoln issued the proclamation, federal troops arrived in Galveston. On June 19, 1865, two months after the end of the war, US general Gordon Granger issued a statement: "The people of Texas are informed that, in accordance with a proclamation from the Executive of the United States, all slaves are free." As the news spread, formerly enslaved people gathered in celebration. A year later they celebrated "Jubilee Day" (later called "Juneteenth") with music, prayer services, and parties. The day was mostly ignored by others until activists like Opal Lee decided to rectify the matter. At eighty-nine, this former elementary school teacher decided to use her retirement to promote Juneteenth as a national holiday. For five years she circulated petitions and staged marches—first in Fort Worth, then in Washington DC. Interest rose, and Juneteenth became more widely celebrated. Finally, in 2021, when Ms. Opal was ninety-four, Congress designated June 19 as a national holiday. Opal Lee was present when President Joe Biden signed the legislation into law.

Consider This: Persistence and patience change things. A champion willing to fight for the right is always needed to make fundamental changes in any country, organization, or business.

THE MAGNA CARTA

May we think of freedom not as the right to do as we
please, but as the opportunity to do what is right.
PETER MARSHALL

The American Dream has been shaped by a few crucial documents that have defined the methods by which people could seek freedom and happiness. The Mayflower Compact, the Declaration of Independence, and the Constitution are usually mentioned. But an event important to the foundation of the United States also happened on June 19, 1215, nearly three centuries before Columbus arrived in the New World: King John of England signed the Magna Carta. Although it had a complicated history, that parchment inspired all of the other freedom documents written in early America. The Magna Carta guaranteed, among other rights, that a king must rule by law and that the king himself is subject to the law.

This document was instrumental in shaping the foundation of America and in many ways influences how we run our households, our clubs, and our businesses today. The US Constitution provides a framework under which our country is governed, defines the powers and limits of the law, and seeks to ensure that the law applies equally to all people. Although the US also has a problematic history in attempts to equally apply rights and the laws among its citizens, the fact that our freedom laws exist ensures that Americans have a right to protest and rebel against ill-used power. As a result, Americans tend to work best in a business, organization, or society that strives to treat all people fairly and works toward the common good. History shows that the American system of government, although not perfect, has provided its people with laws and opportunities to mold our government into a fair and equitable system for all people.

Consider This: Never forget or underestimate the heritage of the American Dream. Remember how the struggles of others won the freedom we enjoy today.

WINTON BLOUNT BUILDS A BUSINESS

Success is really about expertise.

STEVE YOUNG

Sometimes an opportunity presents itself as a gut feeling. After World War II, Winton Blount and his brother Houston decided to revive their family's sand and gravel business, which had almost gone under during the war. When Winton went to Atlanta to purchase surplus army equipment, the auction included attractively priced tractors and scrapers. He bought some equipment with only a gut feeling. Once he took possession of the machines, he had to figure out how to use them. The logical next step was to go into the contracting business. The Blounts took small jobs, learned, and took on larger jobs. They gained enough expertise to bid on and construct a wind tunnel for the air force in 1952. This project gave them insights on how to bid on other technical buildings for the air force and NASA. As America's space program moved into high gear, those building projects were the first of many that required the kinds of specialized experience the Blounts had obtained on previous projects. Projects included an indoor ocean for the navy, nuclear reactors, a cyclotron, and an airline terminal at the Atlanta airport.

Winton's offhand purchase had turned into a substantial business, employing thousands of workers. But construction work is cyclical. So the Blounts diversified into manufacturing machinery and equipment to smooth out the business cycles. As a result of specializing in constructing technically complex buildings, the Blounts secured contracts that offered higher profit margins. Winton Blount used much of his fortune to benefit numerous charities, including the United Charities and the YMCA. He also took leave from his business in 1968 to serve as America's postmaster general.

Consider This: Take the time to become an undisputed expert in solving complex problems (or building complicated buildings). Then you'll stand out as an expert and be able to step up the ladder past your competition.

ALEX HALEY'S ROOTS

Either you deal with what is the reality, or you can be
sure that the reality is going to deal with you.
ALEX HALEY

Alex Haley contributed a new chapter to the American Dream in his bestselling book *Roots*. He showed millions of Americans the value of knowing who you are, where you came from, and the value of your heritage. The pinnacle event for Haley was the airing of the *Roots* miniseries on national TV (which won nine Emmy awards.) But that accomplishment was a long time in the making. After retiring from the Coast Guard, Alex decided to become a writer. During his first year, he eked out a measly $2,000 working sixteen-hour days. At one point, Haley took stock of his situation. He had two cans of sardines and eighteen cents to his name. Sensing that he'd hit his lowest point, Haley put the items in a sack as a reminder. The next day he received a check for an article he had written. Haley kept that sack hanging like a trophy in his library for years.

Haley had made some progress as a writer by the time he started writing *Roots*. He remembers going deeply into debt as he spent much of his time sifting through old records in courthouses: "I owed everybody I had been able to borrow from." Haley missed five deadlines and was bogged down in his attempt to describe Kunta Kinte's journey from Africa to America aboard a slave ship. Somehow he found someone to loan him more money and booked passage on a freighter. Haley spent ten days in the vessel's cargo hold, stripped to his underwear and trying to imagine what it had been like for Kunta. The experience gave him an understanding of his forebears' feelings, and he finally completed the story.

Consider This: Trust in your goals. Hang on during the tough times. Muster the strength needed to overcome the valleys of depression and humiliation. Then rise up to accomplish the task at hand.

A PASSION FOR EXCELLENCE

A certain excessiveness seems a necessary element in all greatness.
DR. HARVEY CUSHING

Many Americans are content with not stepping out of bounds. Peer pressure and cultural mores keep people in check and often prevent them from doing something crazy or fantastic. When Tom Peters and Nancy Austin wrote the book *A Passion for Excellence* about successful American businesspeople, the word "passion" stood out as the best description of the phenomenon they observed in business after business. Passion is that quality that moves a person beyond the ordinary execution. With passion, the objective becomes a personal quest. Extra hours do not mean anything. Skipping meals is a natural occurrence. This is not a half-hearted exercise. For a passionate leader, an important and worthy goal provides a compelling reason to leap into the fray. The fulfillment of that goal is a journey of excitement and joy.

People who have broken out of the ordinary learn to love their participation in life. They often go against the grain. When others shy away from a task, they seek it. They may be the first to volunteer. Then they tackle the task with excitement. That kind of boldness spreads to others, and the person who exhibits that excitement may become what Tom Peters calls a "champion." Champions are the building blocks of many (maybe most) businesses. Often they are business owners. If the owner (or manager) is fortunate, a few employees will catch the enthusiasm and become their own champions. Champions inevitably make mistakes. Sometimes they fail. And sometimes they succeed. Nevertheless, they always seek to make a difference in whatever they do. If they're allowed to progress, they will attract people to their goals. If they are discouraged from making progress, they will go elsewhere.

Consider This: The organization that can tap into the energy of a champion can perform tasks that are impossible to accomplish by ordinary means.

ROSE BLUMKIN'S NEBRASKA FURNITURE MART

Sell cheap and tell the truth, don't cheat
nobody, and don't take no kickbacks.
ROSE BLUMKIN

A 1984 article in the *Wall Street Journal* stated that even at ninety, Rose Blumkin could "run rings around" the top graduates of America's business schools and Fortune 500 CEOs. She emigrated from Russia to the United States in 1917, bribing her way past a border guard and traveling through China and Japan. She remembered, "When I came to this country, I thought I am the luckiest one in the world." The daughter of a poor rabbi, her success was due to a combination of brains, wit, and the determination to make something of herself.

Rose Blumkin began her business career at age forty-three in a pawnshop in Omaha, Nebraska. She ran the shop with her husband until he died in 1950. Then she decided to do something grander. Her idea became the Nebraska Furniture Mart, one of the largest furniture retailers in the US. But its rise to the top did not always go smoothly. Blumkin had to borrow $50,000 on a short-term note to pay suppliers during the Korean War. By holding a special sale, she quickly made $250,000 in cash and paid off the loan. Once out of debt, Blumkin operated on a cash-only basis and provided her customers with a wide range of quality products selling 20 percent to 30 percent below regular retail. One of the first businesses to successfully use the superstore concept, Rose Blumkin sold 90 percent of Nebraska Furniture Mart to Berkshire Hathaway in 1983 for $60 million in a handshake deal. Billionaire Warren Buffett said of her, "I'd rather wrestle grizzlies than compete with Mrs. B and her progeny."

Consider This: It is not trite to say "America is a land of opportunity." Opportunities abound for anyone with guts, brains, integrity, and fortitude.

SONIA SOTOMAYOR MAKES THE DECISION

Although I grew up in very modest and challenging
circumstances, I consider my life to be immeasurably rich.
SONIA SOTOMAYOR

Many stories of achievement begin with reading books. Sonia Sotomayor is no exception. As a curious child growing up in the Bronx as the daughter of Puerto Rican parents, she devoured every Nancy Drew book. Those books made her want to be a detective. And since a detective needs to know many things, she devoured books that took her around the world and through history. After Sonia's father died when she was nine, her mother used her meager income to provide the best educational resources she could afford. She bought a set of encyclopedias, and Sonia read every volume. She was accepted and sent to the highly rated Cardinal Spellman High School. Then a turning point in Sonia's life came from an unlikely source: *The Perry Mason Show* (a TV show about a detective). Sonia realized that the most crucial person in the series wasn't Perry Mason, but the judge who made the ultimate decisions. That settled it. She would become a judge.

After graduating as valedictorian, Sonia was encouraged by a counselor to apply to Ivy League schools. She was accepted to Princeton and entered a world she'd never imagined—full of wealthy and privileged kids. After initially stumbling academically, she doubled down, got help, read, and studied more than any other student. She graduated summa cum laude. Her next step was Yale Law School. Again her vision for the future changed. At one lecture she was convinced that becoming a public servant was preferable to earning big bucks at a prestigious law firm. Her rise through the ranks moved her from assistant district attorney to a United States District Court (appointed by George H. W. Bush), and finally to the Supreme Court (appointed by Barack Obama).

*Consider This: Read to learn. Learn to achieve. Achieve to gain influence. Use
your influence to create a better world*

FIVE GUYS BURGERS AND FRIES

*If we have to worry about the price, we
don't want to be in this business.*
JERRY MURRELL

If all you know how to cook is burgers and fries, your only option is to open the bestselling burger and fries joint in America. Jerry Murrell decided that's what he'd do. So Jerry, with his four sons, started a little burger restaurant they called Five Guys. (Jerry's wife, Janie, served as bookkeeper.) Their idea was to create a restaurant that brought people from far and wide. Jerry noticed the little burger joints where lines were constantly out the door. What separated these joints from the others was their specialization. Just burgers. Just fries. After talking it over with the family, they made a plan. Simple. In 1986 they found a little low-rent location, bought used equipment (which they rebuilt), and gave it the temporary name Five Guys. The first day started slow, but the word got around, and they had a crowd by the day's end.

Why was it successful? Jerry knew how to grill burgers and fry potatoes, so that's all they offered. They selected the most popular potatoes, pickles, cooking oil, and bread to make the best burger. Even the mayonnaise was chosen using a taste test. They all chose the same one, which was expensive. But that's what made the best burger. So their burger price had to be more than an average burger. It didn't matter. People came because Five Guys burgers were the best. As sales increased, the family had to decide where to go next. Working together, they raised money from friends and began an expansion that has grown to more than 1,500 franchisees worldwide and $2 billion in revenues (when this book was published).

Consider This: A simple menu with the best ingredients and excellent service beats cookie-cutter places with mega menus and cardboard food. Control the quality, and watch people beat a path to your door.

CURT CARLSON ADAPTS TO NEW OPPORTUNITIES

Enjoying success requires the ability to adapt.
Only by being open to change will you have a true
opportunity to get the most from your talent.
NOLAN RYAN

The son of Swedish immigrants, Curt Carlson was born into a family that stressed hard work and the importance of family. By the age of eleven, Curt had his first paper route. While in college, he operated a corner newsstand and sold advertising. After graduation he worked as a salesman for Procter & Gamble. One day he noticed a department store giving away coupons for each dollar's worth of merchandise purchased. The idea was to collect coupons and redeem them later for merchandise. That gave Curt an idea. In 1938 he started the Gold Bond Stamp Company. He spent evenings and weekends selling his trading stamps to mom-and-pop groceries in Minneapolis, Minnesota. The concept caught on slowly at first, but soon Curt quit his full-time job to devote time to his new venture.

Just as the Gold Bond business took off, World War II paralyzed the market. But the company managed to survive, and by the 1950s Gold Bond stamps were being offered by stores throughout America. Unsure the trading stamp would last forever, Curt decided to adapt. In 1960 he purchased a Radisson Hotel in Minneapolis. Using that as a start, he built a chain of hotels throughout the United States and Canada. Other Carlson holdings included restaurants, marketing companies, travel agencies, and investment firms. Carlson also supported nonprofit organizations. His company belonged to the Minnesota Keystone Club, consisting of businesses that donated 5 percent of their earnings to selected local organizations. In recognition of a $25 million gift, the University of Minnesota named their Carlson School of Management after him.

Consider This: Working hard and smart can still get you to the top. But that's not the end. When one idea dies out, adapt, choose a new opportunity, and keep going.

BOYS TOWN

He ain't heavy, Father . . . he's m' brother.
BOYS TOWN SLOGAN

While operating a haven for homeless men in Omaha, Nebraska, Father Edward J. Flanagan learned an important lesson. Many of these men had begun life as neglected or abused children. That realization made him want to address the problem at its source—providing neglected young boys with a way to escape inevitable poverty. So, with support from his archbishop, Father Flanagan changed the direction of his ministry and opened a home for such youth.

On December 12, 1917, Father Flanagan began his ministry by taking in five troubled youngsters at a modest home in Omaha. News spread quickly. By Christmas he was caring for twenty-five boys. Judges heard about the effectiveness of this ministry and sent so many boys that only those whose conditions were most desperate could be accepted. At first local residents were generous with donations. Still, some complained about the growing number of delinquent boys in the neighborhood. With support from friends and business owners, Boys Town was erected on a ten-acre farm outside Omaha. On October 22, 1921, Father Flanagan and the boys moved into their new home. The hastily constructed temporary buildings soon housed a growing "family" of more than two hundred boys. Omaha citizens conducted several campaigns to raise support for the town. Finally, in March 1922, the ground was broken for a permanent five-story main building. Thousands of children have experienced the benefits and responsibilities of a loving family through the ongoing ministry of Father Flanagan's Boys Town. Today, Boys Town provides services to more than thirty-five thousand children.

Consider This: Every person has potential. For some, family or circumstances prevents them from finding that potential. For those with the heart and resources, helping others is not a task. It is a welcomed opportunity.

THE COMPANY HERO

I have not failed. I've just found 10,000 ways that won't work.
THOMAS EDISON

In business, as in all organizations, it is helpful to have a role model to follow. Organizational heroes are not easy to come by. When one appears, the most should be made of their expertise. In many businesses the founder is the hero. They took the company from nothing to something with hard work, sweat, and commitment. Often the hero failed at other enterprises only to rise again (and again). One such person was Tom Watson. He tried his hand at teaching, bookkeeping, selling pianos and sewing machines, and working as a butcher. He got involved in unsavory financial practices until he turned his career around in the emerging Computing-Tabulating-Recording industry. His experiences fashioned his famous directives to his employees to "Think" and "Aim High."

Thomas Edison emulated persistence by trying thousands of ways to make a light bulb work before stumbling onto success. Mary Kay lifted her life from a disastrous beginning to become a giant in the cosmetics industry. Milton Hershey failed and failed again in the candy-making business until he hit upon the idea of a chocolate bar. FedEx had a worker who brought in an entire mailbox that refused to open so the contents could be extracted and delivered on time. A police officer helped raise money for a family whose house burned down. Nurses spent uncounted hours treating COVID patients. A minister lived with the homeless to better understand their plight. Recognition of such organizational heroes inspires others. It heightens awareness of possible opportunities to excel. The result is a more motivated and usually happier employee and a more productive organization.

Consider This: Seek out and repeat hero stories about your business or organization. They will inspire and challenge everyone to step up to the standard.

WARREN BUFFETT'S MILLION-DOLLAR BET

Both large and small investors should
stick with low-cost index funds.

WARREN BUFFETT

In his will, Warren Buffett instructed his widow to place 90 percent of his portfolio in low-cost index funds such as Vanguard. Buffett claims that, for passive inventors, this strategy was not madness. It was genius. To prove it, he placed a million-dollar bet. He contended that funds put in a low-cost index fund, specifically the S&P 500, would outearn any hedge fund over ten years. Part of his logic was that hedge funds, where experts choose stocks and investors pay a commission for the service, were too expensive. And, he surmised, very few people can actually do well selecting funds. So he waited for someone to take his bet. Only one brave investor stepped forward: Ted Seides.

The test began on January 1, 2008. That, it turned out, was a bad year for the stock market. The index fund plummeted 37 percent. The hedge fund only plunged 23.9 percent. Buffett's bet was off to a bad start. Then, in subsequent years, the S&P mainly went up. And without fees to siphon off profits, returns grew and grew. The hedge funds, although they did okay, were burdened by fee after fee. In the end Buffett's strategy averaged 7.1 percent per year, while the expertly managed hedge funds managed only 2.2 percent. To put it in dollars, $1 million earned $854,000 with Buffett in ten years while the hedge funds earned $220,000. Clearly Buffett isn't a passive investor. He chooses stocks, buys companies, and invests actively. But for someone without his expertise, a simple, low-cost index fund is a great way to invest hard-earned money.

Consider This: Sometimes simplicity is the best strategy. For example, earning money slowly and steadily is often more lucrative in the long run than gambling for quick returns.

JULY 1

FORD'S V-8

Most people spend more time and energy going
around problems than in trying to solve them.

HENRY FORD

People with vision often butt heads with the more practical world. One person imagines in their mind's eye how something could be accomplished. But convincing others may not be an easy matter. A select few can ignore the naysaying of others and push to make their vision become a reality. For example, Henry Ford wanted to build a V-8 motor with cylinders cast in a single block to outdo the rival 6-cylinder Chevrolet motor. Engineers could design it on paper, but they all agreed that it simply could not be made. "Produce it anyway," was Ford's reply. He put his best engineers in a secret laboratory and told them to get to work. For months and months they experimented with ideas and came to Ford saying, "It can't be done!" But Ford insisted, and the engineers tried additional ideas.

After more than a year of experimentation, there seemed to be no reasonable solution to the problem. The engineers reiterated their first assessment: "Impossible." Ford again said, "Keep trying." Although the engineers remained convinced that the task could not be accomplished, a solution was eventually found, and Ford had his V-8 motor. Some called Ford hardheaded, and they were right! But had it not been for his stubborn determination, Ford would not have pioneered many advancements that revolutionized the fledgling automobile industry. A visionary may see capabilities far beyond what is currently possible. If there were no visions of the future, we would not strive to reach them.

Consider This: The solution to a problem may not be readily available. It may be thousands of man-hours away. But if you can conceive that there is an answer, you can eventually find a way to make it happen.

A GATHERING OF TRAITORS

Follow the path of the unsafe, independent thinker. Expose your ideas to the danger of controversy. Speak your mind and fear less the label of "crackpot" than the stigma of conformity.
THOMAS J. WATSON

A time for decision had come. A small gathering of patriots—some would call them traitors—faced a world-changing dilemma. They knew the choice before them could very well cost them their lives. The date was July 2, 1776. Representatives from thirteen colonies gathered to consider a resolution to declare America's independence from the king of England. If even one of the colony delegations objected, the motion would fail. Most supported the idea, but Delaware's vote was split. One agreed. One disagreed. And one delegate, Caesar Rodney, was absent, trapped in a thunderstorm between Dover and Philadelphia. Nevertheless, the proposal was brought forward by Virginia's Richard Henry Lee. "Resolved: That these United Colonies are, and of right ought to be, free and independent States, that they are absolved from all allegiance to the British Crown."

Adoption of this measure meant the delegates could lose all their status and wealth. They would surely hang if they voted in favor and their actions failed. The document up for vote eliminated slavery. But some states objected, so others compromised. Nevertheless, the Declaration retained "all men are created equal." Intense negotiations continued. As the final vote began, the door to the chamber swung open. Caesar Rodney arrived, wet from head to toe, "in his boots and spurs." He cast the deciding "yea" vote, and the resolution passed. John Adams wrote that July 2 would forever be celebrated with "pomp and parade, games, sports, guns, bells, bonfires, and illumination." But negotiations for final changes in wording meant the official announcement would have to wait for two more days.

Consider This: Every decision is imperfect. But sometimes the best strategy is to move forward as you can while you continue to seek a more perfect way.

MOVING UP THE LADDER

*You simply have to put one foot in front of the other and
keep going. Put blinders on and plow right ahead.*

GEORGE LUCAS

Everyone has heard the phrase, "It's not what you know but who you know
that counts." This bit of folk wisdom has found some verification in studies
about how people move up the corporate ladder. A good relationship with
more senior people can be helpful to your career path. Most managers tend
to promote people they can work with, whom they can trust, and who will be
team players. The employee who ignores the role of business relationships is
probably the same one who will stay in the mailroom the rest of his career. In
a corporate study, Robert Jackall researched the factors that help move people
up the managerial ladder. He understood that once a person reached a certain
level, their managerial ability was taken for granted. After that, there were five
other key factors. The top factor Jackall discovered was Patron Power.

A manager must have a mentor, sponsor, or champion who can pull them
up the ladder. Often, when the mentor moves up, their favorite workers move
up as well. Style is also an essential component for a potential upward move.
The manager must be well organized and give well-conceived presentations and
think fast. Also, the manager must be perceived as a team player. He must have
self-control, manage his stress, and exhibit a smiling and agreeable demeanor
in public. Finally, the manager must look and dress the part. Shakespeare said
we are all actors, and only those actors who can play the part well wind up in
the starring role.

*Consider This: Which of these factors do you need to work on? Are any of them
holding you back?*

THE RISK OF FREEDOM

*The Constitution only gives people the right to pursue
happiness. You have to catch it yourself.*
BENJAMIN FRANKLIN

What does Independence Day have to do with your personal success? On that day, a unique type of government never before seen in the history of the world was formed. And from it, the United States created opportunities like the world had never seen. Americans have the freedom to succeed, to fail, to choose their lot in life. It all started when a few entrepreneurial patriots risked their lives to make it happen. In the summer of 1776, a group of fifty-six men met and fashioned the greatest nation in the world. They knew they were at risk. Patrick Henry boldly declared, "If this is treason, make the most of it." Thomas Jefferson was called upon to form a committee and draw up a Declaration of Independence. Every man knew that a signature on such a document could be a warrant for his death.

War was inevitable. People would die, and the outcome of the revolution could not be predicted. Yet, those patriots held fast to their strong belief in freedom and the rights of individuals. They were willing to take the risk—and willing to hope, work, and fight for victory. On July 4, 1776, after extensive debate, arguments, and modifications, each delegate signed the Declaration. The final document was flawed, as is every human endeavor. In some ways, it didn't go far enough. But it began a process by which every American can enjoy the freedom to choose how to live, what occupation to pursue, and what beliefs to hold. On Independence Day we celebrate those who took this bold step and risked their lives to secure those freedoms for us all.

Consider This: The United States is based on the belief that each person can and should be able to exercise the freedom of choice. What have you done with your freedom?

MONOPOLY

*You do not have to be a rocket scientist or have a
Harvard degree to play Monopoly for real.*
ROBERT KIYOSAKI

It was a bleak winter in 1933. The weather and the economy were terrible. Charles Darrow of Germantown, Pennsylvania, longed for the trips he had made to Atlantic City, New Jersey, but the Great Depression left him with little money for such frivolity. So Darrow concocted a little diversion. Inspired by a game named "Landlord," self-published by Lizzie Magie in 1903, he devised a similar game. His properties were the streets of Atlantic City: Boardwalk, Park Place, Baltic Avenue, Marvin Gardens, and the rest. Darrow called his game "Monopoly." It was all about making and spending money, something everyone wanted to do during the Great Depression. He showed the game to a few friends, and they liked it enough to want copies. So he made a few copies by hand and, thinking that he had a good idea, showed the game to Parker Brothers. But they considered the game too complicated to ever be successful.

Not willing to stop because of a single no, Darrow raised enough money to self-publish some sets and offered them to Wanamaker's Department Store in Philadelphia. Soon Monopoly was the rage of the city. People who normally went to bed by nine o'clock would find themselves still trying to buy Boardwalk at two in the morning. Something about the game was addictive. After the successful showing at Wanamaker's, Parker Brothers took a second look and acquired the rights to the game for $500. Now produced by Hasbro, Monopoly is a worldwide pastime that even boasts an annual "world series" of Monopoly.

Consider This: It's a tricky proposition, but if you have a good product—a book, a game, or a device—one strategy is to self-publish it. If you can prove its viability, you might be able to get a major company to offer you a deal.

SUPER GLUE

Mistakes are the portals of discovery.
JAMES JOYCE

For all the horrors of war, it is also a time of innovation. Necessity, it seems, really does lead to invention. But sometimes the creation gets overlooked, at least for a while. Such was the case in 1942 when Dr. Harry Coover Jr. was trying to create a clear gun sight. He failed to discover the substance he was looking for in his experimentation. Instead, he came up with an exceptionally sticky goo, too sticky to be of any use. The stuff was soon forgotten. Then, in 1951, Coover and Fred Joyner, now working at Eastman Kodak, rediscovered this same substance, cyanoacrylate, while working on another project. This time they realized that a super-strong adhesive might have commercial value. What made it worthwhile is that it required no heat or pressure to bond to anything (and it stuck to almost everything). In 1958 this cyanoacrylate glue was marketed for the first time under the super clever name Eastman #910.

Cyanoacrylate (also called CA Glue) caught on. It was marketed as Super Glue, Loctite Quick Set 404, Permabond, Krazy Glue, Gorilla Super Glue Gel, and Super Bonder. CA Glue quickly caught the fancy of newspapers and radio and television programs looking for exciting stories. On one occasion a radio station put different adhesives to the test to see which could hold up a three-thousand-pound car. You guessed it. Eastman's Super Glue came out on top, holding an automobile up for ten seconds. More and more uses of CA Glue have been discovered over the years. It's been used to close up wounds on the battlefield, hold electronic components together, attach artificial fingernails, fix broken ceramics, quickly bond wood pieces together, and much more.

Consider This: Accidents happen. But sometimes they lead to serendipitous discoveries. Keep your mind open. The next mistake you make may be worth millions of dollars.

MAD LIBS

If you could choose one characteristic that would
get you through life, choose a sense of humor.
JENNIFER JONES

Leonard Stern was given the word "hyperbole" at a school spelling bee. He stammered, thought. And gave it a try. But he misspelled it and lost the round. Humiliated, he went home and studied the dictionary, determined to never make that mistake again. As it turned out, Stern liked the dictionary and decided to learn one new word every day. After growing up and becoming a writer for television scripts, Stern remembers racking his brain one day trying to describe a noise for a *Honeymooners* script he was writing. About that time his friend Roger Price showed up. Stern told him, "I need an adjective." Price started listing bizarre adjectives, and each one made Stern laugh. What if "Ralph Kramden now had a boss with a clumsy nose"? Or a "naked nose"? The odd adjectives stuck into the phrases were hilarious.

Stern and Price had a eureka moment. This would make a fun game. That night they wrote several short stories with important words (adjectives, nouns, verbs) left out. At a party that night, they had people choose random fill-in words, then repeated the stories with those words. Everyone laughed. It was magic. But they didn't do anything with it for five years. Then one day, as they were eating the blue-plate special at Sardi's in New York, they overhead a conversation. An actor wanted to ad-lib a scene, and his agent told him that was a mad thing to do. They had a name! Mad Libs! They showed their idea to every publisher and game manufacturer they could find. None were interested. So they published it themselves. Today more than 110 million copies of Mad Libs have sold worldwide.

Consider This: Ideas will never go anywhere until there is a champion who's willing to do whatever it takes to bring the concept or plan to fruition. Don't give up too soon.

AN WANG

*Success is more a function of consistent
common sense than it is of genius.*

AN WANG

In 1988 Dr. An Wang was elected to the National Inventors Hall of Fame in Arlington, Virginia. He joined a prestigious group of other well-known Americans, including Thomas Edison, Henry Ford, and the Wright Brothers. An was the son of a Shanghai English teacher. After studying in his native China, he came to the United States and entered Harvard. He emerged with a PhD in physics and an idea for a revolutionary way to store information in a computer's memory. An's invention, a doughnut-shaped device called a magnetic memory core, increased the response speed of the computer's memory. IBM bought the device, and it remained the standard computer core memory for two decades.

Here's how it happened. Dr. Wang founded his own computing company with $600 in a walk-up loft in Boston's South End. In 1951, his first year, Wang's sales were a meager $15,000. To inspire his company to grow, Wang continually challenged himself and his employees to innovate and invent. Over the next several decades, his team developed a continuous stream of new computing products, and the company grew steadily. Wang found a niche in the development of word processing and office automation. He extended his operation, Wang Laboratories, into a Fortune 500 company with an annual revenue of more than $3 billion and thirty-three thousand employees. After An died in 1990, the company was absorbed into other companies. But his contributions to computing are remembered by the An Wang Professorship of Computer Science and Electrical Engineering at Harvard University.

Consider This: One invention does not make a company. In the high-tech industry, success results from a long series of good ideas and a leader who inspires continued innovation.

JOHN WILLIAMS

*So much of what we do is ephemeral and quickly forgotten,
even by ourselves, so it's gratifying to have something
you have done linger in people's memories.*
JOHN WILLIAMS

His music is instantly recognizable. When you hear the first two notes from *Jaws*, your spine shivers, especially if you're in the ocean. John Williams grew up in a musical family and studied at Juilliard, dreaming of becoming a concert pianist. Then, hearing pianists such as Van Cliburn in concert, he decided to be a composer instead. He performed in a Hollywood studio band until he got a chance to write music for the big-screen film *Daddy-O* in 1959. Music for several other movies and television series followed. After that, Williams's star began to sparkle with nomination after nomination, including Academy Awards and Golden Globes.

In 1974 a single meeting changed his career. Director Steven Spielberg had heard a Williams recording and asked Universal to set up a lunch meeting. Williams found the twenty-five-year-old Spielberg surprisingly young and tremendously knowledgeable. Spielberg convinced Williams to compose the score for *The Sugarland Express*. Although the movie didn't win any big awards, it began a partnership that produced some of the most memorable films in American film history. *Jaws* became the pair's first megahit. It was followed by other blockbuster films, including *Star Wars*, *Close Encounters of the Third Kind*, *E.T.*, *Raiders of the Lost Ark*, *Schindler's List*, and *Saving Private Ryan*. Spielberg once said that Williams reinvented himself with every film, with music perfectly suited to each story. In his astounding career, Williams composed the quintessential American soundtrack for generations of filmgoers.

Consider This: Our first dream may need to be modified. Perhaps there's another opportunity waiting for us that will take us to heights never imagined.

ORDINARY PEOPLE MAKE AN EXTRAORDINARY NATION

The major work of the world is not done by geniuses. It is done by ordinary people, with balance in their lives, who have learned to work in an extraordinary manner.

GORDON B. HINCKLEY

Although biographies of famous people with exciting stories are fun and entertaining, they're not really the foundation of an exceptional country. Instead, most people who built America were workers from ordinary families who had extraordinary values. For example, parents Tom and Ida were neither highly educated nor wealthy. Tom was a postman, and Ida stayed at home until all her kids were in school, then opened a small flower shop. They smoked multiple packs of cigarettes a day, and both died early because of the habit. Each kid was expected to do their own homework and get good grades. They never purchased a set of encyclopedias, although everyone in the family read the local newspaper, the *Saturday Evening Post*, and *National Geographic*. All six lived in a 774-square-foot two-bedroom house. At times there was little more than a can of soup in the cupboard, and hamburgers were always "extended" by mixing in breadcrumbs.

They were the epitome of a 1950s- and '60s-era middle-class family. Yes, they had flaws, but they wanted to be treated fairly, so they treated everyone with dignity. They attended church every Sunday and prayed before meals. When each kid turned sixteen, they got a job. Only one graduated from college, and he paid his own way. Your family probably differs in many ways, although maybe some of this description is familiar. But everyday families like this have more to do with creating a country of decent, creative, and entrepreneurial citizens than a stadium full of corporate moguls.

Consider This: Ordinary working people provide a solid foundation for any nation. But, for most of the world, families full of care, love, and stability are (and should be) more important than riches, fame, and honors.

7-ELEVEN CREATES A CONVENIENT BUSINESS

The best way to have a good idea is to have a lot of ideas.
LINUS PAULING

In the 1920s few people had that newfangled appliance called a refrigerator. Instead, most people had an icebox—an insulated wooden box with a compartment where you placed a block of ice. The ice kept the food in the chest cold. People went to a neighborhood icehouse to get ice blocks or had them delivered to their door. One icehouse in Dallas was managed by Johnny Green. He had an idea. Since most grocery stores in that era were only open 8:00 a.m. to 5:00 p.m. Monday through Saturday, what if he offered staples that people might need during off-hours or on the weekend? He could use the cold storage area to sell milk, butter, eggs, and soft drinks to his customers. People began to flock to Johnny's store, particularly in the evenings and on weekends, because it was so convenient. Soon the parent company, Southland Ice, took notice. They implemented Green's idea in stores all over town.

As more and more people bought refrigerators, fewer needed ice. As a result, a lot of ice houses closed. But Southland stores stayed profitable because they offered food and drinks. Thus the convenience store was born. First they renamed them Tote'm stores. Then they changed the name to 7-Eleven to reflect their open hours. Today 7-Eleven is the world's largest operator, franchiser, and licenser of convenience stores, with more than seventy thousand units worldwide. The US stores sell more *USA Today* newspapers, *Sports Illustrated* magazines, cold beer, cold single-serve bottled water, Gatorade, fresh-grilled hot dogs, single-serve chips, and money orders than any other retailer in the world. They also sell fourteen million Slurpees every month.

Consider This: What products does your organization already have that could be leveraged to create new sales or reach new customers? Or what talent do you have that could be leveraged into a new service?

ALEXIA COOPER CAPTURES THE SUN'S RAYS

*If you take care of your employees, your
employees will take care of the customers.*
ALEXIA COOPER

Solar energy is a hot industry. New ways of harnessing and storing solar power make it more viable for businesses and homeowners each year. One company that has taken advantage of this leading-edge opportunity is Bell Solar & Electrical Systems, founded by Trevor Bell in 2007. In 2017 Alexia Cooper joined the Bell team as director of operations. In 2020 she became CEO and stepped up to the challenge of leading a company in a male-dominated industry. Because of her commitment to providing opportunities for women, Bell offered paid apprenticeships to women interested in the electrical or solar industries.

Cooper's goal was to make Bell a growing and viable company in this emerging and competitive industry by providing superior experiences to her customers and employees. Their mission was "rewiring the world to build a sustainable future." They were rewarded for representing Bell's highest technical and customer relations standards. For example, Cooper stated that installers "should be rewarded for being on roofs in 110 degrees." She was also committed to providing cost-effective, clean, and sustainable energy for her customers while helping everyone reduce reliance on fossil fuels. As a result of Cooper's leadership and her team's efforts, Bell grew by a whopping 416 percent in 2020 compared to 2019. Cooper focused on providing a technologically superior product for customers and life-changing careers for her team to maintain company growth. Her leadership put her on the prestigious *Forbes* 30 Under 30 list in 2021.

Consider This: Creating and sustaining a business in a competitive field is difficult. But companies that create win-win environments for both workers and customers are the ones that rise to the top.

ALUMINUM FOIL

When you're curious, you find lots of interesting things.
WALT DISNEY

Many products that we consider indispensable today were developed or discovered by accident. That invariably happens when some keen-minded individual suddenly realizes a use for an item initially created for another purpose. Examples are the microwave oven, facial tissues (Kleenex), Silly Putty, the Slinky, the Frisbee, and even the Band-Aid. These products were all derived from some other existing product. Another item that was discovered by accident was aluminum foil.

Before aluminum foil was invented, tin foil was used to wrap candy and cigarettes. It was also used by Edison to create the first sound recordings. Then, in 1910, aluminum foil was invented in Switzerland. It soon replaced tin foil since it was more malleable and didn't spoil the taste of the wrapped food. One aluminum foil manufacturer was the US Foil Company, founded in 1919 by R. S. Reynolds. On Thanksgiving in 1940, the wife of an employee was looking for a pan in which to roast a turkey. When she couldn't locate one, her husband came up with the idea of wrapping the bird in some of the company's foil. Soon this unique use of the product became known throughout the company. After further development of the foil for consumer use, the company (now Reynolds Metals) introduced a commercial version of aluminum foil to the world in 1947. Sales grew quickly until the Korean War, when Reynolds voluntarily limited its foil production to support the war effort. At the end of the conflict, sales of the company's hallmark product again soared, and aluminum foil has since become a staple of virtually every American kitchen.

Consider This: Look for new uses for the products you sell or use today. Listen to how customers use your products. You might discover a whole new industry.

SERVICE DOGS

The average dog is a nicer person than the average person.

ANDY ROONEY

Dogs have been man's best friend for thousands of years. They've been not only companions but also work partners and helpers. Art from thousands of years ago depicts dogs in both Europe and China leading blind people. It's not known how these dogs were trained, but it's clear they were helpers. In modern America, recognition of dogs as service animals took some convincing. The story begins with a young blind man named Morris Frank. Frank was trapped at home in New York City unless someone was available to help him around. He wanted independence. After World War I, he heard about dogs being trained to lead blind soldiers in Europe. He contacted Dorothy Eustis, an American training German shepherds as guide dogs in Switzerland. He traveled to Europe and received training in 1928. When he returned to the States, news reporters heard of Frank's guide dog and followed him as he walked the streets of New York. They snapped pictures of him crossing busy streets and made him and his "seeing eye" dog, Buddy, famous.

But service dogs were not readily accepted at first. No laws required specific certification of dogs or acceptance by the public. Landlords could ban dogs from their buildings, and businesses were not required to allow them into stores. Nevertheless, the number of animal-owner teams grew with the help of organizations such as the Seeing Eye, NEADS, and Can Do Canines. Finally, in 1990, the Americans with Disabilities Act (ADA) was passed by Congress. It defines a service dog as any guide dog, signal dog, or other animal trained to assist people with disabilities. Today service dogs are recognized and welcomed in all businesses and buildings across America.

Consider This: One person's need fulfilled can help many other people. What can you do to create a better world by helping people in need?

GENERAL MOTORS

Give a man a clear-cut job and let him do it.

ALFRED P. SLOAN

More than one thousand companies attempted to enter the automobile business at the turn of the century. About two hundred made commercial products, and only a handful went on to succeed. Unfortunately, as in all new technology areas, the shakeout eliminated all but the most innovative, determined, and able companies. One such manufacturer was General Motors (GM), formed in 1908 by W. C. Durant. Durant brought together several new auto companies, including Buick, Oldsmobile, Cadillac, Oakland (Pontiac), Ewing, Marquette, and Reliance and Rapid (who produced trucks). The Chevrolet Motor Company, formed in 1911 by Durant and race car driver Louis Chevrolet, became a part of GM in 1918. But as so often happens in business, the genius who brought the idea to fruition didn't have the business acumen to take it to the next level. So in 1923 Alfred P. Sloan took the helm.

Sloan reorganized GM. He changed it from a mishmash of acquired companies with different goals and values into one solid business. During the thirty-three years of Sloan's leadership, GM progressed from producing only 10 percent of the world's cars to making over half the world supply in the mid-1950s. Perhaps Sloan's greatest gift to GM was a superior management style, which has been studied and replicated in countless businesses since. Sloan described his style as "decentralized operations and responsibilities with coordinated control." His goal was to balance individual and group management, giving each worker a straightforward task and the responsibility to carry it out. By 1931 GM was the largest auto manufacturer in the world.

Consider This: In every new industry, there will be a shakeout. Those companies that survive will do so because of better ideas and superior management.

CELESTIAL SEASONINGS

Good taste is the flower of good sense.

A. POINCELOT

Just for his own pleasure, nineteen-year-old Mo Siegel picked herbs in the mountains of Colorado and blended them to make an herbal tea. His friends loved the tea and encouraged him to sell the blend. Mo experimented with selling small amounts of his concoction at local health food stores, and customers seemed to like it. Although his small experiment was successful, Mo found that creating a company to produce and sell large amounts of tea was not easy. But the dream of success was fixed in his mind, and it urged him on. Mo and his wife, Peggy, crisscrossed the country, introducing their tea to skeptical store owners. Back home, times were very lean. There was no money to hire herb pickers or people to make the tea bags and print the boxes.

Mo believed that his company would make it. Although he was a college dropout, Mo read profusely. He gained business sense and a success-oriented mindset from reading the biographies of his American heroes: Abraham Lincoln, Walt Disney, Tom Watson, and others. He also had a deep belief in God and had carefully studied the life of Jesus. Work, work, and more work slowly moved the business into prosperity. Mo Siegel was smart enough to realize that he could not know everything. So as his Celestial Seasonings company grew, he hired key people from Coca-Cola, Pepsi, Pepperidge Farms, General Foods, and other successful corporations. Workers were given ownership in the company. Their commitment to excellence in quality and production made Celestial Seasonings a classic success story. At the time of this writing, Celestial Seasonings is the largest manufacturer of herbal teas in North America.

Consider This: Study, work, and think. Learning from the masters, working hard, and thinking smart are always keys to success.

NORM BRINKER

*You have 45 minutes to convince the customer
to come again; that's your objective.*
NORM BRINKER

While only a first grader, Norm Brinker dreamed of owning a horse. His family couldn't afford one, so Norm earned money by picking cotton, delivering newspapers, raising rabbits, and kenneling dogs. Those early businesses taught him both success and failure. Norm's skill and love of riding earned him a spot on the 1952 Olympic equestrian team. Two years later, at the Modern Pentathlon in Hungary, Norm's horse stumbled during a jumping competition, catapulting him out of the saddle. Even though he sustained a broken collarbone, Norm got back on his mount and finished eighth in a field of sixty. This type of perseverance and grit epitomized Norm's entire life.

To pay his way through college, Norm sold cutlery door-to-door. Upon graduation he received several job offers and chose the one that promised to be the most "fun." Norm played an essential role in expanding Jack-in-the-Box fast-food restaurants during the 1960s. In 1964, with a lot of experience under his belt, he decided to open his own restaurant. His first try, Brink's Coffee Shop, was a failure. But after rethinking and studying the market, he came up with a winner. His new restaurant was based on an Old English theme. Steak and Ale was an instant success. It is also cited as the originator of the salad bar. Steak and Ale was so successful that it inspired an entire casual dining industry. Other restaurants in Norm Brinker's universe include Chili's, Bennigan's, Macaroni Grill, Corner Bakery Cafe, On the Border, and Maggiano's Little Italy. Examples of restaurants started by Brinker's protégés include Outback Steakhouse, Houston's, and P. F. Chang's.

Consider This: Persistence, fortitude, and hard work are the foundations of success. So when you're knocked down, get back up and keep fighting.

THE TYPEWRITER

Events are never absolute. Their outcome
depends entirely upon the individual.
HONORÉ DE BALZAC

Christopher Sholes was not the first person to invent the typewriter—in fact, he was the fifty-second. As early as 1843, patents were awarded for writing machines. In 1866 Sholes joined the list. As a printer and newspaperman, he created a machine designed to number book pages. When a friend remarked that his device could be redesigned to type letters, Sholes accepted the challenge. For seven years he worked on versions of a typing machine. Once he had a working prototype, he wrote letters to possible investors on his new device. One of his contacts was a Pennsylvania businessman and promoter named James Densmore. Densmore agreed to pay off Sholes's debt of $600 and provide future financing for a 25 percent stake in the invention. Sholes agreed, not knowing that the $600 represented all of Densmore's liquid assets.

Densmore embraced the new venture with enthusiasm. Realizing that the device needed more mechanical expertise and financing, the pair sold rights to the machine to another company, Remington. Sholes took a $12,000 payment for his share, and Densmore negotiated a royalty that would eventually pay him $1.5 million. Remington promoted the machine but was a little off in its initial marketing of the typewriter. Their sales pitch, "Persons traveling by sea can write with it when pen writing is impossible," didn't sell a lot of machines. Finally they rethought the business advantages of typewriting. With the help of the YWCA, they taught thousands of women how to use the typewriter. Using the skills of newly trained typists, they made a successful entry into the business world.

Consider This: You may not be the first to think of a new idea, but if you keep at it when others quit, you may well be the one who gets the prize.

CHIP AND JOANNA GAINES'S "FIXER UPPER"

I had always had a dream to open up a boutique of some sort.
JOANNA GAINES

Joanna's dad ran a Firestone store, and she appeared in some television ads. One day when Chip came into the store to get tires on his truck, he saw her and said, "Hey, you're the girl in the commercials." Two years later, they were married. Chip and Joanna were entrepreneurs from the start. In 2003 Joanna opened a little store in Waco called The Little Shop on Bosque, helping customers with interior design. As a side business, she and Chip flipped houses. He'd demo and rebuild, and Joanna would design the renovation. Then, after a decade of fighting the ups and downs of the housing/renovation market (and a few personal spats as well), opportunity knocked.

Chip and Joanna's life was about to change. It started with photos of one of their renovations a friend sent to a blog named "Design Mom." The post caught the eyes of a production company working with HGTV. Chip and Joanna were ready for a new adventure. They had over a hundred redos under their belts, and they fell quickly into producing a pilot. Chip was silly and funny. Joanna had Southern charm tempered with self-confident ideas. When the episode aired, viewers loved the give-and-take of this real-life family. The single episode turned into a series in 2014, and ratings shot through the roof. Chip and Joanna's success not only brought Waco into the nation's limelight, but it also launched a juggernaut industry centered around Magnolia Market at the Silos. As Joanna once said, "If I didn't have Chip Gaines in my life, I'd still be dreaming in my head—but not acting out on any of that, not living it out."

Consider This: Be brave. Get out there and start doing something you enjoy. Find a partner. Each person may be strong, but together you can be unstoppable.

THE POTATO CHIP

*Common sense in an uncommon degree
is what the world calls wisdom.*
SAMUEL TAYLOR COLERIDGE

In 1853 George Crum was chef at a resort in Saratoga Springs, New York, when he came up with a new way to fry potatoes. Everyone liked the idea, but some customers told George his sliced potatoes were too thick. He cut them thinner. Even thinner, they said. Finally, he sliced the potatoes so thinly they were almost transparent. He then fried them in deep oil and salted them. Just right! The customers ate them up. Like most legends, there are competing stories about who first devised the chips. Other accounts claim that his sister, Kate Wicks, first fried up the tasty snacks. Nevertheless, once the chips (now called Saratoga Chips) appeared on the scene, their fame quickly spread up and down the East Coast and to the rest of the world.

In the 1890s George Sleeper also contributed to the history of the potato chip. He was a caterer in Massachusetts when he placed potato chips in box lunches. They proved so popular that he built a business around the chips and popularized their use in packaged lunches. In 1921 Earl Wise used the potato chip to get him out of a bind. As a grocer with far too many potatoes, he decided to slice them on his cabbage cutter and make them into chips, which he sold in bags for a nickel each. His idea soon grew into a business. Wise Potato Chips became one of the first producers of processed foods sold in grocery stores. Hundreds of independent chip makers sprang up throughout the United States in the twenties and thirties and after World War II. Many of those enterprises eventually were assimilated into larger food companies.

Consider This: Good ideas do not have to be original. It may be less risky to duplicate someone else's success from another part of the country.

WINNEBAGO'S JOBS

*Thousands of tired, nerve-shaken, over-civilized people
are beginning to find out going to the mountains is
going home; that wilderness is a necessity.*

JOHN MUIR

Citizens watched in dismay as young people from Forest City moved away from the small town and into the big city. It was all about jobs. To counteract the trend, the chamber of commerce decided to develop a new industry for the town. One of those playing an active part was John K. Hanson, a funeral home manager. First, John opened a travel trailer dealership. Next, he worked with a company in California to increase business to manufacture the then-popular "Aljo" trailer. Initially, the company was successful and provided the jobs the community wanted. But within a few years, the company had no assets and thirty-nine unsold trailers. The company cut production and threatened to close. Hanson took charge. After losing the California company's support, he changed the company's name to Winnebago (after a nearby river) and set up a new factory.

With the community's investment in danger, Hanson worked with a committee of local leaders who agreed to manage the new factory for a year. The new company needed credibility. So Hansen applied his knowledge of the furniture business to help the factory build better and lighter furniture specifically designed for travel trailers. The company also developed a Thermo-Panel to insulate the trailer and keep weight down and other "comfort" amenities. Hanson took an active role in the national trailer manufacturers' organizations and created dealer shows and promotions. He also offered incentives to trailer buyers such as free delivery anywhere in the US. By the end of the 1960s, Winnebago was established as a premier trailer manufacturer.

Consider This: One answer to a failing community is to create opportunities. Unfortunately, governments are seldom great entrepreneurs. But they can provide fertile soil where new industries can grow.

MARTHA BERRY'S COLLEGE

Not to be ministered unto, but to minister.
BERRY COLLEGE MOTTO

Martha Berry, the young daughter of a well-to-do family in northern Georgia, went to an old log cabin to read and write on most Sundays. She noticed that mountain children peeked through windows to watch her. Inviting them in, she told them Bible stories. Week after week, more children and even adults came to listen. Martha was impressed by the bright youngsters. But she also knew they had virtually no chance of obtaining an education. So she started a small school in an old church near Lavender Mountain. The church was named Possum Trot. From this humble beginning rose one of America's most renowned educational institutions.

For many years at Martha Berry College, students worked to pay their tuition. None were turned away for lack of funds. Berry even named the gate leading to her campus The Gate of Opportunity and believed that every building on the site should have a spire "to keep people looking up." As needs (and the number of students) grew, Martha searched for outside funding. Martha Berry College inspired the world. It also attracted such benefactors as Andrew Carnegie, Henry Ford, presidents from Theodore Roosevelt to Franklin Roosevelt, the king and queen of England, and many more. Each time a new project was needed, Martha announced, "We are stepping out on a plank of faith." Even today, according to Martha Berry's wishes, Berry College continues to be a different kind of institution, with a solid commitment to "educational quality, Christian values, insistence on the work ethic, and adherence to the principles of American private enterprise: personal responsibility, individual initiative, service to others, courage to take risks, belief in self and in our nation."

Consider This: One person can change the world with imagination and bravery. Could you be that one person?

IRVING BERLIN'S SONGS

*Simplicity is the badge of genius. Simplicity
is the badge of distinction.*

A. A. MILNE

As one of the most published songwriters in America, Irving Berlin must have studied with great composers. Perhaps he learned music theory from European masters or received training at a great conservatory. But no. In reality Berlin had none of those advantages. After only two years of formal education, he took to the streets as an entertainer. He sang in saloons and learned to pick out tunes with one finger on the keyboard. He never learned harmony and could only play in the key of F sharp. Yet in 1907 Berlin began to compose. It was not until 1911 that he had his first big hit, "Alexander's Ragtime Band," which sold more than a million copies in the first few months. Drafted in 1917 for service in World War I, Berlin wrote a soldier's show that included the famous song, "Oh, How I Hate to Get Up in the Morning."

Berlin's songs seem to be spontaneous inspirations. Yet his process of writing was long and painful. He often struggled with lyrics, going through many revisions to get them right. Then, with his limited piano mastery, he would bang out a tune. Somehow, after all the agonizing, the song would begin to flow naturally. Unlike a Gershwin song that can be identified after hearing its first measure, Berlin's songs have never had a distinctive style. Berlin never initiated a new musical trend; he took an existing trend and adapted his music to it. He wrote for the Ziegfeld Follies, Marx Brothers' movies, and Broadway shows. His best-known hits have included "White Christmas" and "God Bless America." In his own simplicity, Irving Berlin has managed to tell the ever-changing story of America in song.

Consider This: You don't have to be complex to be good. Simplicity goes a long way and has staying power that no fad will ever match.

FRANK LLOYD WRIGHT'S FALLING WATERS

Form follows function—that has been misunderstood. Form and function should be one, joined in a spiritual union.
FRANK LLOYD WRIGHT

Critics said he was past his prime. His best years were behind him. But Frank Lloyd Wright wasn't through. Wright grew up in Wisconsin. His lifelong concept of beauty and function came from his love of its landscape, its trees, hills, and valleys, its turn of seasons, everything. After his father left the family in 1885, Wright struggled to earn his college education. To cover expenses, he took a job as an assistant to the well-known architect Joseph Silsbee. That set Wright's path. He dropped out of school to work for Silsbee, moved on to another architectural firm, Adler and Sullivan (the father of the skyscraper), and continued to learn from the masters. Finally, he left Adler and Sullivan in 1893 to follow his own path. First making a name for himself with his prairie-style houses, Wright stepped into the international scene by securing a commission from the Japanese Emperor in 1915.

As the Great Depression hit and commissions dried up, Wright was approaching seventy. Many saw his light starting to wane. Not so. Wright was only catching his breath for a renewed sprint that would make him the quintessential American architect. His resurgence began with a commission for a residence from a famous Pittsburgh family, the Kaufmanns. The daring house he designed, "Falling Waters," was built between 1935 and 1937 and is now one of the most famous houses in the world. He designed the house to sit on top of the falls. It would blend into nature. The results were stunning. Falling Waters brought Wright new international fame and catapulted him into a new season of designing many other iconic buildings for another three decades.

Consider This: Is your work finished? Are you too old to continue? Think again. The best ideas may be yet to come. Relight your torch, and step up to the task.

RENEWING DISNEY

As long as you act as if you're coming from
behind, you have a shot at staying ahead.
MICHAEL EISNER

Walt Disney created much more than a company—he created a unique vision of the American Dream. Many of America's values and goals have been shaped by Disney's stories. These skillfully crafted tales have given generations of Americans hope in good over evil and the prospects of a better tomorrow. After Disney died in 1966, his entertainment empire languished. Walt's vision was so crucial that the company deteriorated without his leadership. By the 1980s hardly anyone expected the Disney Company to recover. This led to a shareholder revolt in 1984. Walt's nephew Roy took action. Along with the Bass brothers, they put Michael Eisner in the chief executive's seat. Eisner, a former president of Paramount with a solid track record, brought innovative ideas back to Disney. Drawing on the vast treasury of Disney films and characters, Eisner revived Disney's television presence, promoted the Disney theme parks, and reinvigorated Disney movies. Disney was crawling back to the top.

Bob Iger succeeded Eisner in 2000 and brought his own creative juices to the studios. He brought Pixar, Marvel, Twentieth Century Fox, and Lucasfilm Ltd. into the fold to strengthen the brand. He also fortified the Disney Animation Studios and opened Hong Kong and Shanghai Disney parks. With Eisner's fresh vision and strong leadership. Disney seemed unstoppable until the 2019 pandemic hit. During that severe economic slowdown, Iger stepped down, and Bob Chapek took the reins in 2020. Although Disney took a significant financial hit during the downturn, its strength, imaginative genius, and history helped it roar back into viability.

Consider This: The exit of a strong founder may signal the beginning of the end. In fact, the market is so unforgiving that innovative companies must have superior leadership to survive in both good and bad times.

NASA'S FEMALE HUMAN COMPUTERS

*I feel my job is fun, and that's why I go back every day
and why I keep learning things—because it's fun.*

SUE FINLEY

In 1939 as the world edged toward war, Barbara Canright took a job at California's Jet Propulsion Laboratory (JPL) as the first female "human computer." She calculated pages and pages of figures to determine the propulsion needed for the (then new) jet airplanes. Later, when World War II began, she calculated the thrust required to launch fourteen-thousand-pound bombers. In 1953 Janez Lawson became the first African-American woman hired by JPL. She became a specialist in programming the IBM 701 computer, whose calculations and programs helped launch satellites, lunar missions, and planetary explorations. Katherine Johnson also joined the team in 1953 as a physicist, space scientist, and mathematician. She provided calculations that enabled Alan Shepard's first flight into space, John Glenn's Earth-orbiting flight, and Apollo 11's moon-landing trajectory. Katherine's story was featured in the movie *Hidden Figures*.

More and more human computers were hired as the need expanded. In 1958 Barbara Paulson made calculations critical to launching Explorer 1, the first successfully launched US satellite. Sue Finley, who also began in 1958, recently served as a subsystem engineer for NASA's Deep Space Network. She also wrote the C code that helped launch the first Mars rover. These human computers and scientists provided much of the critical calculations needed to design and launch missiles and spacecraft in NASA programs from its beginning to today. Their pioneering work has been instrumental in helping NASA explore the universe.

Consider This: Women had to fight to be recognized for their intelligence and ability to excel at the most challenging scientific work. Why not hire the best and brightest no matter who they are?

RICHARD SNYDER'S COOL MILLIONS

Fortune favors the prepared mind.

LOUIS PASTEUR

Being in the right place at the right time helps, but you must also be prepared to act quickly when opportunity knocks at your door. Richard Snyder worked as an executive in the climate control division at Singer when rumors circulated that the company might sell off the division to concentrate on the more glamorous aerospace industry. Snyder saw an opportunity to buy the division. To be ready if Singer did decide to sell, he quietly began to arrange the necessary financing. During the next seven months, Snyder talked to ninety-four banks and venture capital companies. During the 1981 recession, Climate Control sales were poor, but its book value was $54 million. Snyder could never find the money to buy it at that price. So he waited. Then, Singer decided to sell the failing business and offered it at $27.5 million. Snyder's plan was implemented, and he quickly arranged the necessary loans.

The new company was named Snyder General. The enterprise slashed expenses, accelerated its inventory turnover, and dramatically reduced the average amount of time needed to collect payments from customers. Within three years Snyder had paid off the original loans. Operating his own company motivated Snyder to expand his business. He encouraged his executives—many of whom had been lured away from the competition—with high earnings that were keyed to the company's growth. He also acquired smaller companies to enter new climate control markets. Richard Snyder took a dead-end business and, through motivated management, turned it into the darling of the industry.

Consider This: Do you want people to perform? Give them the incentive to do so. Make them feel that they are a vital part of the organization. Make their success keyed to the bottom line.

JACK TELNACK OF FORD

> Whenever you see a successful business, someone
> once made a courageous decision.
> **PETER DRUCKER**

In 1980 Jack Telnack, chief designer for Ford Motor Company, was given the opportunity to create a new American automobile. It would be the car that would lead Ford into the 1990s. In the 1960s, before coming to Ford, Jack had designed powerboats for the Trojan Boat Company. Perhaps it was these sleek, stylish lines of a boat that crept into the design of the new Ford car. The new vehicle, as Jack envisioned it, had to be efficient and had to give the appearance of speed even when standing still. Jack was also aware that good looks are not everything, that the car's appearance had to enhance its function; otherwise it would be a sculpture and not a vehicle.

As head of a 550-person staff, Telnack no longer drew designs himself. Instead, he provided inspiration, leadership, and guidance. He sought out the best ideas in automobile design and promoted their use in the new car. Starting with a clean sheet of paper, the automobile that would become the Ford Taurus began to take shape. "It was a very well-calculated risk," Telnack said. "We wanted the customers to feel a bit uncomfortable with the design." This approach enables a new design to last longer without becoming too commonplace. Being careful not to go too far in front of public taste, the design team created a new look for Ford. The look they came up with was so successful it was soon reflected in other models. Indeed, the novel design of the original Taurus set the standard for other automakers to follow into the twenty-first century.

Consider This: Form must follow function. It's great to be good-looking, but it's incredible to be both good-looking and functional.

STEW LEONARD

*A business absolutely devoted to service will have only one
worry about profits. They will be embarrassingly large.*
HENRY FORD

Stew Leonard's is called the "Disneyland of Dairy Stores." Its success attracts
executives from other companies who want to learn what makes his stores so
successful. His legend started in 1969. Progress built a highway right through
the middle of the Leonard family farm. Instead of crying over spilled milk,
Stew decided to take advantage of the traffic by setting up a small dairy store.
He borrowed ideas from two of his heroes, Dale Carnegie and Walt Disney.
Leonard learned the virtues of "cleanliness, quality, and family fun" from
Disney. From Carnegie, he learned, "Successful people are the few / Who
focus in and follow through" and "Lower the price / Sell the Best / Word of
Mouth / Does the rest."

From a small start, his store expanded to more than thirty times its original
size. When it reached one hundred thousand square feet, it had become the
largest dairy store in the world. Carved into a three-ton granite boulder outside
the store are Leonard's Rules, which state, "Rule 1: The customer is always
right! Rule 2: If the customer is wrong, reread Rule 1." Entertainment provided
for customers has included a glass-enclosed dairy plant, a cow that moos at the
press of a button, a petting zoo, and a singing eight-foot robot dog. The store's
walls are covered with employee diplomas from Dale Carnegie. Pictures from
customers worldwide show Stew Leonard bags at the Kremlin, atop the Great
Wall of China, and from the floor of the Pacific Ocean. All of this hoopla has
translated into staggering success. As a bonus, Stew Leonard's has been named
one of the "100 Best Companies to Work For" by *Fortune* magazine for ten
years in a row.

*Consider This: People want to have a good time, even when shopping. They
want to feel like they are at Disneyland, and they want to be treated like royalty.
Give them that, and they will come in droves.*

THE FLIGHT OF *VOYAGER*

Flight without feathers is not easy.

PLAUTUS

America is a land of invention. We're a people searching to go where no one has gone before. We want to do what no one has done and imagine what no one has imagined. Jeana Yeager and Dick Rutan imagined a pioneering aeronautical feat. Jeana worked first as a draftsperson before she decided to take up flying. It was at an air show that she met Dick Rutan. He and his brother owned the Rutan Aircraft Factory in Mojave, California. Jeana had been flying for ten years, and Rutan convinced her to come to Mojave as a test pilot. One day as Jeana, Dick, and his brother Burt were having lunch, the conversation turned to the possibility of setting up an aircraft sales business. They had the background, but how could they develop a concept that would make people pay attention?

Jeana, Dick, and Burt began considering the long-distance flying record. The previous record for distance was 12,532 miles, set by a B-52 bomber in 1962. They would not only try to beat that record, but they would also double it on a nonstop flight around the world. With a bit of backing from parts and materials manufacturers, the Rutans and Yeager designed their plane. The result was *Voyager*, which weighed only 1,860 pounds empty but would weigh 9,400 pounds when fueled and loaded for takeoff. The plane was slightly damaged on takeoff, and the round-the-world trip was complicated by a typhoon and unexpected storms. Jeana Yeager was badly bruised in the turbulence, and at times the pilots became disoriented due to exhaustion. Still, they persisted. Their record-breaking flight was a success. American ingenuity had done it again.

Consider This: Progress is never made by doing the same old thing. Set out to accomplish something new.

CYBILL SHEPHERD

*I think the measure of your success to a certain extent will be
the amount of things written about you that aren't true.*
CYBILL SHEPHERD

If Cybill Shepherd appears gutsy in her many acting roles, it's appropriate. Named after her grandfather Cy and her father, Bill, Cybill grew up in Tennessee, where she excelled in school and athletics. At age sixteen, she entered and won the Miss Teenager Memphis title, and at eighteen, she won a contest for Fashion Model of the Year. Cybill suddenly became a hot property as the new cover-girl sensation. Director Peter Bogdanovich, who was looking for a lead for his movie *The Last Picture Show*, saw one of those covers. So he went to New York and convinced Cybill to take the role. The pair collaborated on several movies, and Cybill's star rose rapidly among the Hollywood crowd. Then came the crash as Cybill fell on hard times with the critics. *Rolling Stone* reported that "her fall from grace was steep and rocky."

Cybill became a liability and was shunned by producers. When Bogdanovich tried to get her a lead role in the 1976 movie *Nickelodeon*, Cybill was unmarketable. She left Hollywood and returned to Memphis, where she appeared in regional stage productions. In those productions, she gained more acting experience and new confidence in her abilities. Cybill's star was relit in 1984 with the debut of the sassy television detective show *Moonlighting*, which costarred Bruce Willis. After a somewhat slow start, the show was ranked in the Nielson top twenty by the end of its first season. In 1986 the show received sixteen Emmy nominations, and in 1988 Cybill Shepherd's commemorative star was placed on the Hollywood Boulevard Walk of Fame.

*Consider This: When everyone is against you, it is easy to give up. It takes guts to
fall back, improve your technique, and reenter the fray.*

FRED SMITH OF FEDERAL EXPRESS

Information about the package is as important as the package itself.
FRED SMITH

Education is much more than simply learning facts. Facts don't provide insight. Facts don't promote risk-taking. Looking back on your life, have there been times when you had the gut feeling that something would work when everyone else thought it would not? Were you right? As a student at Yale, Fred Smith wrote a paper outlining the need for a nationwide delivery company that specialized in time-sensitive goods. According to Fred's research, such a company might have a substantial market. The paper got a C, but Fred didn't forget the idea. After graduation and a stint in the Marine Corps, Fred decided to put his idea to the test. He remembers, "My four years in the Marine Corps left me with an indelible understanding of the value of leadership skills." So, he bought into an aviation service in 1969 and commissioned two consulting firms to study the feasibility of overnight express delivery. What the companies told him confirmed his earlier research.

With his feasibility study in hand, Fred Smith raised $80 million, including some family funds, to start his new venture on June 1, 1971, in Little Rock, Arkansas. Large amounts were spent on advertising. This included full-page ads and television commercials. Operations began on April 17, 1973, serving twenty-four cities. The company almost went under several times. Fred kept pushing. With catchy advertising phrases such as, "When it absolutely, positively has to be there overnight" blasted onto the airwaves, the company finally became profitable in 1976. By 1980 earnings totaled nearly $60 million, and Federal Express had become the dominant force in the overnight courier business.

Consider This: When your ideas are rejected or ridiculed, rethink. Maybe they're right. Then again, perhaps they're wrong. Keep investigating until you're convinced your idea is sound.

AUGUST 2

MISTY COPELAND

Be strong, be fearless, be beautiful. And believe that anything is possible when you have the right people there to support you.

MISTY COPELAND

Misty Copeland grew up in a blended family of mixed race, with African-American, German, and Italian heritage. She was born in 1982 to a mother who was a former Kansas City Chiefs cheerleader, and a father who was mostly absent. At age seven Misty saw a movie about gymnast Nadia Comăneci. She remembered, "I fell in love with her fierceness and grace." She wanted to be like Nadia. But how? Misty lived with her five siblings in a cramped hotel room with no prospect of becoming her own person.

Then an opportunity came in the form of ballet lessons. Starting at age thirteen (much later than most kids), she took to dance immediately. "It gave me a voice, made me feel powerful." Within two years she was winning competitions. In 2000 she was named National Coca-Cola Scholar by the American Ballet Theatre (ABT). She won a Leonore Annenberg Fellowship in 2008 and began appearing in major roles by 2012. In 2014 she made ballet history as the first African American to star in a lead role in ABT's *Swan Lake*. In 2015 she appeared as Juliet in *Romeo and Juliet* and was named principal dancer, the first African American to achieve this level in ABT's seventy-five-year history.

Misty attributes her accomplishments to successful Black women mentors and ABT director Kevin McKenzie. Her competence extends beyond the stage. She's written books, received an honorary doctorate and other awards, and was named National Ambassador for the Boys & Girls Clubs of America. Her life has been featured on the *Today* show, and she was appointed to the President's Council on Fitness, Sports, and Nutrition by President Barack Obama.

Consider This: Find that thing that is yours alone. Something you can give your life and energy to without hesitation. It is your calling. With determined practice and skillful support, you'll rise to the top.

THE HULA HOOP

Fads are born to die.

KEN HAKUTA

One of Wham-O Manufacturing Company's megahits was a financial failure. Its story began when a friend brought an Australian exercise hoop to childhood friends Rich Knerr and Spud Melin. The two were already marketing several sports articles (including the Frisbee) and thought the hoop looked like fun. They dubbed it a Hula Hoop, trademarked the catchy name in 1958, and promoted the new plaything in parks. Sure enough, kids gathered around for a look and then ran to their local store to buy one. Wham-O gave away "seed" hoops on beaches and college campuses to get the craze going. The company's marketing plan was effective, and the Hula Hoop took America by storm. But there was a problem with its success.

Although they had applied for a patent, more than forty competitors entered the market, drawing on the promotion that Wham-O had already begun (and paid for). It was too late and too expensive to force the competitors out of business. Although millions of Hula Hoops were sold, the fad was short-lived, and in the end the company lost money on the toy. But the advertising placed Wham-O in the public eye, and they became a household name. The Hula Hoop experience also prepared the firm to better protect its following popular product, the Super Ball, invented in 1965 by Norman H. Stingley. The Hula Hoop was brought out again several years later. Although it was not as popular as its initial release, Wham-O made money the second time around. Other successful Wham-O products include Silly String, the Slip 'N Slide, the Hacky Sack, and the Boogie Board.

Consider This: A loss may really be a success in the long run. It can give you experience and exposure and prepare you for the next challenge.

DELL COMPUTERS

You don't have to be a genius or a visionary or even a college graduate to be successful. You just need a framework and a dream.
MICHAEL DELL

New ventures are often conceived on the leading edge of technology. Such has been the case for many companies in the microcomputer industry. Even with billion-dollar companies such as IBM and AT&T leading the way, the window of opportunity often opens wide enough for even an ill-financed college student to make it big. Michael Dell prepared himself for later opportunity when he was young by selling newspaper subscriptions and working in telemarketing.

When his family bought a personal computer, Michael adored it. He took it apart to understand every component of the device all the way down to the chip level. He knew computers were the future, and he wanted in on the action. But his parents insisted that he enroll in the premedicine program at the University of Texas at Austin. That didn't quell his dream. He set up a computer business in his dormitory, placed ads in computer magazines, assembled the computers, and shipped them to customers. Michael's company, PC Limited, soon grew so large that he convinced his parents it could be a full-time business. Within several years his computer sales were more than $100 million annually. Michael's company, now named Dell Computers, kept costs down and quality high. In 2009 Dell was bought by Perot Systems, entered the IT services market, and expanded. Dell repurchased his company in 2009 and continued to grow to become one of the most influential computer manufacturers in the world.

Consider This: Watch for the window of opportunity to open. It's at that point that anyone with brains and determination can successfully compete against the big guys.

THE GOLDEN RULE STORES

*I cannot remember a time when the Golden Rule was not my
motto and precept, the torch that guided my footsteps.*
JAMES CASH PENNEY

Today, when you enter a modern department store, you may think about how it's run by a gigantic and complex conglomerate. Yet every business was at one time a single person's idea. The giant corporation of today is an extension of that original idea. An example is the store founded by James Cash Penney. He was born in Hamilton, Missouri, in 1875, the son of a Baptist minister. Penny raised pigs and watermelons during his early life, and also ran a butcher shop. But his shop refused to supply meat to hotels that sold liquor (an era when the Temperance movement was active), and his butcher shop failed. So he turned his eye toward retailing dry goods. In 1902 he bought a one-third share in a store located in Kemmerer, Wyoming.

Using experience gained from working in that store, he launched a chain called the Golden Rule stores. He chose that name because they were based on the concept of treating all people with the kindness we expect, that is, the Golden Rule as taught by Jesus. Every store had a giant Golden Rule sign hanging on a prominent wall. Penney believed that every person was a "human dynamo, capable of accomplishing anything to which he aspires." He despised debt, drinking, and smoking, and he demanded zeal, enthusiasm, and loyalty from every employee. Penney claimed that applying the Golden Rule made his stores (now named JCPenney) a success. By the time he died in 1971, Penney's stores had annual sales of more than $4 billion and were the nation's sixth-largest merchandiser.

*Consider This: Do you apply the Golden Rule to your work? Do you demand zeal
and enthusiasm from yourself and your employees?*

C. E. WOOLMAN AND DELTA

Quality begins with people.
C. E. WOOLMAN

An airline many people travel on for holiday visits and business trips traces its beginnings to the lowly boll weevil. This story begins in the early 1900s. An agriculture district agent, Collett Everman Woolman, battled the destructive boll weevil bug in an OX5 Jenny biplane rigged as a crop duster. His dusting operation was a rousing success, which led him to consider commercial uses for the airplane. Woolman left the agricultural service in 1924 to join the newly formed Huff Daland Dusters company. Soon he was made vice president and field manager. Since the dusting business was seasonal, Woolman worked to secure mail routes. In 1929 he came up with another way to earn money. He offered passenger service. The company was renamed Delta Air Service and served customers in the Mississippi Delta region.

In 1945 C. E. Woolman was named president of Delta and served in that position until he died in 1966. Under his leadership the company became one of the industry's largest and most respected airlines. Woolman's credo was found in his adaptation of the Golden Rule. He reworded it specifically for Delta Air Lines: "Let's put ourselves on the other side of the counter. We have a responsibility over and above the price of a ticket." Woolman knew the value of each customer's loyalty and pressed Delta employees to provide a high standard of service. He emphasized that all the airlines had similar airplanes, so the difference had to be in quality of customer service. He believed "any individual or business that is completely honest in all its dealings is likely to succeed." And Delta did.

Consider This: Never forget, businesses are made up of people with feelings, beliefs, and a desire to belong to something good, honest, and worthwhile.

JIM THORPE—RUNNING ON BORROWED SHOES

> I never was content unless I was trying my
> skill . . . or testing my endurance.
> **JIM THORPE**

Everyone knows how critical running shoes are to athletes. Nike, Adidas, Asics, and others make that clear in every advertisement. Every slight edge helps you become a champion. And that's what makes the story of Jim Thorpe, a Native American and member of the Sac and Fox Nation, so incredible. He attended the 1912 Olympics games with bright hopes. What he accomplished in the face of adversity is incredible. Thorpe was a two-time high school football star in the Pop Warner League before qualifying for the Olympics as part of the American track-and-field team. At the Olympics he competed in the pentathlon and decathlon events for a total of fifteen competitions. He won medals eight times.

On the first day of the competition (the pentathlon), he won medals in four of the five events. Then something happened. A few minutes before the start of the second day's competition, his shoes vanished. In 1912 there were no sports shops to order a quick pair. So his friends and coach scrambled to find two (mismatched) shoes, one from a garbage can. They weren't even Jim's size. Thorpe squeezed one foot into a shoe that was too little. He wore extra socks on the other foot to tighten up the fit of a too-large shoe. That day he won the 100-meter hurdles. After that he placed third and fourth in the pole vault and javelin (his worst events.) He then ran a blazing 1500-meter race and won. His victories—all in the borrowed shoes—gave him two gold medals. In his NFL career that followed, Thorpe was chosen for the 1920 All-Decade Team and the National Football League Fiftieth-Anniversary All-Time Team, among other honors.

Consider This: When life situations try to steal your goals, put on whatever running shoes you can muster and give it your best shot. Don't let circumstances slow you down. Go for the gold.

BILL MOOG'S BUILDINGS

Leadership is the capacity to translate vision into reality.
WARREN G. BENNIS

Bill Moog was an engineer at Cornell Aeronautical Laboratories (later Calspan Corp.) when he invented a servo valve, a control mechanism used on various machines. The company tried to market the device but received just one order for three valves. Since Cornell figured such a small order was not worth its effort, management let Moog personally handle the project. He cranked out the devices in his spare time. The company gave up on selling the device because orders trickled in too slowly. Seeing an opportunity, Moog and his brother Arthur, along with Lewis Geyer, pooled $3,000 to begin Moog Valve. The founders worked eighteen-hour days in an old dirt-floor airplane hangar for more than a year to fill orders. When new employees started coming on board, Bill made it his goal to make the company a great place to work.

The buildings at Moog Inc. were designed with plenty of windows, clean environments, and piped-in music in the cafeteria. Having felt intimidated by inspection policies at other places he had worked, Bill instituted a self-inspection system. This allowed each employee to act as his own inspector. In addition, the company created massive technical training opportunities to help its employees gain advanced skills, and it offered grants for college tuition. Job security became a chief concern, and provisions were made against layoffs. But the exceptional work environment did create one major problem for Moog Inc. Word got out about Moog's working environment. As a result, they routinely attracted thousands of applicants each year for a handful of available positions. From these humble beginnings in Elma, New York, Moog Inc. now has (at last count) manufacturing plants in twenty-six countries.

Consider This: A good environment provides a company with a loyal, dedicated, and productive workforce.

THE LEO BURNETT AGENCY

*Creative ideas flourish best in a shop which preserves
some spirit of fun. Nobody is in business for fun, but that
does not mean there cannot be fun in business.*
LEO BURNETT

For the past fifty years, the Leo Burnett advertising agency has created some of the best-known and most remembered ad campaigns the world has ever seen. These include the Jolly Green Giant, Sunkist's Charlie the Tuna, The Pillsbury Dough Boy, The Keebler Elves, The Maytag repairman, "Fly the Friendly Skies of United," and countless others. The agency's personality mimics the personality of its founder, Leo Burnett, who demanded more than just creativity in ads. The ads had to sell the product, and to ensure that they would, Leo spent time getting to know his clients and concentrating on providing just the right feel for the product. He encouraged his representatives to become members of the client's family. They were taught to think like the client, understand the products, and become consumed with the desire to make the client successful.

Leo practiced what he taught. One corporate legend that illustrates how deeply Leo concentrated on a project involves his encounter with a custodian's closet. One day, with a yellow pad in hand, Leo left his office and headed for the men's room. Being engrossed in thought, he accidentally opened a janitor's closet, went in, and locked the door behind him. After some time people began to ask, "Where's Leo?" Finally he carved a hole in the door with his penknife and got someone's attention. Leo was presented with the door as a gift at the agency's Christmas breakfast that year. Although Leo Burnett died in 1971, his vision continues to drive the company.

Consider This: Creativity just for creativity's sake is not worth much. But creativity that solves a specific problem is worth gold.

COCA-COLA'S BEGINNINGS

A Coke is a Coke and no amount of money can get you a better
Coke than the one the bum on the corner is drinking. All the
Cokes are the same and all the Cokes are good. Liz Taylor knows
it, the President knows it, the bum knows it, and you know it.

ANDY WARHOL

At the turn of the century, Five Points was the meeting place in Atlanta, Georgia. Anything new in town was discussed there, especially at Joe Jacobs's Drug Store. Therefore, Joe's pharmacy was a natural place for Dr. John Pemberton to test his new beverage formula. Willis Venable had a leased soda fountain in the store, and Pemberton asked him to mix one ounce of his syrup with five ounces of water and ice. Venable drank the concoction, smacked his lips, and suggested a second round. But as he began putting water in the glass, he accidentally pulled the lever for soda water. His eyes lit up at the pleasing flavor and effervescence when he tasted the second mixture.

Pemberton explained that his concoction consisted of extracts from the coca plant and cola nuts. Thinking a name with two *C*s in it would be memorable, he called his new drink Coca-Cola. On May 8, 1886, Coca-Cola went on sale in Joe Jacobs's Drug Store. Three weeks later the first advertisement appeared in the local newspaper and described Coca-Cola as "Refreshing! Exhilarating! Invigorating!" Coca-Cola was not the first soft drink in the marketplace, but it offered a new and pleasing taste. Pemberton had a great product, but he didn't possess the resources to make the beverage a success. He lost money on Coca-Cola in its first two years, and just before he died, Pemberton sold an interest in the product for $1,750 to Asa Candler. Candler soon bought up the remaining interests in the drink and took Coca-Cola from obscurity to success.

Consider This: Even the best idea may take years and the right businessperson to crack the marketplace and become an industry leader.

CORPORATE LORE

Company cultures are like country cultures. Never try to change one. Instead, try to work with what you've got.

PETER DRUCKER

In his book *Business as Unusual: The People and Principles at Herman Miller,* Hugh De Pree describes Herman Miller, Inc.'s struggle in expanding from a small family business in the 1940s into a major corporation today. The office furniture manufacturer is based on Christian religious values and traditions. When the company's rapid growth began to strain those original values, Peter Drucker was asked to suggest methods to keep the enterprise on track. He recommended that new employees be educated about the founders and their early struggles and how their philosophy came into being. When an enterprise is small and young, its employees know its history because they were a part of it. They see the founder and often relate to him on a first-name basis. Like the creativity of Walt Disney in every early Disney animation project, De Pree had to make his intentions known to his employees. His message was, "Courage, integrity, humility, service—these are the hallmarks of leadership, and these characteristics must be at the core of Herman Miller."

As a business grows, however, the impact of the company's beliefs and mission may be lost on the average employee. Company leaders often play the role of "corporate evangelist" or cheerleader to keep corporate lore alive. Well-known corporate cheerleaders include Alfred Sloan, Henry Ford, Thomas Watson, John Deere, Walt Disney, Stanley Marcus, Trammel Crow, and Bill and Dave Packard. Leaders of a large organization cannot know every employee. But it's essential that the leaders' stories and experiences—in the form of corporate lore—be told frequently to workers to remind them of their beliefs and goals.

Consider This: Give people some tangible message, perhaps a parable, on which to hang their corporate beliefs. One truly inspirational story that describes the company's goals is worth a thousand company rules.

LANE CEDAR CHESTS

Even the woodpecker owes his success to the fact that he uses his head and keeps pecking away until he finishes the job he starts.

COLEMAN COX

In 1912 Edward Hudson's father told him to start making cedar chests in an old box plant that the elder Hudson had just purchased. The twenty-one-year-old youngster didn't even know what a cedar chest was, but he followed his father's instructions. Edward got help from his former high school woodworking teacher and ordered $50,000 worth of equipment. John Lane, Edward's father, went through the ceiling, but the terms for the machinery were good, and the plant went into production. The resulting product was handsome and well made. But sales of the chests were sluggish, so Edward started going on sales calls himself. After being turned down by several furniture stores, he came up with the idea of a fanciful cedar chest display. When he showed this concept to the stores, they bought Edward's vision and his furniture, and sales increased.

Seeing how well this original promotion did, Lane used other schemes to promote the chests. By studying the market, Lane discovered that many young women cherished the European tradition of the trousseau or marriage chest. That insight changed how his furniture was advertised. Now he promoted them as a line of "hope chests." Another idea was supplying dealers with millions of hand-size versions of the Lane Love Chests. These were given as gifts to graduating high school girls. At one time, two-thirds of all girls graduating from high school received a miniature Lane Love Chest, which was promoted as "the gift that starts the home." After World War II Lane added other furniture items to its product line and continues to be a successful marketer of fine furniture.

Consider This: A product may not be profitable because it is not sold correctly. Go into the marketplace and see how the product can most benefit people, then sell it with that information in mind.

MADELEINE L'ENGLE'S STORIES

You have to write the book that wants to be written. And if the book
will be too difficult for grown-ups, then you write it for children.
MADELEINE L'ENGLE

Born in 1918, the only child of strict parents, Madeleine L'Engle spent much of her childhood in the privacy of her room, where she often escaped into the world of books. Because of her father's health, the family moved to Switzerland when Madeleine was twelve. She attended an impersonal boarding school and was known only as "Ninety-seven." At first, Madeleine had a negative view of herself. Then, after discovering the plights of people in the Bible, she began to relate to the underdogs God used. As an escape from her isolation, Madeleine began to write stories. She finished her first at age five. She developed a love for storytelling and continued using that medium for expression and escape. In her stories she created friends who helped her work out problems that others had to solve in regular life.

As an adult and with more insight into the real world, Madeleine continued her writing. In retrospect, her early stories were silly. But they helped her learn skillful tools of drama and narrative. In 1959 she sent a manuscript to a publishing house. "This was a book I was sure of," she remembers. It was about a twelve-year-old girl who had problems in school. She saw herself as ugly, dull, and clumsy but soon discovered spiritual powers in the universe that were on her side. The book was rather unusual and was rejected by forty-two publishers. But the forty-third accepted the manuscript, and *A Wrinkle in Time* went on to win the prestigious Newbery Medal, a top award for children's literature.

Consider This: Every person has the talent to share with the rest of the world. Even those who have a difficult childhood can grow up to be the best in their field.

CODE TALKER SECRETS

I . . . do hereby designate August 14 . . . as National Navaho Code Talkers Day, a day dedicated to all . . . Native Americans who gave of their special talents and their lives so that others might live.

PRESIDENT RONALD REAGAN

The strategy of war is to achieve an advantage over the enemy. So highly complex machines (like the Enigma machine) are often used in sending and deciphering messages. One of the most successful American strategies during World War II was using Native Americans as Code Talkers. The army trained these men how to use their own languages to communicate secret messages about troop movements, times and places, and strategies. Because their languages were impossible for enemy soldiers to understand, Code Talkers provided a valuable communication tool. Soon the navy and marine corps recruited their own Code Talkers. In fact, many tribes participated, including Cherokee, Crow, Fox, and Comanche. And in World War I the Choctaw nation formed an early version of Talkers in a strategic telephone squad.

During the battle for Iwo Jima, one hundred Navajo Code Talkers successfully transmitted more than eight hundred messages for the Marines over several weeks. During the landing of the Fourth Infantry Division on Normandy in 1944, thirteen Comanche Code Talkers kept lines of communication open from the battlefield to command headquarters. These soldiers fought side-by-side with other soldiers, dodging bullets like everyone else. They were not hidden in an out-of-fire radio hut. Some were killed. Because their role in the war was top secret, the public knew nothing about their pivotal role. But on August 14, 1982, President Ronald Reagan recognized the role of Code Talkers by declaring a National Code Talker Day.

Consider This: Serving without recognition is a high honor if the cause is just. But honor is befitting all who risk life and limb to serve others.

GEORGE S. CLASON—THE RICHEST MAN IN BABYLON

*Part of all you earn is yours to keep. Learn to live on less
than you make and save the balance for yourself.*
GEORGE S. CLASON

When a work of fiction hangs around for more than a hundred years, sells millions of copies (in twenty-six languages), and is still a top-selling book, there must be something in it worth noting. Such is the case of a book by George S. Clason. It came about because of the stock market crash of 1929. At that time people were buying stocks by borrowing money. This unwise strategy not only destroyed individuals but it almost destroyed the entire American economic system. One result of the downturn was its effect on Clason's map-printing business. Although maps were popular as automobile travel increased in the 1920s, the Great Depression abruptly ended that market. So Clason began printing pamphlets on the hot topic of regaining personal financial independence. Instead of creating boring how-to guides, he put investment theories into short stories. These were eventually compiled into the book *The Richest Man in Babylon.*

Briefly, this book follows the lives of two friends, Bansir and Kobbi, in ancient Babylon. They reflect on their lives and realize they have nothing to show for their many years of work. So how is it then that their friend, Arkad, who started out just like them, became the richest man in Babylon? They ask him, and what follows is practical financial and lifestyle advice that has been the foundation of many, if not most, financial gurus and investment books for the past hundred years. Author Og Mandino called Clason's story "the greatest of all inspirational works on the subject of thrift and financial planning," And the proof is in the pudding. Clason used his own principles to eventually not have to worry about money at all—just like Arkad in the book.

Consider This: Most financially secure people get rich slowly and steadily instead of quickly. This is because they follow the advice of the wise instead of gambling their future to slipshod financial schemes or high-priced investments.

LEARNING FROM MISTAKES

An error gracefully acknowledged is a victory won.
CAROLINE GASCOIGNE

Tom Watson Sr. was the guiding hand in the success of IBM for forty years. He knew the risks associated with business and the value of learning from mistakes. One year a young executive took responsibility for a project that cost more than $10 million. The idea failed. When the young man was called in, he offered his resignation. "You can't be serious," said Watson. "We've just spent $10 million educating you!" When Thomas Edison conducted experiment after experiment to invent the electric light, he made thousands of "mistakes" before success. Levi Strauss made the mistake of selling his entire supply of dry goods, leaving him with only canvas to make pants. Gail Borden failed at numerous ventures before he invented condensed milk. Milton Hershey failed more than once in the candy-making business before finding success with the Hershey bar. SpaceX's frequent failures to land a rocket nearly made them a laughingstock until it worked.

Almost every enterprise has experienced its share of mistakes. Yet mistakes are a tool of learning. Although repeating mistakes is foolish, a legitimate try that turns sour should be accepted as part of the process of moving forward to a better idea. The old adage is right: "If you are not making mistakes, you are not making progress." Those who keep trying (and learning) make the most significant advancements in any venture. We have a natural tendency to avoid trial and error and often find risk-taking to be unsettling. Yet taking calculated risks is often rewarded. As Edward J. Phelps so aptly stated, "The man who makes no mistakes does not usually make anything."

Consider This: Are you so afraid of making mistakes that you shield yourself from success?

ALICE ZHANG AND VERGE GENOMICS

The most important thing about starting and running a successful company is persevering . . . It's all about grit.
ALICE ZHANG

Creating a new, effective drug isn't easy. In fact, it's tough. Sometimes ninety percent of a pharmaceutical company's research fails to find a usable drug. And each failure costs a lot of money. So drug research is both difficult and costly. Nevertheless, that's the kind of career Alice Zhang decided to pursue. Born in Maryland to Chinese parents, she visited China for the first time at age twelve. She was promptly arrested and expelled with her parents for pro-democracy activism. She later returned to China to work with AIDS patients, increasing her expertise and interest in medicine. While in college she interned at the National Cancer Institute and Saeed Tavazoie Lab at Princeton, working in genomics (studying the structure, function, evolution, and mapping of DNA sequences). After attending a UCLA-Caltech Medical Scientist Training Program, she left to start her own company, Verge Genomics.

The mission of Verge is to discover ways to develop drugs using technological advances in artificial intelligence (AI). Instead of the old, lengthy discovery methods, Verge uses AI to explore possible medicines. Specifically they look for drugs to treat neurodegenerative diseases like ALS, Parkinson's, and Alzheimer's. AI takes advantage of computing power to quickly consider vast numbers of possible compounds. This machine-learning technique combines information from previous studies, patients' lab results, known drug uses and interactions, and other sources to formulate potential drugs. The idea is to learn. Repeat. And learn more. This cutting-edge algorithmic approach is not a slam-dunk. But it can lead to a faster and better design of drugs for specific uses.

Consider This: The successful synergy of combining two diverse areas (in this case, biology and computer science) can lead to advancements that neither expertise could accomplish individually.

TWINKIES

*Trust your hunches. They're usually based on facts
filed away just below the conscious level.*
DR. JOYCE BROTHERS

Although seldom considered as American as motherhood and apple pie, a packet of Twinkies in a lunch box is an American tradition. The delicious Twinkies treat was invented by Jimmy Dewar during the Great Depression. (Isn't it amazing how many things were developed during tough economic times?) As plant manager for Continental Bakeries, Jimmy considered ideas to keep his business profitable. One day he noticed the shortcake pans used during the strawberry season remained idle the rest of the year. While mulling ways to use those pans to make a low-priced snack, Jimmy also came up with an idea to inject the snack with a filling.

About that time he went on a business trip to St. Louis. There he saw a billboard advertising Twinkle Toe Shoes. A spark of an idea flashed in his brain. "Twinkies" was an excellent name for a snack. It had a neat "snack" sound. The "twin" part of the name meant there'd be two snacks in a package. That was the right size (at the time) to sell for a nickel. Thus the idle pans found a need. They were used to make a shortcake-like snack with an injected filling. Twinkies quickly became popular. A big boost was received when Twinkies were featured on a popular television program, *The Howdy Doody Show*. One of the stars, Clarabell the Clown, passed the snacks out to the audience as the host, Buffalo Bob Smith, sang the Twinkies song. How big a part of the American culture has the Twinkie become? Some wedding cakes are made of Twinkies, and former first lady Rosalynn Carter was caught eating one in a candid photograph.

Consider This: The best advertising available for any product is when it becomes a part of the culture.

SHERWIN-WILLIAMS PAINT

*The world hates change, yet it is the only
thing that has brought progress.*
CHARLES KETTERING

At times you must stick to your convictions. This can be particularly difficult when your beliefs run counter to long-standing traditions. For example, paint has been around for thousands of years, as exemplified by cave paintings as prehistoric murals. Egyptians used pigments to decorate their houses and tombs as long ago as 1000 BC. Fast-forward to the nineteenth century. House paint was sold in a base color with pigments available for custom mixing. But the average nineteenth-century American rarely used paint. Most houses were left unpainted, but if a home was painted, the owner usually had to rely on a painter to mix the desired color or be content with white. It was almost impossible to purchase two batches of paint that matched exactly.

In 1870 a paint company named Sherwin, Dunham, and Griswold had a tough decision to make. One of the partners, Henry Sherwin, had developed an idea to create ready-mixed paints, but the other owners were against it. They were sure that people wanted to mix their colors at home—to get the tint just right. Sherwin disagreed, the original company was dissolved, and Sherwin found another partner, Edward Williams. Their new firm, Sherwin-Williams, embarked on a lengthy research project to perfect a way to premix paint consistently and conveniently. The company's ready-mixed paint was introduced in 1880 and signaled a revolution in do-it-yourself painting. Soon few American houses were left unpainted, proving that Henry Sherwin was right after all— homeowners didn't like the hassle of mixing their own paint.

Consider This: Some people cannot see advancement. Some will not consider a change. But those who imagine the future are often those who create it.

VICKS VAPORUB

If I have a thousand ideas and only one turns
out to be good, I am satisfied.
ALFRED NOBEL

Sometimes success comes from putting two and two together. It sounds simple enough. The problem is determining which two to combine. For years, treating the common cold has been a problem. It has long been known that some relief could be gained from opening the nasal passages with various aromatic medications and vaporizations. From ancient times, poultices, plasters, herbal vapors, and the like had been touted as effective cold remedies. But most of those "cures" had unpleasant side effects. They smelled horrible and frequently irritated the skin. Using vapors in conjunction with steam often resulted in facial burns. So for many years, druggists searched for an effective ointment with none of these drawbacks. Many experimented with various salves, but few were any good.

Then, sometime in the 1890s, Lunsford Richardson, a druggist in Selma, North Carolina, came up with an idea. Desperate to find relief for his croupy baby, he used menthol, a little-known drug from Japan, in an ointment base to create a salve. When the ointment was applied to the chest or nose, the body's heat vaporized the menthol. This permitted the medicated vapors to be inhaled for hours. He first called his invention Vick's Croup & Pneumonia Salve. The ointment became one of several items sold under the brand name Vicks Family Remedies. The name came about because Richardson had purchased his drug business from Dr. John Vick, his brother-in-law. Plus, he thought "Vick's" would be easy to remember. Eventually the salve was renamed Vicks VapoRub. The 1919 flu epidemic tripled the sales of Vicks VapoRub and made it a household name.

Consider This: The ingredients for success may already be out there simply waiting for someone to put them together.

JOHN GOODENOUGH AND THE LITHIUM-ION BATTERY

I have learned to be open to surprises . . . to not have preconceived
ideas or close your mind from listening to what might work.
JOHN GOODENOUGH

Did your pocket just ring? Cell phones are everywhere. But they wouldn't be anywhere or they'd be impractically heavy if it weren't for the lithium battery. There'd be no Tesla automobiles, iPads, earbuds, or any other lightweight electronic devices. So how did this battery marvel come about? The lithium-ion battery became practical because of a spark of an idea in the mind of John Goodenough. John studied math (Yale, 1944) and later got a PhD in physics (University of Chicago, 1952). Academics didn't come easy for John. He suffered from dyslexia and struggled to learn to read and write. But his mind had no problem imagining what others could not. He took a position at MIT and worked on computer memory (RAM) and magnetic materials, then went to Oxford in 1976 to work in electrochemistry and batteries, and finally to the University of Texas in 1986.

The first lithium battery was patented by Exxon from work done by Stanley Whittingham. But it had severe problems—like catching fire. Goodenough's innovation, a lithium-cobalt-oxide cathode (the "positive" side of the battery) made it more practical. Next, a scientist in Japan created a better "negative" side. Finally, in 1991, Sony picked up on the combined ideas and marketed the first battery using Goodenough's advancement. This battery launched the revolution in lightweight electronic devices we're enjoying today. In 2019 the Nobel Prize in Chemistry was awarded to John B. Goodenough, M. Stanley Whittingham, and Akira Yoshino, for their work on the lithium-ion battery. Today, Li-ion batteries have become an indispensable part of our everyday lives. They are found in almost every electronic device.

Consider This: It sometimes takes a village to create practical breakthroughs. So contribute what you do best, and work with others to make the whole better than the parts.

READER'S DIGEST

*Don't dodge difficulties; meet them, greet them, beat
them. All great men have been through the wringer.*

A. A. MILNE

Good ideas may meet with success initially, then hit a roadblock when everything looks good. In fact, many ideas are laid to rest at that point. DeWitt Wallace's dream would have been buried long ago if not for his determination to overcome obstacles. Wallace had an idea for a small publication that would be entertaining and informative. At the time, there were many good magazines on the market, but a reader would have to spend a small fortune to buy them all. So Wallace put together a dummy magazine that used condensations of previously published articles. He named his prototype *Reader's Digest*. Unable to secure backers for the venture, Wallace and his fiancée rented an office. She set up their own small publishing concern. On their wedding day the couple sent out mimeographed circulars seeking subscriptions. When they returned from their honeymoon two weeks later, they had received 1,500 charter subscriptions.

The first issue of *Reader's Digest* was dated February 1922. Everything went well as other magazines readily gave them permission to reprint articles. But as subscriptions increased, the other magazines began to see *Reader's Digest* as competition, and sources for pieces dried up. In 1933 Wallace started commissioning articles for other magazines, securing the rights to reprint them later. He was widely criticized, but the concept kept his publication alive. The practice was discontinued in the 1950s, but *Reader's Digest* had become a continuing success by then. Although not as widespread as it once was, the *Digest* continues to be published in multiple languages worldwide, even while other publications have fallen by the wayside in favor of digital media.

Consider This: Even when your dream does not become a reality the first few times you reach for it, keep trying. Persistence is often your most powerful ally.

LIFE SAVERS

Without promotion, something terrible happens . . . nothing!
P. T. BARNUM

McDonald's restaurants may never have become so prolific without Ray Kroc. Charles Doolin bought the recipe for Fritos corn chips from a man needing money to return to his home in Mexico. Although Christopher Sholes invented the modern typewriter, promoter James Desmore turned it into a profitable product. The Life Saver has a similar story. In 1912 Cleveland candy salesman Clarence Crane looked for a summer substitute for his melting chocolate candies. He decided to produce a mint. To make his mints stand out among the competition, he designed them round and with a hole in the middle. He found a local pill maker who could produce the mints in quantity and wrap them in a cardboard tube. Their shape made the name "Life Saver" a natural.

An advertising salesman named Edward Noble picked up a package of the mints at a New York candy store. He was so impressed with the candy, the shape, and the name that he immediately went to Cleveland to try to sell advertising for the product. Crane wasn't interested since the mints were just a summer sideline. But Crane suggested that if Noble liked the product so much, he should buy the rights to make the mints. A deal was struck. Noble raised the capital to launch the venture with Roy Arlen. But a significant problem with the candy was its inability to stay fresh in the cardboard tube. That was solved by enclosing the mints in a tinfoil wrapper. Placed next to cash registers as impulse buys, the mints sold quickly and soon became a national success.

Consider This: You may not be an inventor, and that's okay. More often it's the inspired promotion of a good product that really makes the difference.

DUKE KAHANAMOKU

*Just take your time—wave **comes**. Let the
other guys go, catch another one.*
DUKE KAHANAMOKU

A tall bronze statue of Duke Kahanamoku stands on Waikiki Beach with colorful flower leis adorning his arms. The legendary Hawaiian surfer was born in 1890, a minor royal (his grandfather was a high chief) when Hawaii was still a kingdom. He was named after the visiting Duke of Edinburgh. Kahanamoku lived most of his life in and around the ocean's waves. As a teen he designed his own sixteen-foot surfboard (most are about nine to ten feet long). He perfected a way to propel it using a flutter kick known as the Kahanamoku kick (later used by freestyle swimmers). Using his personalized kick, he set a world record swimming across Honolulu Harbor in 1910.

Duke qualified for the 1912 Olympics, where he set records in 50-, 100-, and 200-yard freestyle events. The *New York Times* reported that "at one time [he held] every freestyle record up to a half-mile." He won his first Olympic gold in the 100-meter freestyle and silver in a 200-meter relay. He won two gold medals in the 1920 Olympics. At thirty-four, he came in second in the 100-meter Olympic race, beat by legendary actor and swimmer Johnny Weissmuller. "It took Tarzan to beat me," he said.

Because of his fame, Duke served as an ambassador for Hawaii. He introduced the surfing sport to beach boys everywhere. In 1925 he rescued eight people from a capsized boat while battling thirty-foot swells, making trip after trip into the waves using his surfboard. The event made news worldwide, and surfboards soon became standard gear for lifeguards around the globe. After retirement Duke became sheriff of Honolulu. In 1963 he began a foundation to help teens in water sports, police work, and international relations.

Consider This: Talent alone will not change the world or make you famous. But talent, heart, and courage can make your star shine long after you are gone.

THE ZIPPER

I don't want to see the zipper in the back of the
monster suit. Like everybody else who goes to the
movies, I want to believe the monster is real.
ERIC STOLTZ

Many inventions can be traced back to ancient Greece, Egypt, or Arabia. The toothbrush, cosmetics, the razor, and many other valuable items were simply improved upon as technology advanced. The zipper is different. In 1851 Elias Howe patented an "Automatic, Continuous Clothing Closure." Unfortunately, this early, crude zipper was never marketed. But some years later, in 1893, Whitcomb Judson improved on the idea and patented a "clasp-locker" device. Judson made boots with these clasp-lockers taking the place of the buttons and shoelaces on high-top boots. Judson and his partner, Lewis Walker, attempted to promote the clasp at the 1893 World's Fair, but no one was interested. The only substantial order they received was from the post office, but the bags equipped with the fastener jammed so often that they were soon discarded. Like many first tries at inventions, it needed improving.

Then, in 1913, an engineer named Gideon Sundback improved on Judson's idea. He created a more reliable fastener, much like those in use today. His zipper was first employed by the military, then found its way to civilian clothing by the 1920s. But early versions had to be unstitched each time the garment was washed and then resewn because of a rusting problem. The public needed more to convince them of the value of this new device. Enter Goodrich. In 1923 they introduced a line of galoshes called Zipper Boots. Because of these popular boots, the fastener became widely known as a zipper. Steady improvements in the design and materials used to manufacture zippers made them a standard part of clothing by the 1930s.

Consider This: Any good idea can be improved on. Just because an idea fails the first time it is applied is no reason to give up. If you don't improve upon an idea, someone else probably will.

THE MICROWAVE OVEN

You want experimentation. Every once in a while, you stumble upon something that blows your mind.
JEREMY STOPPELMAN

Since World War II, the pace of American life has increased so dramatically that it appears we are trying to create an instant society. Consumers demand instant service. Many stores offer instant credit. Instant potatoes, instant stock market quotes, and point-of-sale displays for instant buying decisions. A significant component of our fast-paced society is the microwave oven, which essentially has provided people with the first new way to cook food since the fire. Although it was bound to be discovered eventually, the microwave oven was invented by accident by Percy Spencer.

Spencer left school after the fifth grade but always had an "itch to know." He worked jobs that taught him about electricity, wireless technology, and math. During World War I he served as a radio operator, where he continued to study electricity. After the war he went to work at the American Appliance Company (later named Raytheon), where he became a skilled engineer with a knack for tinkering with physics. During World War II he experimented with a magnetron device used in radar systems. One day he noticed something peculiar. As he was testing a magnetron, he realized that a candy bar in his pocket had melted. Spencer exposed other foods to the magnetron's presence to find out what had taken place. Popcorn popped, and an egg exploded, half-cooked from the inside out. Building on that research, Raytheon developed a commercial microwave oven. But because of the bulkiness of vacuum-tube technology (pre-transistors), it was expensive, and few were sold. Spencer introduced a much smaller home model in 1952. The stage was set for a revolution in how Americans cooked. Percy Spencer died in 1970 at age seventy-six with more than 150 patents to his name.

Consider This: Many new ideas are developed by accident. But it's the individual who possesses the itch to learn more who make astounding discoveries.

TETSUYA FUJITA, MR. TORNADO

Today the technology is there to give early and, normally,
ample warning when a powerful tornado approaches.
When a tornado strikes, all of us are at risk.
SPENCER BACHUS

When a tornado hits the American landscape, meteorologists classify its strength. An F0 tornado is weak, with 40- to 72-mile-per-hour winds. It creates light damage, maybe blowing tiles off a roof. An F1 has winds up to 112 miles per hour. The F2, F3, and F4 are progressively stronger. An F5 tornado has violent winds surging from 260 to 318 miles per hour, and it causes incredible damage. Houses are lifted from their foundations and disintegrated. Cars are thrown hundreds of feet. Many lives can be lost. The Fujita Scale (F-Scale) was introduced in 1965, and a recently developed Enhanced Fujita Scale (EF-Scale), based on observed damage, was adopted in 2007. The Fujita Scale was named for the Japanese American Tetsuya "Ted" Fujita.

Fujita was born in Kitakyūshū City, Japan, in 1920 and moved to the US in 1958, where he subsequently became an American citizen. As a professor at the University of Chicago, he studied meteorology. Following his personal fascination with tornados, he dug deeply into their structure, origins, and strength. As an original "storm chaser," he mapped the paths of the tornados, took aerial photographs, and learned to read a storm's debris pattern to determine its strength. His 1965 study of a cluster of tornados in a midwestern storm led to his F-Scale. Soon, the entire world adopted the F-Scale to estimate the severity of the damage left in the wake of a tornadic storm. Beyond his work on the scale, Fujita also first described microbursts and downdrafts and their danger to aviation. Today the pioneering work of Mr. Tornado is the foundation for analyzing and classifying thunderstorms, tornados, and hurricanes.

Consider This: If you have a passion for something, perhaps you can use that to discover knowledge about the subject that is unique and useful.

THE REAL UNCLE SAM

This nation will remain the land of the free only
so long as it is the home of the brave.
ELMER DAVIS

There really was an Uncle Sam. The person who was the model for that venerable character was a true American hero named Samuel Wilson. Born in 1766, Wilson was a youthful patriot who served as a drummer boy late in the American Revolution. After the war Sam opened a meatpacking company in Troy, New York. He was a fair businessman and was known throughout the community as Uncle Sam. When soldiers were stationed nearby during the War of 1812, Sam supplied them with meat. The crates sent to the army were stamped on the side with the initials "US" indicating they were for the United States army. This was before those initials were in common usage. But when asked what the initials stood for, one of Sam's employees said they were the initials of his boss, Uncle Sam. Thus, soldiers referred to the meat as being from Uncle Sam.

The press picked up on the Uncle Sam name as it gained popularity among the troops. In fact, American soldiers soon started referring to themselves as "Uncle Sam's men." A cartoon version of Uncle Sam first appeared in 1820 and depicted the character wearing a black top hat and tailcoat. Red pants were introduced during Andrew Jackson's presidency, and a beard was added during Abraham Lincoln's term in office. During the Civil War, artist Thomas Nast made Uncle Sam tall and thin, modeling the character after Lincoln. The modern version of Uncle Sam was created by artist James Montgomery Flagg. He created the World War I poster with the now-familiar caption, "I Want You for the US Army."

Consider This: In a world where daily news distresses the soul, patriotism, as depicted in the character of Uncle Sam, can lift spirits as a symbol of hope, fair play, responsibility, and a call to service.

THE AUTOMOBILE RADIO

Now let's use our nutpickers on this problem, and then
we'll decide what it is we have to do. Then let's do it.
PAUL GALVIN

In 1928 Paul Galvin had success building and selling radios. Then Black Friday devastated the American economy in 1929. As a result of the stock market crash, large manufacturers began dumping radios on the market. Galvin's retailers stopped orders and wanted to ship back products. Galvin found himself saddled with large shipments from suppliers for parts he could no longer use. He traveled from Chicago to New York to work out a deal with one of his suppliers, and while there he heard about people putting radios in cars. They charged about $250, and each installation was a custom job. Galvin thought about how his company could develop a lower-price automobile radio, one for the mass market, on his way back to Chicago.

The men at Galvin's shop tried designing a car radio. There were significant problems. Early automobiles couldn't accommodate the bulky tuner, battery, and speaker. Plus, the antenna had to be placed in the headliner, requiring the liner to be torn out and replaced. Installation could take two days. Still, they experimented. After convincing a banker to give him a loan, Galvin's men installed a radio in the banker's car—but the vehicle caught fire thirty minutes later. Galvin later went to a radio convention. Having no exhibit booth, he drove his car around the convention center. At the same time, his wife convinced potential customers to take a demonstration ride. Little by little, the car radio was perfected, and one morning while shaving, Galvin came up with a new name for his product: "Motorola."

Consider This: In the face of disaster, some people will quit. Others will seek new ideas and new ways of meeting the challenge. Which option would you choose?

MARVA COLLINS

Once children learn how to learn, nothing is going to narrow their mind. The essence of teaching is to make learning contagious, to have one idea spark another.
MARVA COLLINS

Educated in a one-room schoolhouse in Atmore, Alabama, Marva Collins learned about teaching from caring and inspiring teachers and principals and her own common sense. After teaching for two years in Alabama, she moved to Chicago and continued her teaching career. Marva followed the recommended Chicago school system curriculum for fourteen years but became increasingly frustrated with its impact on students. She believed stories like "Run, Spot, Run" had no real meaning for children. They weren't stimulating or exciting and didn't inspire kids to read. So she added *Aesop's Fables* and other classic children's stories to the classroom fare.

Marva told her students that they were the "brightest in the world." While children in other classes struggled to learn thirteen words in a basal reader, her students wrote stories about the brontosaurus and tyrannosaurus. Unfortunately, colleagues belittled Marva's techniques, and she was eventually harassed out of the public school system. Convinced that her ideas about education were valid, Marva opened Westside Preparatory School, taking in problem children. She taught Shakespeare, Dickens, and other classics. Her students memorized quotations and poems, solved real mathematical word problems, and openly discussed life issues. Marva's students responded with a hunger for knowledge. When her first class of "misfits" took standardized achievement tests, they ranked five grades above the national average. Her successes were the subject of a television movie, *The Martha Collins Story.*

Consider This: What could we accomplish if we were truly inspired and pushed to meet our real potential?

ANNE SULLIVAN

*People seldom see the halting and painful steps by
which the most insignificant success is achieved.*
ANNE SULLIVAN

The story of Helen Keller is well known. She was born a healthy baby, but as a young child she was stricken with a disease that left her blind and deaf. Her parents could not communicate with her or control her, and Helen grew up like an animal. Finally, in desperation, the family called for help, which arrived in the form of Anne Sullivan. Anne had the understanding and love to bring Helen "back into the real world." How was it that she could perform such a miracle when Helen's parents and countless doctors had failed to make any progress? Where did Anne find such love and patience?

The story begins in the early 1870s at the Tewksbury Almshouse, a Massachusetts poorhouse. A young and almost blind girl was abandoned by her family to live in that dismal facility. Her miserable existence was relieved when members of a commission toured the home. She asked them for help, and they sent her to Perkins School for the Blind. There she had surgery to help her eyesight. Since she'd grown up in poverty and had little schooling and no social graces, she had a tough start. But the teachers saw something in her. She was exceedingly bright. Over time she excelled and became her class's valedictorian. In her graduation speech, she said, "Let us go cheerfully, hopefully, and earnestly, and set ourselves to find our especial part. When we have found it, willingly and faithfully perform it; for every obstacle we overcome, every success we achieve tends to bring man closer to God." That girl was Anne Sullivan.

Consider This: Everyone needs care and love. Without them, there can be no worthwhile dreams. What personal mountains could be moved if people really showed a nurturing love for one another?

THE CHICKEN MAN

Baldness. Handsome in a man, beautiful in a chicken.

FRANK PERDUE

Chickens are so common and plentiful that it seems they should be a commodity business. After all, one chicken looks like another. Or does it? One chicken company has made a big name for itself by growing chickens a cut above the rest. Arthur W. Perdue entered the chicken business in 1920 using savings from a previous job. He started small, with fifty chickens. In that same year, Arthur's son, Franklin Perdue, was born. Arthur's chickens produced superior table eggs, and young Frank learned a great deal by observing his father's careful attention to detail. Focusing on quality and cost gave Arthur a good profit in a low-profit-margin business. From the beginning the Perdues always looked for ways to improve their business and their chickens. They learned that contented chickens produced more eggs. They learned how to develop better feeds. By 1970, they had learned the value of "quality message" advertising, much of which featured Frank himself.

"It takes a tough man to make a tender chicken," said one Perdue ad. "I'm not about to compromise when it comes to my legs and breasts," quipped another. Frank declared, "If you can find a better chicken, buy it!" In 2007 Perdue introduced an antibiotic-free chicken under the Harvestland brand. All of its brands were antibiotic-free by 2014. Perdue grew to become one of the most successful chicken producers in the US, selling literally hundreds of chickens each minute of every day. Most recently, it was the third-largest producer of broilers in the US. Perdue's formula for quality and innovation has produced considerably more than chicken feed.

Consider This: If the chicken business can be innovative, your business can be innovative. How can you improve the quality of your product? How can you make your message memorable?

EASTERN ONION

Whatever you can do or dream, you can. Begin it.
Boldness has genius, power, and magic in it.
GOETHE

It doesn't take a college degree to be successful. Mary Flatt was a testament to that. She'd tried her hand at several businesses by the time she was thirty. They all failed. Looking for new opportunities, she and her husband, Jim, and their two kids moved to Las Vegas with no money or jobs. Fortunately, Jim found permanent employment at a casino, but Mary skipped from one position to another. One day Mary was at a party when a Western Union singing telegram was delivered. Mary felt the presentation was flat. She believed that singing telegrams should be fun, exciting, and even outrageous. An idea was born.

Mary scraped together $1,200 to get her idea off the ground. At first Jim thought the idea was harebrained and gave Mary no support or encouragement. Still, Mary continued with her plans. Songs were written for almost every occasion, from birthdays to "Happy Divorce Day," and friends helped make costumes for the venture, which Mary cleverly named Eastern Onion. The first week, five grams were sold, and Mary was on her way. Although the business made virtually no profit during its first ten months, a big break came when stories about Eastern Onion's novel telegrams appeared in the local newspaper. With the free publicity, sales began to increase. Then, when the company was featured in the national press, Mary Flatt started getting calls from people interested in obtaining franchises. At one time Eastern Onion franchises stretched from coast to coast, in most major cities. Most recently, you could still send an Eastern Onion singing telegram in Atlanta, San Francisco, New Orleans, Minneapolis, and Reno.

Consider This: Many people have failed and failed again. But if they keep trying, they increase their chances of finding that one idea that will make it big.

WILMA RUDOLPH, THE POLIO VICTIM WHO WON THE GOLD

Never underestimate the power of dreams and the influence of the human spirit. We are all the same in this notion: The potential for greatness lives within each of us.

WILMA RUDOLPH

Wilma Rudolph was an example of how an undying belief in oneself could be the catalyst to overcoming problems. Polio took a toll on Wilma as a child. For six years she wore leg braces and could not walk, but she believed the braces would someday come off. The doctor was doubtful Wilma would ever walk correctly, but he encouraged her to exercise. Wilma didn't understand that she might be permanently handicapped. She thought that if a bit of exercise was good, a lot must be better. When her parents were away, Wilma took off the braces and tried again and again to walk unaided. Finally, when she was eleven, she told her doctor, "I have something to show you." Wilma removed her braces and walked across the room. She never put them on again.

Wilma wanted to play sports. After some false starts at basketball, she made a bold move. She confronted her coach, saying, "If you give me ten minutes a day, I will give you in return a world-class athlete." The coach laughed uncontrollably but agreed to give Wilma the time. When basketball season was over, Wilma turned to track. By age fourteen she was on the track team, and by sixteen, she was encouraged to prepare for the Olympics. Wilma Rudolph won a bronze medal at the 1956 Olympics and three gold medals at the 1960 Games. In 1961 she was named the Associated Press Female Athlete of the Year. And in 1990 she became the first woman to receive the National Collegiate Athletic Association's Silver Anniversary Award.

Consider This: Belief in yourself and hard work can make you a world-class individual in whatever area you choose. What will you have if you give up? What can you have if you keep on trying?

HENRY AARON

*My motto was always to keep swinging. Whether I was
in a slump or feeling badly or having trouble off the
field, the only thing to do was keep swinging.*

HANK AARON

Few people garner recognition merely for being good at something. Glory comes to people who are the best. Being the best means giving more of yourself, doing more than is expected, and producing more than everyone else. When most people believe it's time to quit, those who ultimately succeed go a little farther. When young Henry Aaron suited up as a rookie for the Milwaukee Braves, he wanted to make a name for himself in major league baseball. But so did every other rookie. To be remembered, Henry would have to do something spectacular. "Hammerin' Hank" Aaron did just that. He eclipsed Babe Ruth's long-standing home-run record of 714 in 1974, then tallied a major league record of 755 homers by the time he retired in 1976.

Looking back on what gave him the ability to achieve those marks, Henry recalled a priest. As one of Henry's twin babies lay very ill early in his career, Father Seblica came into his life. The priest was very caring and showed great concern for the family. The two became friends and handball rivals. Years later, when Henry was having trouble getting a child accepted into a private school, Father Seblica worked vigorously on the youngster's behalf. When Henry asked the priest what kept him going, Father Seblica replied, "I do what I can, and then some." Henry took that motto onto the playing field. He did all he could—and then some. That's when Henry Aaron began his climb to the top. History provides excellent examples of what you can accomplish when you seek to go further than you believed you could.

Consider This: Are you satisfied with what you're doing? Why not go even further? Do all you can, and then some.

THE REST OF THE STORY

*In times like these, it helps to recall that there
have always been times like these.*
PAUL HARVEY

Paul Harvey was born in 1918 in Tulsa, Oklahoma, and his father died when Paul was just three years old. Because he showed an interest in radio, Paul's high school English teacher pushed him to take a job at KVOO, a local radio station. Occasionally, Paul was allowed to do some announcing. Sometimes he read the news from the wire, and he even filled in a few times by playing his guitar. Paul gradually moved up the ranks, from station gofer to spot announcer, newscaster, and manager. "I hung around the studio every minute I wasn't in school," he remembers. Then, in 1944, Paul began two fifteen-minute news commentaries from a Chicago-based radio station. After that people recognized his voice, punctuated by a memorable staccato delivery. He added a segment in 1946 called "The Rest of the Story," where he told an anecdote that had a surprise ending. In 1976 the ABC network spun off that segment into its own series.

Paul Harvey always championed his traditional values of God, country, family, a strong work ethic, and rugged individualism. He spoke with a homespun style that, to many, made him the spokesperson for middle America. No one saw him as a big-city journalist—he was just a next-door-neighbor kind of guy telling a story. Paul's efforts have earned him numerous honorary degrees and won him some of the most prestigious awards in the communications industry. With his distinctive style and instantly recognizable delivery, Paul Harvey drew millions of listeners into his stories. He told it like it was and then ended his broadcast by wishing his listeners a "good day!"

Consider This: Be straightforward in your speech. Be clear in your explanations. Say yes or no more often than you say "maybe."

MILTON HERSHEY

I didn't follow the policies of those already in the business.
If I had, I would never have made a go of it. Instead, I started
out with the determination to make a better nickel chocolate
bar than any of my competitors made, and I did so.
MILTON S. HERSHEY

Some people see failure as a sign to give up. Those who eventually become successful see failure as a stepping-stone and another lesson in the business school of life. So they just keep on trying. Milton Hershey's father was an itinerant speculator, moving from place to place and investing in every kind of business with little success. Milton, born in 1857, attended seven schools in eight years and never made it past the fourth grade. He first worked for a printer, was fired, and then was apprenticed to a confectioner. In 1876 Milton opened his own candy business in Philadelphia, but he couldn't make a profit. Next he went to Denver and opened a candy store. It also failed. Milton made another attempt in New York City, which failed in 1886.

Finally, Hershey returned to his hometown of Lancaster, Pennsylvania, and began making caramels. The candy came to the attention of an English importer, who placed a big order. The caramel business prospered, and Hershey built a modest factory on the site that eventually encompassed sixty-five acres. In 1893, inspired by German chocolate makers at the World's Columbian Exhibition, he started The Hershey Chocolate Company and produced his own chocolate. By 1900 he had sold his caramel business (for $1 million) and was concentrating solely on making chocolate. In 1909 he and his wife Catherine opened the Hershey Industrial School for orphaned boys. Hershey refused to advertise (a policy the company adhered to until 1970), believing that quality would sell his wares.

Consider This: Failure can be a valuable part of learning. Unfortunately, some see it as a dead end, while others see it as an opportunity to learn a valuable lesson.

PETER MCCOLOUGH OF XEROX

The secret of success in life is for a man
to be ready for his opportunity.
BENJAMIN DISRAELI

After World War II, C. Peter McColough attended Harvard Business School and took a job as a salesman for a chemical company. He loaned his résumé to a friend who wanted to copy its format. The friend happened to show McColough's résumé to a corporate recruiter, who (as recruiters are apt to do) kept the résumé in mind. As a result of that tenuous connection, McColough was offered a job at Lehigh Coal and Navigation. After working at the company for several years, he was approached by another recruiter, who told him of a position at the Haloid Company, a photographic and camera concern.

McColough was not impressed as he toured Haloid's facilities. The vice president's bookshelf was an orange crate painted green, he recalled. But he remembered seeing a Rube Goldberg–like xerographic device called the Model A. The gizmo made dry photostatic copies with much cranking, buzzing, and humming. Amazing. McColough talked to Haloid's president, Joseph Wilson, about the device and became fascinated with it. He saw potential in a machine that could make high-quality copies in large numbers. He had to make a tough decision. He decided to move from his well-paying job at a stable company to an enterprise in its infancy. In 1954 he became the Haloid general manager of its reproduction service center in Chicago. In 1959 he became the general sales manager. In 1961 Haloid was renamed Xerox. McColough became the company president in 1966, and as he expected, the Xerox copy machine forever changed how businesses operated.

Consider This: Do you hear opportunity knocking? Do you have the courage to open that door? Are you ready to take advantage of what may be offered?

TOO MUCH PLASTIC

There's so much pollution in the air now that if it weren't
for our lungs, there'd be no place to put it all.
ROBERT ORBEN

Plastic is a fantastic invention. It's used for everything—from throwaway bags to toys to medical devices. Unfortunately, the success of plastics has also caused problems. It's hard to get rid of. An estimated 14 million tons end up in our oceans each year. This contaminates the ocean wildlife and ends up in the seafood humans consume. In fact, we humans have a history of polluting our own environment. The industrial revolution filled cities with smoke, smog, and dangerous airborne chemicals until it got so harmful that factory emissions were controlled. Historically, rivers worldwide were drains for sewage and industrial waste until the stench and pollution killed fish and caused rampant disease. Then it was addressed. The plastic pollution of the oceans is now threatening humanity.

Many organizations are addressing ocean pollution. One such organization is 4ocean. It started when two American surfers, Andrew Cooper and Alex Schulze, were vacationing in Bali. They noticed how badly the beaches were filled with plastic. Cooper asked a lifeguard, "How come nobody's cleaning up this trash?" The answer was they tried every day, but it kept coming back. When Cooper and Schulze returned to Boca Raton, Florida, they invested their life savings and started a business to promote ocean cleanup. By supporting their initiative through sales of online products, they're responsible for cleaning up almost 20 million pounds of waste from global beaches. The trash is then delivered to recycling centers or repurposed to create new products from the garbage. In 2018 they were awarded *Surfer* magazine's Agent of Change Award. 4ocean and other organizations continue to address the issue of ocean cleanup.

Consider This: There is only one Earth. Unfortunately, as civilization progresses, our innovations sometimes create pollution. The responsible strategy for every new invention is to pair it with a solution that cleans up any mess it makes.

AN IDEA-NURTURING WORK CLIMATE AT 3M

*As our business grows, it becomes increasingly
necessary to delegate responsibility and to encourage
men and women to exercise their initiative.*
WILLIAM MCKNIGHT

Most one-product companies have their heyday and then fade quickly from the marketplace. The companies that continue to be successful for decades foster innovation. That is not easy for large companies, where the corporate bureaucracy often stifles creativity. But because of principles laid down by early company president William McKnight (1929–49), innovation became a top priority for 3M. Since many 3M products are soon copied by competitors, 3M always needs new ideas to keep making profits. To encourage its workers to participate in creative thinking, 3M developed a series of policies to create an atmosphere conducive to discovering new product ideas. Some of the results of this thinking include waterproof sandpaper, Scotch tape, Post-It Notes, Scotch-Brite scouring pads, and NextCare health-care products.

Top management acknowledged each success with pride and great fanfare. They also accepted failure with constructive concern that promoted a try-again attitude. Management allowed new ventures to develop without the pressures associated with daily production. Instead, researchers and marketing staff were encouraged to mingle and feed on each other's ideas. When a new product looked worthwhile, the person who developed it was given a great deal of responsibility in taking the product to the marketplace and giving it a chance to succeed. Today 3M supports 8,500 scientists at fifty-four innovation centers worldwide. From that resource, it has received more than one hundred thousand patents.

Consider This: In almost every organization, there are innovative and creative individuals. To take advantage of this brainpower, management must create a business culture that allows experimentation, failure, and rewards for success.

GEORGE KRESS

Life is like riding a bicycle; you don't fall
off unless you stop peddling.
CLAUDE PEPPER

George Kress became a millionaire and then put his money to work helping other people. Inspired by a Norman Vincent Peale sermon, Kress established the Green Bay, Wisconsin, Chapter of the American Foundation of Religion and Psychiatry. Through that organization, people of the region receive help with such problems as alcoholism, family abuse, and marital conflicts. Kress summed up his belief in the following way: "Two characteristics are important to develop. The first is integrity. You'll need lots of help to make it; people have got to like and trust you or you won't get anywhere. The second is dedication; you have to be willing to make your work a priority."

In the early part of the century, Kress earned his money by creating and selling wooden boxes through the Green Bay Box & Lumber Company. He attended the University of Wisconsin and earned a BA in accounting. But in 1925, when his father's horse-collar and wooden-box business took a turn for the worse, Kress had to put an accounting career on hold to rescue the family business. Throughout the Great Depression, Kress and his wife nursed the family enterprise, and it survived. When the repeal of Prohibition created a demand for shipping boxes, Kress recognized an opportunity: corrugated boxes would be ideal for shipping bottles. In 1933 the Green Bay Box Company began manufacturing corrugated boxes. Although Kress died in 1997, his vision for continual product improvement keeps the company at the forefront of packaging today.

Consider This: Those who hang on during tough times are often in the right place to meet new demand when the market revives.

AMERICA'S 9/11 HEROES

America was not built on fear. America was built on courage, on imagination, and an unbeatable determination to do the job at hand.

HARRY S. TRUMAN

September 11, 2001, changed America. Not since Pearl Harbor had our country been so brazenly attacked. This time the events were seen live on television. The Twin Towers collapsed, the Pentagon burned, and United Airlines Flight 93 crashed. Yet amid the chaos, heroes emerged. Firefighters and police officers rushed to rescue people in the collapsing buildings. Other Americans rushed to help. Blood banks filled up with people wanting to donate blood. Volunteers, sometimes having no idea what they could do, stepped forward. And the members of Congress stood in unity on the steps of the Capitol, singing for America. Singing for the lost. Singing for hope.

Although there are many stories of heroism, one that captured the hearts of all Americans was the incident aboard Flight 93. The plane took off from Newark Airport on its way to San Francisco. About forty-six minutes into the flight, a group of hijackers stormed the cockpit. The pilot struggled but was overpowered. The hijackers took control. They pointed the plane toward the Capitol Building in Washington, DC. Some passengers happened to get messages on their phones about the Twin Towers in New York and the attack on the Pentagon. Knowing their lives were all but over, they rallied to retake the airplane. Little is known of the actual events, but the passengers confronted the hijackers and caused enough turmoil that the plane crashed into a field near Somerset, Pennsylvania, instead of hitting the US Capitol Building. Those heroic Americans gave their lives to save others.

Consider This: Tragedy brings people together. But wouldn't it be better if we realized the freedoms, liberties, opportunities, and privileges we have every day? Shouldn't we stand together, helping all Americans in our corporate quest for life, liberty, and the pursuit of happiness?

MALCOLM FORBES

When what we are is what we want to be, that's happiness.

MALCOLM FORBES

Malcolm Forbes loved life, and he particularly loved the life of a capitalist. In fact, Malcolm was often called a "cheerleader for capitalism." Who else would name his Boeing 727 corporate jet *Capitalist Tool*? Who but a capitalist could afford a Boeing 727? Although he received a substantial inheritance from his father, Malcolm became a success in his own right. He was decorated during World War II, founded two weekly newspapers, and produced an award-winning history magazine before taking over the family enterprise. After Malcolm joined Forbes, Inc., the family empire grew much larger than Malcolm's father could ever have dreamed.

Malcolm Forbes claimed that a person can't be successful unless he loves what he is doing. In fact, if someone loves what he is doing, then he is succeeding, since that is really the meaning of success. The "income" a person derives from life is the opportunity to do those things that are the most fulfilling. One of Forbes's most significant breaks in life may have been one of his failures. In 1957 when he was running for governor of New Jersey, he was "nosed out in a landslide." That was the year he became editor-in-chief of *Forbes* magazine. Plunging into the life of a publisher, he became caught up in the joy of running the business, and his joy turned into an enormous success. During his life Forbes was the leader of a New York motorcycle pack, became the first person to complete a hot-air balloon trip across the United States, and celebrated his seventieth birthday (in 1989) with a $2 million party in Morocco. Malcolm Forbes enjoyed life.

Consider This: How can a person be successful if they are not happy? Success is fulfillment. And it may or may not be related to material goods.

MARY KAY

People and pride are the two foremost assets
in building a successful business.

MARY KAY ASH

In mid-1963, after a successful career in direct sales, Mary Kay Ash retired—for a month. During that brief span she wrote a book to help women survive in the male-dominated business world. Sitting at her kitchen table, Mary Kay made two lists. One list contained the good things she had seen in companies. The other featured the things she thought could be improved. When she reviewed the lists, she realized that she'd inadvertently created a marketing plan for a successful company. So with her life savings of $5,000 and the help of her twenty-year-old son, Richard Rogers, she launched Mary Kay Cosmetics on Friday, September 13, 1963.

Mary Kay's goal was to provide women with an unlimited opportunity for personal and financial success. She used the Golden Rule as her guiding philosophy and encouraged employees and sales force members to prioritize their lives: God first, family second, career third. Because of Mary Kay's steadfast commitment to her goals and principles, Mary Kay Cosmetics grew from a small direct-sales company into the largest direct seller of skin-care products in the US, with the nation's bestselling brand of facial skin care and color cosmetics. By 2020 the company had more than 3.5 million independent beauty consultants worldwide. But being a beauty consultant takes energy, determination, and skill. Those who succeed are rewarded with a viable and lucrative business. Mary Kay Cosmetics' unique combination of enthusiastic people, quality products, innovative marketing concepts, and an ambitious set of goals turned the founder's idea into an American business success story.

Consider This: Nothing is easy. If it was, everyone would be a success. Instead, what you're looking for is an opportunity that provides you with the training, support, and product that can help you turn your enthusiasm and hard work into something beautiful.

BIRDS EYE FROZEN FOODS

I am best described as just a guy with a very large
bump of curiosity and a gambling instinct.
CLARENCE BIRDSEYE

Clarence Birdseye had an excellent idea for quick-freezing food storage, but marketing the concept was not easy. After preparing more than a million and a half pounds of frozen food in 1928, General Foods found they had no place to sell its products. They had not created a viable marketing plan and were running out of time and money. So they looked around for help. After coming up short several times, they finally joined the Postum Cereal Company. Postum took the name General Foods Corporation and began a plan for marketing the Birds Eye–trademarked frozen foods. First it selected Springfield, Massachusetts, as a test site and installed free freezers in eighteen grocery stores there.

For forty weeks the General Foods marketing team gave away free samples. They conducted research in homes and spoke at clubs, schools, and anywhere else they could gather a crowd. This research paid off. It convinced them there was a market for frozen foods, but the road to success still eluded them. They attempted to expand their frozen-food business to consumers for four years. They could still make an impact in the New England states. Then, in 1934, they changed their strategy and began marketing frozen foods to institutions. Results were promising. By 1940 Birds Eye brand products were being distributed nationally. With the onset of World War II, the need to conserve metals resulted in increased consumer preference for frozen foods over canned products. By the end of the war, most Americans had become used to the convenience of frozen foods. The expansion of the market has continued ever since.

Consider This: Finding the right way to market a good idea often takes many trials—and sometimes years and a little good luck.

DOING BUSINESS ONE-ON-ONE

No typewriter is as warm as the human voice, and no phone
call can take the place of eyeball-to-eyeball contact.

J. B. FUQUA

J. B. Fuqua was one of the most successful businessmen in America. If you listened to him talk enough, he'd tell you that part of his success was the result of doing business one-on-one. When he started in business, J. B. went to Augusta, Georgia, to create a radio station. Without knowing a soul, he found several people interested in the idea. He talked them (face-to-face) into providing the funding. Once, when J. B. attempted to buy theaters from two brothers in Georgia, he heard that one sibling would be leaving town and would not be back soon. J. B. immediately took an airplane to see the brothers. The three drew up a contract on a yellow writing tablet that evening. It was a $20 million deal. J. B. later said that if he had not met with the brothers that night, the contract might have never happened. When he heard about a bottler who wanted to sell but had tax problems, J. B. showed up at the man's office at eight o'clock the following day. He worked out a deal to buy the business using the other man's money.

Dealing directly with people means that J. B. Fuqua often answered his own phone. "It might be Santa Claus," he said. Being so accessible meant Fuqua seldom missed an opportunity. An idea that a secretary might think is nonsense could be worth a million dollars to a person who knows what to do with such an idea. After reaching his goal of becoming a millionaire, Fuqua continued making deals "for sport." He successfully led Fuqua Industries for more than forty years and eventually retired to spend much of his time serving on the boards of various philanthropic organizations.

Consider This: Are telephone or Zoom meetings effective? Sometimes they're necessary. But if you want to have the best chance of closing a deal or explaining a concept, talk face-to-face (in person) with your client.

CONRAD HILTON

Success seems to be connected with action. Successful people keep moving. They make mistakes, but they don't quit.
CONRAD HILTON

Conrad "Connie" Nicholson Hilton grew up in San Antonio, New Mexico. His first job was as a clerk in his father's general store. He learned business lessons about buying at a bargain and selling at a profit. But his eye was on banking. In 1913 he raised money from local ranchers to start a bank, only to be cheated by a shady partner. Then World War I got in the way. As an army lieutenant, Hilton served in France and made lifelong friends. After returning home he looked for a bank to purchase. With an oil boom in progress in Texas, he decided to look there. He traveled from town to town but found nothing he liked. When he arrived in the small town of Cisco, he decided to take his chances there.

He tried to negotiate a deal to buy the local bank but ran into another shady businessman. Frustrated, he sat in the lobby of the local Mobley Hotel and watched oil workers scrambling to find a room for the night. The hotel rented each room for eight hours, three times a day. Intrigued by the busy activity, Hilton found the owner. After examining the hotel's books, he negotiated a handshake deal to buy the place. He contacted family and friends to raise needed cash, describing the hotel between a flophouse and a gold mine. The deal was struck, and Connie Hilton was in the hotel business. After bringing in his army buddies as partners, he found other hotels to buy, refurbish, and reopen. In 1925 he built a brand-new hotel named the Dallas Hilton. Now there are Hilton hotels all over the globe.

Consider This: There's no substitute for action. You can dream many dreams, but until you jump into the fray, you'll never see any of them come true.

DAN BRICKLIN'S SPREADSHEET

VisiCalc took 20 hours of work per week for
some people and turned it out in 15 minutes and
let them become much more creative.

DAN BRICKLIN

Dan Bricklin played with microcomputers before most people had ever heard of one. He entered MIT in 1969 to study mathematics but switched to computer science. While at MIT Dan helped design an online computer calculator. After graduation he went to work for Digital Equipment Corporation, where he gained experience working on word processing programs. In 1977 Dan entered Harvard to work toward an MBA. His familiarity with computers placed him in the right place to solve a nagging business problem: automating spreadsheet calculations. Dan had to calculate everything by hand in his business courses, laboriously writing down hundreds of numbers and meticulously calculating sums, differences, and percentages. It was easy to make mistakes. Sometimes sums didn't agree. Recalculating took time.

As a result of his frustration, Bricklin began to create a software program that would do for numbers what a word processor did for words. He linked up with a friend, Bob Frankston, to design a commercially functional program that would accomplish such a task. In 1979 they started Software Arts, Inc. and introduced their program as VisiCalc. Once VisiCalc became available on the Apple II computer, it caught on like wildfire. In many ways VisiCalc was responsible for Apple's own success. Customers often would go to a computer store wanting VisiCalc, ask what type of machine the program ran on, and then buy an Apple computer. VisiCalc was the first "hit" microcomputer program and dominated the business computer market until challenged by new programs Lotus 1-2-3 and Microsoft Excel. In 2001 Bricklin received an honorary doctorate from Newbury College.

Consider This: Cross-pollination among disciplines such as science and business may result in ideas that will advance them both.

THE SUPER BOWL

Winning the Super Bowl the first time is an unbelievable thrill.
ROGER STAUBACH

To virtually every professional football player and fan, winning the Super Bowl is the ultimate achievement. But the annual Super Bowl game is a relative newcomer to a sport whose first professional contest was played in 1895 in Latrobe, Pennsylvania. The first Super Bowl was played seventy-two years later in January 1967. This match featured the champions of the National Football League (founded in 1922) and the American Football League (founded in 1960) as a test to see which league's winner was better. The NFL's Green Bay Packers won that first game. In subsequent years—especially after the two leagues merged in 1970—the Super Bowl has garnered more media coverage than any other professional sporting event. Why? Because it parallels our own ambitions to compete and succeed.

One of football's most heralded players is Hall of Fame quarterback Roger Staubach of the Dallas Cowboys. He remembers the ups and downs that led to his second NFL championship ring in Super Bowl XII. Dallas struggled against itself and the Denver Broncos in the early minutes of the game. They fumbled the ball three times deep in their own territory. Somehow Dallas escaped without giving up any points but also missed three field goals. The team was jittery and could have fallen under the weight of its mistakes, but the players refused to fold. Instead, Dallas capitalized on Denver's errors and held them scoreless until the third quarter. Then, keeping its collective cool, Dallas played with dogged determination and defeated Denver 27–10 to win its second Super Bowl.

Consider This: Winners have their share of mistakes and bad breaks. Don't let mistakes make you stumble. Instead, look for opportunities to move forward and run toward the daylight.

MARY CROWLEY

Real wisdom is looking at the world from God's point of view.
MARY CROWLEY

Her husband was too lazy to work, so Mary had to get a job. She'd never been employed before, and the country was in the throes of an economic depression. The day before beginning her job search, Mary stood in front of a mirror and practiced twelve ways of asking for a position. The following day, dressed in her finest clothes, she entered what appeared to be the most prosperous department store. "I want to see the owner," Mary said. "Won't do you any good," came the reply, but Mary found the owner's office anyway. "I've picked this store to work in," she said. When told there were no jobs, Mary said, "Just let me work one Saturday. If I don't sell enough to more than pay my salary, you won't have to let me come back." The owner agreed, and by that afternoon, Mary had outsold every other person in the store.

After her first marriage was dissolved, Mary met and married David Crowley. While raising her family, she continued her sales career and became a top producer for Stanley products. An importer asked Mary to help him sell home-decorating items, and Mary recruited a force of more than five hundred women. She put together a training program using Proverbs as her "degree in business administration." To encourage her top sellers, she planned a trip to reward them. In the trip that Mary had planned, she learned that her boss included a cocktail party against her wishes. In the ensuing disagreement with her employer, Mary was shown the door. After a good cry, she picked herself up. She began Home Interiors, which became one of America's most successful direct-sales organizations. Crowley died in 1986, and her company fetched an astounding $1 billion when sold in 1994.

Consider This: You have to stick with what you believe in. If you compromise your beliefs, there is no way you can devote yourself fully to your goals.

CHUCK HOUSE AT HEWLETT-PACKARD

Take risks. Ask big questions. Don't be afraid to make mistakes;
if you don't make mistakes, you're not reaching far enough.
DAVID PACKARD

Sometimes the boss is wrong. Sometimes, when you know you're right, you've got to go ahead and do what you know will work. In his book *Intrapreneuring*, Gifford Pinchot III profiled Chuck House of Hewlett-Packard. Chuck worked in the oscilloscope division of the company but had an inkling that there were other uses for Hewlett-Packard's scopes beyond just those for which they were sold. When Hewlett-Packard started working on a project for the Federal Aviation Administration, he got a crack at helping to find another application. The development team had hoped to build a better monitor for use in control towers. They came up with a monitor half the size and weight and twenty times faster than existing equipment. But the monitor didn't meet the FAA's requirements, and the project was scrapped. Chuck still had hope for the monitor and persuaded his boss to spend an additional $2,000 to show it to some potential customers.

Chuck thought he might have a winner and got permission to put several other people on the project. But during HP's annual review, the project received a thumbs-down from marketing and management. Dave Packard himself said, "When I come back next year, I don't want to see that project in the lab!" Nevertheless, Chuck's boss let him go "underground," and he finished his two-year project in less than a year. When Packard returned to the lab the following year, the monitor had already shown that it would be successful in the marketplace. HP gave Chuck House a Medal of Defiance to celebrate his victory over the system.

Consider This: All the corporate wisdom in the world cannot take the place of one person who believes in a project and will champion it to success.

MRS. FIELDS'S COOKIES

Good enough never is.

DEBBI FIELDS

Debbi Fields baked a delicious chocolate chip cookie that everyone liked. Based on the recipe on the back of the Nestle's chocolate chips bag, Debbi put her own heart and soul into her version of the recipe. Friends couldn't get enough of the yummy goodness. So, with their encouragement, she borrowed $50,000 and opened a small cookie store in Palo Alto, California. It took Debbi a while to discover the secret of making her business a success. Part of that discovery was that she was not selling cookies but heart. To this day Debbi believes that what people really want in her store is caring. Debbi learned that she had to go into the mall and give away samples to bring people to her store. She had to use the finest ingredients to ensure the best cookies, and she had to price the cookies so that people could buy them for less than it would cost to make them at home. Debbi's company, Mrs. Fields Cookies, wants its customers to experience a warm feeling of quality and caring in every cookie. That is why their cookies are served warm. In many cases, cookies that are not sold within two hours are given to local charities.

Anyone who enters a Mrs. Fields store is greeted by a friendly salesperson who will help them have a brighter day. As her company expanded, Debbi chose managers not only for their ability to run the store but also for their ability to have fun. Believing that the cookie business should be more like a Disney spectacular than a bakery counter, she was determined to give people a little of the fantasy that makes life fun.

Consider This: Selling is more than just ringing up a sale. It is a Broadway production: welcoming customers with a warm hello, convincing them to believe in and enjoy your product, and sending them away with a smile.

ROBERTO GOIZUETA AND NEW COKE VERSUS CLASSIC COKE

*Perhaps no other corporate leader in modern times
so beautifully exemplified the American dream.*

JIMMY CARTER ON ROBERTO GOIZUETA

Roberto Goizueta was born in Havana, Cuba, in 1931. He graduated from Yale and began working as a chemical engineer for Cuban Coca-Cola in 1954. When Fidel Castro's communist regime came into power, Goizueta's family fled to the United States. He continued working for Coca-Cola in Miami, then in the Caribbean, and finally at their headquarters in Atlanta, Georgia. Goizueta built a reputation within the company as a relentless and meticulous worker. His accomplishments earned him advancements, and in 1979 he was elected Coke's vice chairman. Later in 1979 he became president and soon warned, "We're going to take risks."

Everyone wants to be remembered for their successes. Still, Roberto Goizueta had to live with one of the century's most publicized marketing miscues: New Coke. Before introducing the new formula to their signature drink, Coca-Cola conducted extensive research. They wanted to develop a better-tasting cola in response to the Pepsi Challenge taste tests. But they failed to recognize the powerful consumer loyalty commanded by the original product. When New Coke was introduced, there was an immediate backlash from Coke's most loyal customers. Goizueta then made the bold move to backtrack and reintroduce the original formula as Classic Coke. Instead of letting the New Coke fiasco take him or his company down, Goizueta recovered from the mistake and took Coca-Cola to new markets and record sales. During his sixteen years at Coke's helm, he increased the company's value from $5 billion in 1981 to nearly $150 billion in 1997.

Consider This: You're going to make mistakes. It's what you do with them that counts. First change your direction. Then move forward to correct the mistake as quickly as possible.

RENOVATORS SUPPLY

*Genius is the very eye of intellect and the wing of
thought; it is always in advance of its time.*
WILLIAM SIMMS

In 1974 Claude and Donna Jeanloz had begun to restore an old home in
Massachusetts when they discovered a problem common to most renovators:
a lack of authentic fixtures. Tracking down source after source, it took them
four years to get the items they needed. It occurred to them that other home
renovators would also have a hard time finding things for use in restoration.
So Claude and Donna decided to start a small mail-order catalog business to
address that need. Their catalog carried hard-to-find plumbing and electrical
fixtures as well as doorknobs and hinges. Working with other suppliers, the
couple created a central clearinghouse for virtually everything people involved
in a home renovation would need.

There is often a limited window of opportunity for an idea to be successful. For Renovators Supply, the timing was right, as many baby boomers were
moving into inner-city areas to reduce commuting time and costs. Houses were
being renovated in virtually every major US city. As their company grew, the
Jeanlozes sold advertising in their catalogs to manufacturers. In addition, they
introduced supplemental catalogs specializing in accessories to add finishing
touches to the restored houses. Business boomed, and the couple opened a
series of retail stores called Renovators Supply, where people could come in
and quickly obtain the most common renovation materials. Over the years
they acquired other companies (Millers Falls Company) and expertise (CNC
Manufacturing) to keep up with the market's needs. They also kept up with
marketing trends by transitioning from catalogs to e-commerce.

*Consider This: What kinds of hard-to-get items do lots of people want? Keep an
eye on the horizon for possible new trends. If the timing is right and you can provide what others need, you could be the subject of the next success story.*

H&R BLOCK

We like to test things . . . no matter how
good an idea sounds, test it first.
HENRY E. BLOCH

Henry Bloch studied mathematics in college and completed his degree while in the US Air Force. After serving as a first lieutenant and navigator on a B-17 Flying Fortress during World War II, he returned to Kansas City, Missouri. At first he went to work for a brokerage firm. Then, after a year of working for other people, Henry decided to find his own American Dream. He borrowed money from his aunt to join his brother Richard in opening the United Business Company. This enterprise performed bookkeeping and managerial services for local clients. In addition, the brothers provided free income tax preparation as an additional service. The tax preparation business was so helpful their clients started telling their friends about the Blochs. This resulted in a steady growth and by 1954 the number of people wanting tax preparation help was so great that the Blochs had to work long hours seven days a week to keep up.

Henry saw that the income tax preparation business could support itself exclusively. In 1955 he and Richard formed a new company called H&R Block, Inc. (an easier spelling of the family name). The enterprise expanded rapidly via a franchise arrangement. H&R Block offices soon became familiar sights at shopping centers and Sears stores throughout the country. Block was one of the first businesses to introduce computers for tax preparation, which allowed processors to be quicker and more efficient. They also helped the IRS pioneer the use of e-filing. In 2017 they introduced "augmented intelligence" to better understand customers' complex and unique tax situations. Today H&R Block annually prepares more than twenty million tax returns.

Consider This: Rapid expansion and franchising work best for businesses with a single purpose and an easily replicated formula.

QUINCY JONES'S NEW CAREER

Every day, my daddy told me the same thing. "Once
a task is just begun, never leave it till it's done. Be
the labor great or small, do it well or not at all."

QUINCY JONES

In 1974 doctors discovered that Quincy Jones had two brain aneurysms. "Please, God, not now," he cried. Quincy had played trumpet for years, and he still had too many dreams to let it all end now. One of America's top Black jazz artists, Quincy had performed on Broadway and still had a promising career ahead of him as a trumpeter. But unfortunately, medical problems forced him to face the reality that he could not return to his beloved instrument. Instead, he would have to apply his musical talents elsewhere. Jones even planned and attended his own memorial service where Richard Pryor, Marvin Gaye, Sarah Vaughan, and Sidney Poitier gave eulogies. But the service was way too premature.

Quincy Jones didn't die. Instead, he channeled his formidable musical ability into composing, directing, and producing, and soon began to attract the attention of some of the entertainment industry's most influential people. His attention to detail is legendary. He worked and worked to make the music right, then worked some more to see if he could make it perfect. Jones produced and conducted the "We Are the World" recording, and he wrote the scores for *Roots*, *The Color Purple*, and many other films. He also produced *Thriller* with Michael Jackson, one of the most successful record albums of all time. Steven Spielberg summed up Jones's intensity of life in a *60 Minutes* interview: "He takes a minute and finds two minutes of enrichment out of one minute of living."

Consider This: Life is what you put into it. It is what you dream and how hard you work to make those dreams come true. What you make of your life is no one's responsibility but yours.

ESTÉE LAUDER

*If you put the product into the customer's hands, it
will speak for itself if it's something of quality.*
ESTÉE LAUDER

She'd cracked the American market, but the European market, particularly Paris, seemed out of her reach. Estée Lauder (born Josephine Esther Mentzer in Queens, New York) was never one to accept defeat. Hence, she came up with a rather imaginative plan. At her Galeries Lafayette display one day, she "accidentally" spilled some of her Youth Dew fragrance. The scent wafted throughout the store and enticed the women shoppers to discover its source. Unconventional, yes. But typical for someone who was dead set on getting her way. Lauder had conquered another continent. But this victory was only one of her achievements. Estée started her cosmetics empire in a stable behind the family home. During World War I her uncle, John Schotz, had come to the US from Hungary and set up a chemical laboratory in the stable. There he perfected a velvety skin cream. Young Estée Mentzer watched with awe and learned all there was to know about the process.

By the time she was in high school, Estée was making her own creams and testing them on every girl she could recruit. After marrying Leonard Alan Lauder in 1933, she continued her experiments in the kitchen. She sold her creams (calling them "jars of hope") at beauty shops in New York. Estée insisted on creams of the highest quality. To expand her sales, she hounded the cosmetics buyers at the best department stores in the country—Saks, Neiman Marcus, and others—and even visited each store to personally train the sales-women. Estée Lauder placed her early advertising dollars into samples and giveaways and pioneered the concept of gifts with purchases.

Consider This: The product is only half the story. Success comes to those who market relentlessly, sell their stories thousands of times, and continue to spread their message zealously even when others have stopped.

CHARLIE CHAPLIN, THE "LITTLE TRAMP"

Let us strive for the impossible. The great achievements throughout history have been the conquest of what seemed the impossible.

CHARLIE CHAPLIN

Charlie Chaplin will always be remembered for creating the Little Tramp, a character he portrayed in dozens of movies. He is also remembered for his comedic insight and the precision, cleverness, and seeming ease with which he performed on film. But studies of Chaplin's life and work have brought his genius into focus. He was a virtuoso of hard work, frustration, and messy creation. Virtually all of his films were made with no script. Chaplin started with the germ of an idea. From that, he began filming a scene, not knowing where it would lead. Repeating the process again and again, with some changes each time, he would build on that scene and imagine a storyline. It wasn't finished yet. Chaplin would often reshoot entire scenes when he would think of one additional bit of information relevant to the story evolving in his head.

The resulting scenes seemed fluid and effortless to the viewers whereas they were actually ground out little bit by little bit. When inspiration stopped, so did the entire production. The crew and actors would sit around for days with nothing to do until Chaplin thought of a new idea. As a result, he had numerous and heated confrontations with studio chiefs and financial backers who felt he was using too much film and wasting the crew's time. Most actors and directors would have folded under pressure or been fired. But success breeds hope, and Chaplin gave investors and studios hope. Sure enough, Charlie Chaplin's films were among the era's most successful. His genius was not doing it right the first time, but doing it enough times to finally get it right.

Consider This: Our society (or job) often gives us one chance to get things right. If you have any control, never be satisfied with the first good result. Keep going until the finished product is excellent.

VIKING FREIGHT DELIVERS

*The greatest pleasure in life lies in doing that
which others say cannot be done.*
VIKING FREIGHT'S MOTTO

Dick Bangham and friend Jim Haapoja were working for Memorex when they were bitten by the need to follow their American Dream. In 1966, starting with a Chevy pickup and an old Pontiac, the pair began a delivery service. Often working sixteen hours a day, they survived on a few small delivery contracts. Finally the business caught on, saw profits, and gave them hope for additional growth. They prepared for expansion. Dick and Jim met with bankers and transportation experts. Unfortunately, they got the same message over and over again. Their plan was impossible. No company could become a successful common carrier because there were too many insurmountable regulations, unions, and slim profit margins. But the two continued to pursue their dream. They didn't give up.

Using loans, leases, and internally generated capital, Bangham and Haapoja steadily expanded Viking Freight. Bangham insisted on extensive training for all employees, promotion from within, and upward career planning. All new employees spent a full day at the company's headquarters (known as Viking University) to learn the "Viking Way." Viking became one of the most envied common carriers in the western United States and received numerous excellence awards from the trucking industry. It always told its employees, "Viking doesn't pay your wages, the customer does. Viking simply takes the money and divides it up between the employees, the suppliers of equipment, and services, and tries to keep enough to continue growing. Without customers, there would be no money to divide." FedEx bought Viking Freight in 2001, but to its former employees, its legacy represents the fulfillment of a genuine American Dream.

Consider This: Never forget who the most important person in our business is: the customer.

PILLSBURY'S BEST

Act; act now; act effectively; act for the greatest good.
He belonged to the type of man who "does things."
HORACE HUDSON, OF JOHN PILLSBURY

John Pillsbury came to St. Anthony, Minnesota, in 1855 and was soon joined by his nephew Charles. Since the new community needed tools and supplies for building, Pillsbury opened a hardware store. By 1869 Pillsbury was successful but was looking for other opportunities. The area's milling industry was in poor condition and losing money. When the mill owners looked for a partner to save them, most investors turned them down as a hopeless cause. Charles Pillsbury saw an opportunity. He bought a one-third interest and began to apply his enthusiasm and hard work to bring the mills back to profitability. Although he knew little about actual milling, he had a keen understanding of business. He bought new machinery to produce better flour and took a personal interest in improving the daily milling operation. By 1872, Pillsbury had bought out its partners, and the business was renamed C. A. Pillsbury & Company.

Not happy to only be profitable, Pillsbury sought to have the best and most modern mills available. His relentless desire to create the biggest and best mills in the country led him to purchase several other local mills. In each one, he increased productivity by implementing the most modern machinery and time-saving procedures. "Pillsbury's Best" flour began to establish a reputation as one of the best brands available. Charles traveled to Europe in 1888 and obtained special "secret" devices that made the new mill, named "A," the largest and most modern mill in the world. The foundation of the Pillsbury company was based on innovation and a constant desire to produce the world's best product.

Consider This: An organization is not successful only because it provides a necessity. What makes an organization successful is leaders who have a vision for excellence and work hard to make success happen.

TERADYNE

Concentrate your resources to win. You have a chance to lose because you might pick the wrong objective. On the other hand, if you don't concentrate, it's a sure loss.

ALEX D'ARBELOFF

Teradyne, Inc. got off to a rough start. Nick DeWolf and Alex d'Arbeloff sat in DeWolf's living room in 1960 and began to draw up plans for a new company. Each was an engineer who had the itch to create their own business. Together they successfully raised $250,000 and rented space over a hot dog shop in Boston. Their first product, on which they had spent their whole bankroll, was a go/no-go diode tester. When the gadget was ready, they began showing it to potential customers. Everywhere they went, they were turned down. Friends even took them aside to express their sorrow that the new company wasn't working out.

DeWolf and d'Arbeloff were discouraged but refused to give up. The pair knew the tester was something their customers needed, but they had to convince the customers of that need. They persisted. Sales slowly increased until the company began making a profit. Then, in 1969, the bottom dropped out of the semiconductor industry. Teradyne held on. They put their heads together and came up with new ideas to diversify into other kinds of equipment. DeWolf eventually left the corporate life, but d'Arbeloff continued to head the firm. d'Arbeloff saw his ideas tested in the unforgiving corporate crucible. He attributed his success to his Three R's management style: (1) Recruiting people from universities; (2) Retaining them by giving them the freedom to operate; and putting them on the (3) Right projects. The trick was to pick strategic projects and then devote sufficient resources to make them work. Today Teradyne, Inc. manufactures systems to test electronic and computer components in factories worldwide.

Consider This: Know your customers well enough to provide them with precisely the products they need.

WHITE CASTLE HAMBURGERS

*Know that you'll learn more from your
mistakes than your successes.*

BILLY INGRAM

While many of the largest hamburger restaurants fight it out by redesigning their sandwiches over and over again, one company has been consistently successful by keeping its burgers the same for decades. In 1921 E. W. Ingram and Walt Anderson opened the first White Castle in Wichita, Kansas. Anderson was an experienced fry cook, and Ingram knew real estate. They borrowed $700 to open their first restaurant and carefully selected the White Castle name to symbolize the restaurant's commitment to purity and cleanliness. The entrepreneurs' innovative idea became the world's original fast-food hamburger restaurant chain. Like many of the most successful fast-food chains, White Castle has remained a family business, with the Ingram family continuing to own all stores.

White Castle's success isn't based on a big burger. Its burgers, also known as sliders, are small, and the 100 percent USDA steam-grilled beef patties are served on buns about the size of a square dinner roll. In 1947 one store operator, Earl Howell, introduced the five holes in the patty. Hardly anyone buys just one White Castle burger—most customers buy them by the bagful. White Castle customers are very loyal. A Chicago customer once waited outside a new store for fifteen hours to buy the first hamburger sold at that location. Some couples have even been married at White Castle restaurants. Once, two adventurers took a pair of sliders to Antarctica and were photographed while enjoying the burgers at the South Pole. White Castle burgers continue to be known as "the crave heard round the world."

Consider This: You don't need to compete head-on with a company that dominates an industry if you have your own unique style, service, or product. Sometimes being different is the right move.

SCRABBLE

Nothing is invented and brought to perfection all at once.
THOMAS COLE

To Americans, family time is often game time. Most games are sold during holiday periods, and the two games that sell best are Monopoly and Scrabble. Both were invented during the Great Depression when people, who otherwise would have been at work, had time to devote to playing games. In 1931 Alfred Butts, an unemployed architect, developed a game consisting of one hundred wooden tiles, each with a letter of the alphabet printed on one side. The game's object was to select letters from the pool of tiles and form a word, with each word receiving a score based on the number of tiles used to form it. Alfred worked on his game for a decade, perfecting it and changing the way it was played. He added a playing board and gave each letter a point value. The board allowed players to create words in much the same way as filling in the blanks on a crossword puzzle.

In 1948 Butts decided he was satisfied with this game. He and his wife chose to market it under the name "Scrabble." The couple set up a workshop to produce the playing board and pieces. Selchow & Righter noticed an early version of Scrabble and agreed to manufacture the boards. They thought the game was interesting but probably nothing more than a fad. As the years passed, orders continued to increase, and in 1953 Selchow & Righter acquired exclusive manufacturing rights. More than fifty years after its debut, Scrabble continues to be one of the top-selling board games in the world.

Consider This: Do you have some invention to promote? The best way to sell it to a company is to prove that it will sell. Is your company looking for the next million-dollar seller? Keep your eyes open for the small idea that could turn into a huge success.

ROBERT GODDARD

For every action, there is an equal and opposite reaction.
NEWTON'S THIRD LAW OF MOTION

When Robert Goddard began working on the problem of sending a rocket into space, he soon realized that the weight of such a vehicle's fuel would be tremendous. Further, the fuel would be expended quickly, leaving a heavy empty container attached to the spacecraft. Goddard's solution was to create a multistage rocket. As soon as the fuel in the initial stage was consumed, the fuel tanks and motor for that stage would be jettisoned, and the rocket would continue its climb with less weight to bear. It was a brilliant idea that ultimately enabled NASA to send men to the moon. But Goddard would never see his concept put to use. He'd patented the multistage rocket in 1914, nearly four decades before such a vehicle was constructed.

Robert Goddard's pioneering vision for rocketry is an example of American ingenuity that has placed the US at the forefront of the technological age. In a 1907 article in *Scientific American*, Goddard explained how gyroscopes could stabilize airplanes in flight. In 1919 he wrote a book titled *A Method of Reaching Extreme Altitudes*. The press ridiculed Goddard, who was at that time head of the physics department at Clark University, saying he didn't have even a high school understanding of physics. Nevertheless, Goddard continued his research by winning occasional small grants. But even with such meager resources, he was able to construct the first liquid-fueled rocket in 1926. While the US government generally ignored his work, Germany used Goddard's ideas to create the V2 rocket during World War II. Although Goddard died in 1945, his concepts for rockets and space travel are still used today.

Consider This: If you're on the cutting edge of discovery, don't be surprised if people ridicule your ideas. Stick to what you know is right, and the truth will eventually be recognized.

ELI WHITNEY

*I do the very best I know how, the very best I can,
and I mean to keep on doing so until the end.*
ABRAHAM LINCOLN

Eli Whitney grew up on a small farm in Massachusetts before the American Revolution. Knowing that his family's acreage wasn't large enough to split between him and his brothers, he left home to seek his fortune. Although he had little formal education, Eli learned enough to enter and graduate from Yale University. Later, after taking a tutoring job in Georgia, he used his farm background and mechanical aptitude to help a friend solve the problem of separating seeds, hulls, and foreign material from cotton. As a result, the cotton gin invention helped the South rise from poverty to prosperity. Still, Whitney's design was quickly copied, and he saw little profit.

Although the cotton gin changed an industry for the better, Whitney is best known for his second great invention. He understood that a manufactured product's success rests on the manufacturer's ability to make it better, faster, and cheaper than everyone else. He also realized that a product must be mass-produced for the manufacturer to make a good profit on his investment. Knowing that the fledgling US government needed a domestic supply of rifles, Whitney devised a plan to make the weapons with interchangeable parts. Standardization of parts allowed the various components to be spread among several workers rather than a single gunsmith. This greatly reduced manufacturing time and costs. No bank would risk the capital to fund his concept, but the government was eager to back the rifle project. Whitney's idea became the pattern for American manufacturing that gave US businesses a competitive edge over their entrenched European counterparts.

Consider This: Learn and use the knowledge you have acquired to devise a better plan the next time around.

RENT-A-WRECK

*Whenever you see a successful business, someone
once made a courageous decision.*
PETER DRUCKER

When Dave Schwartz graduated from UCLA, he decided to go into the used car business. After all, he'd been buying and selling cars to work his way through college and enjoyed the work. After raising a little capital, he opened Bundy Used Cars in the Los Angeles area, near the Santa Monica Freeway. Times were tough, and the bills piled up faster than the sales slips. It wasn't long before Dave owed more than he was worth, almost a quarter of a million dollars. It seemed everyone's answer was to take it on the chin and declare bankruptcy. The thought was too much for Dave. He believed he could turn his business around. If he could just hang on, maybe a break would occur.

Fate stepped into his used car lot in the form of a young woman wanting a car. Dave sold her one, but it broke down the next day. He offered a refund, but the customer had a better idea. She only needed the car for three months. Would it be possible to rent a car? Dave cut a deal with the customer. He then considered how to turn the concept into a new revenue stream. He started advertising used vehicles for short-term rentals. Soon they became a sizable portion of his business. A local newspaper columnist gave Dave's car lot some publicity and coined the phrase "Rent-A-Wreck." People were impressed with Dave's honesty and the value of his vehicles. He rented cars to the rich, the famous, and anyone who wanted a bargain. One Volkswagen Beetle brought in more than $30,000 in rental fees during its lifetime. Before long, Rent-A-Wreck franchises had popped up in major cities all across the United States.

Consider This: Combining good value with a bit of mystique can produce good business and solid profits.

COLLARING THE MARKET

Nothing in this world is so powerful as an idea whose time has come.
VICTOR HUGO

At the turn of the century, men's fashion clothing was more like a strait-jacket than a comfortable garment. In particular, shirts were an annoyance. Designers tortured men with shirts that buttoned up the back and had various kinds of stiff, attachable collars. The collars we see men wearing in old photographs or period movies may look stylish and debonair, but in reality they caused rashes and contributed to headaches and stiff necks. There had to be a way to devise a more comfortable dress shirt. In fact, there were probably many potential ways to resolve the problem. But the profits go to those who can turn a good idea into a real solution. In this case, that someone was John Van Heusen. In 1919 Van Heusen developed a way to fuse cloth on a curve. This allowed him to make a detachable "soft-folding collar" that mimicked the traditional stiff collar. It kept its shape without wrinkling and was a more comfortable fit.

The detachable collar was a success. Van Heusen, with partner John Bolton, sold the rights to the invention to the Phillips-Jones shirt company. Van Heusen and Bolton became millionaires from the royalties generated by sales of the collar, but Van Heusen kept on inventing. Another of his inventions was the nonslip shoulder strap for women's lingerie. Then, when one-piece shirts began to dominate the market, the name "Van Heusen" was transferred to the entire shirt. Now marketed by the Phillips-Van Heusen Corporation, the Van Heusen brand continues to be one of the most recognizable names associated with business and dress shirts.

Consider This: Find out what's bothering people and develop a solution to make the problem go away.

BISSELL CARPET SWEEPERS

*To give real service, you must add something which cannot be
bought or measured with money, and that is sincerity and integrity.*
DONALD A. ADAMS

In 1876 Melville Bissell and his wife, Anna, operated a crockery shop in Grand Rapids, Michigan. Each time they received shipments of glass or china, the contents had to be removed from packing sawdust. Because the carpet sweepers of the day had little effect on the bouncy sawdust particles, the resulting mess required almost a day to clean up. Melville, who liked to tinker, considered how to devise a solution. After some experimentation, he built a better sweeper. His customers and friends noticed the device and asked where they could buy the invention. After so many inquiries, Melville decided there was a market for his sweeper. To manufacture his invention, he hired residents of Grand Rapids to make the parts at home. Anna then sold the sweepers to local retail stores. As the company grew, they needed more space to manufacture products. So in 1883 they built their first factory. Unfortunately, it was soon destroyed by fire.

Melville and Anna had to mortgage all their assets to build another plant. Then they learned that a particular Bissell model was defective. Melville recalled the entire output and destroyed the machines. But that disaster, and the Bissells' response to it, solidified the company's reputation for integrity and reliability. Customers could be assured that the Bissell Company stood behind its products. Melville died in 1889, and Anna assumed overall management responsibilities, becoming one of the country's first female corporate leaders. Under Anna's guidance the company continued to grow, becoming one of the most recognized names in the carpet sweeper business, a distinction it still holds today.

Consider This: A disaster can be turned into an asset if the response is correct.

MAXWELL HOUSE COFFEE

That coffee is good to the last drop.

THEODORE ROOSEVELT

Many Americans look forward to that first cup of coffee in the morning. They owe much of the satisfaction they derive from their daily ritual to the person who helped set the standard for consistently tasty coffee. Joel Cheek was a salesman for a Tennessee wholesale grocer in the 1870s. One of the items he sold that never seemed to be up to par was coffee. Because of variations in coffee beans, roasting methods, and blending, the same brand of coffee would sometimes be too weak, too strong, or too bitter. So Cheek set out to make a better and more consistent coffee. He experimented with different types of beans and carefully monitored the blending process until he had developed his ideal coffee. Cheek wanted a coffee that not only tasted good but would also taste the same each time it was brewed. He took his blend to Nashville's famous Maxwell House Hotel, where it proved to be so popular with customers that it soon became the house's specialty.

The popularity of Maxwell House Coffee grew steadily, and in 1907 Cheek served a cup of his blend to President Theodore Roosevelt. "That coffee is good to the last drop" was the president's reaction. The description stuck and has been used as the advertising catchphrase for Maxwell House Coffee ever since. Today the selection of beans and the roasting and blending techniques are still an essential part of the Maxwell House tradition. In addition, rigorous taste-testing ensures that the company's coffee continues to live up to its reputation for good taste and consistency.

Consider This: Give Americans a really good-tasting product, and they will eat—or drink—it up.

CASTRO CONVERTIBLE

Even a little child can do it.
CASTRO CONVERTIBLE ADVERTISEMENT

Bernard Castro arrived in New York from Italy in 1919. The fifteen-year-old could not speak English but managed to get a job with a travel agency. He took English courses at night and soon found a better job with an upholsterer. In 1931, when Bernard decided to go into the interior decorating business, he borrowed money to get started. When the Great Depression hit, Bernard owed everybody. He went to his creditors and promised to pay one or two dollars a week until his debts were settled. He explained that if he were closed down, the creditors would never get their money back.

Many of Castro's customers wanted heavy sofa beds reupholstered and often asked if he could "slim them down." That always meant losing the bed. Castro began to experiment with ways to build a lighter sofa bed, but World War II was in progress, and metal was scarce. Drawing his inspiration from bunks aboard ships, Castro believed that wooden slats could be used to make a sofa bed. When the war ended, he patented a lightweight metal version. An idea for marketing the new bed came one day when Castro went into his living room and found that his four-year-old daughter, Bernadette, had opened the sofa bed. In 1948 he filmed his daughter opening the bed and bought expensive commercials on television to promote the device's ease of operation. At first, the commercials seemed to have no impact, and Castro considered withdrawing the promotion. But after the commercials had been airing for three months, orders began to pour in. That single commercial was aired more than thirty-thousand times.

Consider This: Success seldom happens quickly. You often must be patient if you are to see positive results.

LIZ CLAIBORNE

Render a service if you would succeed.
This is the supreme law of life.
HENRY MILLER

With an increasing number of women entering the workforce during the 1970s, there was a growing need for better women's office apparel. Until the seventies, most women's clothing was considered either too conservative or too fashionable to be worn in an office setting. The growing gap in the women's apparel market did not escape the eye of Elisabeth Claiborne Ortenberg. She'd been a designer at Youth Guild for sixteen years when the company closed. Elisabeth's husband had also begun phasing out his consulting business. They knew the time was right, so in 1976 Liz and her husband started a design company, Liz Claiborne, Inc. She was joined by a production partner, Leonard Boxer, and Jerry Chazen. The foursome's new enterprise was an immediate success, with revenues totaling more than $2 million in their first year. By 1978 sales reached $23 million.

The Claiborne concept provided stylish, up-to-date women's apparel and added a unique service for retailers. A Claiborne representative would show individual retailers how to display, promote, and sell the Claiborne line, as well as how to keep customers coming back for more. The Claiborne concept utilized sketches, photos, and printed materials to demonstrate precisely how to promote the company's products in the store. In addition, it taught the sales staff how to correctly display clothing and explain to customers which blouse went with which skirt. The unique sales-training approach worked well, and the success of Liz Claiborne, Inc. was assured. In 1986 Liz Claiborne, Inc. became the first company founded by a woman to make the Fortune 500 list.

Consider This: If you provide your customer with a better way to make a profit and include a service that others do not offer, you'll make a name for yourself.

BARBARA YARBROUGH ELEMENTARY SCHOOL

A good teacher can inspire hope, ignite the
imagination, and instill a love of learning.
BRAD HENRY

School districts don't name a school after just anyone. They are named after presidents, famous astronauts, and politicians. Barbara Yarborough Elementary school in Midland, Texas, is named after a teacher. And not just any teacher. Barbara Yarbrough was a tough, no-nonsense teacher whom students loved for sixty-two years. In her mid-eighties, when most people were retired, she still greeted children as they came into her classroom. And those students remembered her for life. When they had families of their own, they invited her to dinner and even took her with them on trips. For them, she was a life-changer. A life-inspirer. A love-giver. A tough cookie.

But Barbara didn't have an easy start. Her grandfather was a blacksmith on a plantation, and her grandmother was enslaved. Her mother died when Barbara was nine. Her father became an alcoholic. As a result, she was in charge of caring for her younger brother. For five years she had to survive on the street, homeless. But she had aunts who helped her stay in school. "School saved me," she remembered. At her school, she had teachers who cared. They looked past her dirty clothes and her anger at life and gave her structure and a place to feel safe. Under their care, she excelled. After graduation she earned a BA in arts education. She became a teacher in what she calls "the greatest ministry on earth." School had given her back a life, and in turn, she dove into her teaching career to carry forward the love that had turned her life around.

*Consider This: Education is more than learning facts. The best education is learning about life, love, integrity, and responsibility. And teachers who teach **those** facts are the ones who make our country good and strong.*

BOB HOPE

I have seen what a laugh can do. It can transform almost unbearable tears into something bearable, even hopeful.

BOB HOPE

The American Dream has not come without a price. Countless thousands of young Americans have defended our freedom in wars on distant shores. These soldiers were often lonely, lived in blistering heat or frigid cold tents, ate "K ration" food out of cans and boxes, and wondered if the people back home remembered them. The United Services Organization (USO) remembered them. And so did Bob Hope. For more than half a century, the veteran comedian entertained American troops worldwide, keeping them laughing while keeping their dreams alive. In commemoration of his unflagging efforts, Congress named Bob "America's Most-Prized Ambassador of Good Will."

Like any good businessman, Bob knew his fortune came from the people. His job, much like a salesman's, had been to communicate with the audience throughout his career. He made people feel at home and made them want to buy his "product." During his early days in radio, one show's producers didn't think Bob needed a live audience to perform. But Bob knew that it was people who made his act work, so he ushered in a sizable group from an Edgar Bergen show and never did another live broadcast without an audience. Fans were Bob's customers, and he loved them. "When I open the refrigerator door and the little light goes on, I do ten minutes," he once quipped. At army bases and on college campuses, Bob Hope not only entertained; he sold America. He once told a group of university students, "America's greatest natural resource has always been her people. In times of crisis, this nation always finds the leaders to guide her through."

Consider This: In tough times, laughter can help us put our lives back into perspective and help us hold on to our dreams.

YA-HOO CAKE

*If you're trying to create a company, it's like baking a cake.
You have to have all the ingredients in the right proportion.*
ELON MUSK

Talk about an American Dream . . . Jim Read had been a good salesman, so good that his commissions were getting out of hand. As a result, he was fired by his company. At the age of forty-five, he was having trouble finding another job. To while away his idle time, Jim started experimenting with recipes in the kitchen and made a few cheesecakes. He thought briefly about going into the catering business but dismissed the idea. Then one night Jim had a dream that would change his life. In his dream he saw himself assembling the precise ingredients for a special cake: cherries, chocolate chips, pecans, even the exact amount of baking soda needed. When Jim awoke the following day, he promptly made the cake of his dreams.

A neighbor tried the concoction and yelled, "Ya-hoo, that's a terrific cake!" (That's how folks talk down in Texas.) The neighbor promised that if Jim baked the cakes in the shape of the Lone Star State, he would buy one hundred. Jim thought with that kind of initial order, maybe the cake business had something to offer after all. So Jim and his wife traveled to flea markets to test the idea. They gave away free samples of the cake, usually signing up new customers in the process. People soon began to pass along hints about baking, how to buy fresh ingredients, and how to wrap the cakes to keep them fresh. During their first year in business, the Reads sold 5,400 cakes, and Ya-hoo cakes were on their way to success.

Consider This: Your dreaming mechanism is more innovative than you think. So maybe you should pay more attention to what you dream about.

KENNETH HARRIS AND JAMES WEBB

Science is not a collection of facts; it is a process of discovery.
ROBERT ZUBRIN

As a teenager Kenneth Harris worked as a high school janitor, scraping gum from the underside of desks. Then opportunity knocked. He entered a NASA high school internship program. His experiences inspired him to earn a BS in mechanical engineering in 2014 and a master's in engineering management in 2017. While in his early twenties, Harris had an opportunity to work on the James Webb Telescope. Since he already had a great job managing an electronics lab at the time and saw a lucrative future there, he turned it down. He met with one of his mentors, who told him, "You're crazy." Harris quickly reversed his plans and accepted the new position.

The experiences and credibility he gained working on the James Webb Telescope was a career-changing as well as a life-changing experience. The telescope project provided him with leadership roles and priceless scientific credibility. Plus, Harris had been a part of a project that would shape scientific thinking for generations. The Webb detects light from the dawn of the universe, 13.5 billion years ago. Information scientists gathered by using the telescope will likely change what we know about our origins and how the universe works. Harris has also worked on various satellite systems and has been instrumental in developing measures to protect them from cyberattacks. He hopes to become an astronaut and work on the moon or in a space lab in the future. As one of the nation's top innovators, he was named to the *Forbes* 30 Under 30 list in 2020.

Consider This: Opportunity sometimes only knocks once. So carefully consider your prospects, and choose the path that offers you the most promising potential.

MERCK AND CO.

Profit is not the legitimate purpose of business. The legitimate
purpose of business is to provide a product or service
that people need and do it so well that it's profitable.

JAMES ROUSE

The E. Merck drug company was founded as a family business in Germany
in 1668. Many years later, to expand his operations, George Merck arrived
in New York in 1891. He brought with him the already prestigious company's reputation. Initially, Merck obtained drugs and chemicals from Europe
and distributed them in the New York City area. His son, George W. Merck,
took over the firm in 1925. A Harvard graduate, young George entered the
family business in 1915. In 1933 he built a research laboratory in Rahway,
New Jersey. This became the company's first excursion into pharmacological
research. One of their first innovations was a synthesis of vitamin B. Other
discoveries followed.

George often used the word *serendipity* to describe the firm's research.
Many times one area of research led to the discovery of other more valuable
treasures. For example, while pursuing a drug to treat a rare liver disease,
Merck scientists found vitamin B12. Similarly, when working with cortisone
as a treatment for Addison's disease, researchers discovered the drug's anti-
inflammatory properties. George W. Merck explained his service philosophy:
"We try to remember that medicine is for the patient. It is not for the profits. The profits follow, and if we have remembered that, they never fail to
appear. The better we have remembered it, the larger they have been." Under
his leadership, the company expanded its sales from the 1924 level of $5.2
million to $94.1 million in 1950. Most recently, Merck ranked sixty-ninth in
the Fortune 500.

*Consider This: Profits are the by-products of providing a solution to human needs
or desires. Therefore, spend lots of time looking for a good product, then profits
will follow.*

REYNOLDS ALUMINUM

*Learning and innovation go hand in hand. The
arrogance of success is to think that what you did
yesterday will be sufficient for tomorrow.*

WILLIAM POLLARD

No one saw the true potential of aluminum except R. S. Reynolds Sr. His company (US Foils) had produced packaging material and foils since 1919 but was buying all of its aluminum from outside sources. In 1928, seeing the potential of aluminum, Reynolds created Reynolds Metals Company to produce aluminum foil. Then, in 1939, he asked a French aluminum company official why Germany was buying so much aluminum. He was told that the lightweight metal was used to make "doorknobs, truck bodies, and other things." Reynolds suspected it was actually being used to build airplanes. With war looming on the horizon, Reynolds realized aluminum would soon be in short supply. He informed Congress of his concerns but was dismissed as an alarmist.

Reynolds finally convinced Senator Lister Hill that the US needed its own aluminum production capability. With a loan of $15 million, he built a plant in Sheffield, Alabama. He began producing aluminum in less than six months. A government commission initially predicted that aluminum production would be sufficient to meet America's needs for two years. Still, ninety days later, as its value to the war effort became apparent, aluminum became the first metal to be declared in shortage. After World War II the government wanted to scrap several plants. Reynolds, confident that aluminum was the metal of the future, purchased them. With aluminum foil and siding as their keystone products, the Reynolds Metals Company continued to expand. They produced the first aluminum pipe in 1960 and the first aluminum beverage can in 1963. Reynolds Metals was acquired by Alcoa in June 2000.

Consider This: At times the experts don't know what they're talking about. If you know your industry better than anyone else, believe in yourself.

THEODOR SEUSS GEISEL

Think left and think right and think low and think high.
Oh, the thinks you can think up if only you try!
DR. SEUSS

Theodor Geisel got his first chance to write humor for a Dartmouth College publication named *Jack O'Lantern*. He was fired after he was caught drinking. Nevertheless, he continued contributing under the name Seuss. After a brief time at Oxford University, Geisel returned to New York to begin a career as a cartoonist. He built a reputation in magazines like *Life, Vanity Fair,* and the *Saturday Evening Post.* That led to a position in advertising with the Standard Oil Company, where he spent fifteen years. His work there opened up a new opportunity. Viking Press asked him to illustrate a children's book named *Boners.*

After that experience Geisel decided to write his own children's book. He called it *And to Think That I Saw It on Mulberry Street,* using the pen name Dr. Seuss. He submitted it to a publisher and was turned down. He tried again and was turned down again. After twenty-seven submissions, Viking Press finally published it. The book was well-liked but wasn't a hit, so Geisel continued with his cartooning career. When World War II came along, he worked on animated training films. After the war he turned again to children's books. His new story, *Horton Hears a Who,* solidified his reputation as a children's storyteller. That led to a challenge. Houghton Mifflin and Random House asked him to write a children's book using only simple children's primer words. Geisel wrote and wrote. Sometimes he wrote the same line in his new story a hundred ways and chose the line that worked best. The result was Dr. Seuss's *The Cat in the Hat,* the story that catapulted him into children's book stardom. In a recent list of the 250 bestselling children's books, 47 were by Dr. Seuss.

Consider This: Concentrate on what you do best. Building a reputation can lead from one opportunity to another. Each step forward gives you a chance to have a breakout moment.

GEORGE WASHINGTON CARVER

Education is the key to unlocking the golden door of freedom.
GEORGE WASHINGTON CARVER

George Washington Carver was born into slavery at the end of the Civil War (1864). When he was still an infant, he and his family were kidnapped by slave raiders. Although he was returned to his former owner's farm, he never saw his mother again. Moses and Susan Carver raised George on their farm, teaching him to read, write, and garden. His expertise in gardening made him the "plant doctor" to nearby farmers. At eleven he left to attend an all-Black school in Neosho, Missouri. A childless couple, Andrew and Mariah Watkins, took George in. He learned about medicinal herbs and developed a deep religious faith from them. He later moved to Minneapolis, Kansas, and graduated from high school in 1880. Rejected at Highland College because he was Black, he went to Simpson College. This Methodist school accepted all qualified applicants. He then went to Iowa State University, where he became the first African American to earn a bachelor of science degree. He continued and earned a master's degree.

In 1896 George Washington Carver was appointed director of agricultural research at Tuskegee Institute in Alabama. Surrounded by poor farmers, he dedicated himself to making a better life for all Southerners. When the boll weevil destroyed the South's primary cash crop, cotton, Carver encouraged planting other crops such as peanuts and sweet potatoes. He developed more than four hundred products from those plants and introduced a new era of agriculture to the South. Disliking waste, Carver developed profitable uses for farmers' "trash," including dyes, soaps, and fertilizers. He never patented any of his discoveries but offered them free to help improve the quality of life for his fellow man. To Carver, success meant helping others succeed.

Consider This: Selfish people search for their own success. Generous people find success in helping others achieve their goals.

RICHARD SEARS

There is only one boss. The customer. And he can fire
everybody in the company from the chairman on down,
simply by spending his money somewhere else.

SAM WALTON

Like many young men in the late nineteenth century, Richard Sears believed that becoming a telegraph operator was the ticket to a prosperous career. It was, but not in the way he'd imagined. In 1886 Richard was working as a station agent in North Redwood, Minnesota, when a shipment of watches arrived. The timepieces were for a local jewelry store, but the store refused the shipment. That gave Richard an idea. He contacted the Chicago company that had sent the watches and offered to sell them himself. They agreed, and he telegraphed his fellow station agents up and down the line. Within weeks his inventory was sold out. Sensing the possibilities, he moved to Minneapolis and set up the R. W. Sears Watch Company. Richard moved to Chicago in 1887 and continued selling through station agents.

Everything was going fine until people began to return the watches for repair. Sears advertised for a watchmaker, and the ad was answered by Alvah C. Roebuck. In 1888 Sears opened his business to the public and published a catalog. Knowing that his primary target, the farmer, was a tough sell, Sears relied on three principles to bolster the reputation of his fledgling mail-order concern: (1) customers were given an absolute assurance of honesty; (2) all items sold were covered by a money-back guarantee; and (3) prices were kept low enough to justify ordering by mail. Even after Richard Sears retired in 1910, his original ideas were vital factors in the early success of Sears, Roebuck and Co.

Consider This: Providing exemplary service to the customer is not a new idea.
But for many years, growing and popular businesses have employed excellent
service to keep customers happy.

CAPTCHA AND AI

I believe this artificial intelligence is going to be our partner. If we misuse it, it will be a risk. If we use it right, it can be our partner.
MASAYOSHI SON

When using the internet, you may encounter the statement, "I am not a robot." Of course you're not. But the statement exists because nefarious robot programs, or "bots," mimic legitimate human users. A bot can attempt millions of passwords a day to break into a secure site. If there is a way to make money on the internet (e.g., play poker, get into someone's bank account), they'll find it and become good at it. In 2000 when Yahoo was the most significant player on the internet, spamming bots were creating millions of email accounts daily. Yahoo wanted to stop it, so they mentioned the problem to computer science students at Carnegie Mellon University. Luis von Ahn, a first-year PhD student, accepted the challenge.

Because Yahoo needed to distinguish humans from robots, Ahn came up with a test. It had to be simple enough for humans but too complex for computers. So Ahn devised CAPTCHA, a Completely Automated Public Turing test to tell Computers and Humans Apart. The first test generated squiggly, angular, and distorted letters. Humans could read them, but computers couldn't. Yahoo implemented the test and stopped the bots. Unfortunately, computers got smarter. A new generation, known as reCAPTCHA, involved pictures. Humans could identify images such as crosswalks better than computers. But computers, using AI, caught up again. (A side effect was that the test taught computers how to "see" driving hazards and become better at self-driving.) Year after year companies fine-tuned CAPTCHA and continued to develop new identity tests such as dual log-on and biometric procedures. The struggle between humans and bots will likely continue for many years.

Consider This: AI challenges daily life with cutting-edge opportunities. Human imagination and continual learning will forever be needed to keep pace.

MEL BLANC

We didn't make pictures for children. We didn't make pictures for adults. We made them for ourselves.

MEL BLANC

"What's up, Doc?" Entire generations have grown up listening to Mel Blanc's famous voices. In fact, some of the world's most beloved cartoon characters speak with his voice. Mel's virtual monopoly of Warner Bros. cartoon voices began in the 1930s, but getting to the top was tough. Growing up in a musical family, young Mel aspired to a career in the theater. But his first break came in radio, where he did "funny stuff," including creating various novelty voices. At that time the Warner studios were using spare actors to provide voices for cartoon characters, and Mel thought the performers' work was "god-awful." Every two weeks he applied for the job but was turned down. Finally, the man who kept refusing to hire Mel died, and a new man was put in charge. Treg Brown put Mel to work, and the chemistry started cooking. In 1938 "wascally wabbit" Bugs Bunny was introduced, followed by Daffy Duck, Elmer Fudd, Yosemite Sam, and numerous others.

Mel had a versatile voice, but he still had to work at it. When a new character was being conceived, Mel would experiment with several voices, seeking to match the character's sound with its physical makeup. He paid close attention to diction to make the voice understandable. Warner Bros. stopped making cartoons in-house in 1963 and ceased all cartoon production in 1968. In the late 1970s many of Warner's most famous cartoon characters were revived. Mel Blanc earned as much for speaking a single sentence in his later years as he did for making an entire cartoon years ago.

Consider This: Don't use just anyone to do the job at hand. If you find someone really interested in doing it well, you may be creating a classic.

BETTER FARMING FROM ALLISON KOPF

Agriculture is the most healthful, the most
useful, and most noble employment.
GEORGE WASHINGTON

In the late 1960s, besides the looming problem of the atomic bomb, people worried about the "population explosion." Publications like the 1968 book *The Population Bomb* predicted that, by the 1970s, millions of people would be starving to death worldwide because agriculture couldn't keep up with the world's needs. It predicted, "Nothing can prevent a substantial increase in the world death rate." Many believed life would be unsustainable when the world's population reached four billion. Fortunately, these predictions didn't come true. But feeding today's eight billion people continues to be a considerable challenge. That's why forward thinkers like Allison Kopf are essential. Agrilyst, a company she founded in 2015, provides farmers with techniques to grow the crops needed to feed the world's growing population.

Kopf grew up in the black-dirt region of New York, in a community full of farmers. But she had no idea she'd work in that industry; her interests were in science and technology. In college she developed skills in technology and team leading. She was also the only woman in her physics class. After graduation she returned to New York and got a job at BrightFarms, a hydroponic grower and greenhouse builder. While there she combined what she'd learned about greenhouses with her technology background to form a new company to develop a cultivation management platform for farmers. Agrilyst used data analytics and AI innovations to provide farmers with more efficient and less costly ways to farm nonprocessed produce like lettuce and tomatoes. In 2016 Technical.ly Brooklyn named Kopf "Entrepreneur of the Year."

Consider This: Keep your eyes open for how you can use your interests and experience to create something new and innovative for the marketplace and the world.

DOVEBAR

All you need is love. But a little chocolate
now and then doesn't hurt.
CHARLES M. SCHULZ

When Leo Stefanos stepped on to the ground in New York after arriving from Greece, he must have wondered if he would ever succeed in his new country. Decades later, his son Mike stood in the same place and introduced Leo's answer to America's constant craving for chocolate and ice cream, the DOVEBAR. More than one million frozen treats were sold by street vendors that first year, which would have made Leo proud. The idea for the confection arose one day when Leo saw his young son racing recklessly down the street in pursuit of an ice cream truck. Leo knew that was dangerous and decided to make his own ice cream bar in hopes of keeping Mike closer to home.

Since he owned a candy shop that also sold premium ice cream, Leo went into the store's back room and cut a few blocks of his best ice cream, which he dipped into rich chocolate. Leo intended the treat for his family, but the bars eventually became a popular item at the Dove Candy shop. Mike grew up, earned a CPA degree, and then joined his father in the candy shop in 1977. After Leo died, Mike began to think of ways to expand the family business and introduced DOVEBARs to specialty stores and country clubs in the Chicago area. In 1984 he presented the DOVEBAR at the Fancy Food Show in Washington, DC. He began to receive orders from around the country. Other companies have tried to replicate Dove's success and their product, but they haven't been able to replicate Mike's high-quality ingredients. And even though this means a DOVEBAR costs more than other confections, it continues to be popular because it is the best.

Consider This: Many people care about quality and will pay a premium price rather than accept a so-called bargain.

DR PEPPER

I can't do coffee, but I can do Dr Pepper.

CHER

As the third-largest soda brand (behind Coke and Pepsi), Dr Pepper has always had a bit of an attitude. It began at Wade Morrison's Old Corner Drug Store, located in the railroad hub town of Waco, Texas. At that time sodas were created by mixing carbonated water with flavors such as birch bark, sarsaparilla, and fruit extracts. Charles Alderton, Morrison's pharmacist, liked to experiment with flavors. So when he came up with a fruit flavor he liked, the store put it on the menu. "Shoot me a Waco" was how customers ordered the new drink. The actual name's origin is somewhat of a legend. A popular version of the story is that Alderton had eyes for a sweetheart whose father was named Dr. Charles Pepper. So Alderton named the drink after the dad, hoping to impress the lady. It didn't work, but the drink's name stuck.

Once Dr Pepper became popular, other stores wanted it, so Alderton started selling Dr Pepper syrup. In 1891 Robert S. Lazenby of the Circle "A" Ginger Ale Company bought Dr Pepper and began bottling it. He took his drink to the St. Louis World's fair in 1904 and introduced it to people from all over the US. Although the original soda didn't contain caffeine, it was added in 1920 to compete with other sodas of the era. The "Drink a bite to eat at 10, 2, and 4" campaign sold Dr Peppers all across America, promoting its picker-upper effects. As its popularity widened, Dr Pepper became the largest non-cola beverage in America. Over the years it fought off numerous knockoff brands with similar tastes. Still, it continues to hold on to its niche market as "the most original soft drink ever in the whole wide world."

Consider This: Take a current fad and experiment with new ways to improve it. Who knows, maybe you'll create the next new thing.

CLEAN UP WITH S.O.S. PADS

There are so many wonderful things in your everyday experience,
lucrative opportunities, glorious occasions, that do not exist for
you because you do not have the vision for discerning them.

EDWARD KRAMER

Sometimes the things that can catapult us to success are the things that begin as sidelines. We devise an answer to a problem and then discover that many other people could use the same idea to solve their problems. That is what Edwin W. Cox experienced in 1917. As a Wear-Ever Aluminum saucepan salesman of aluminum cookware, he was mediocre. He just couldn't get housewives to listen to his presentation. That's when Edwin thought of using a gimmick. He decided to offer each potential client a free gift as a reward for letting him do his sales pitch. Of course, the gift had to be helpful for the housewife and had to solve some cooking-related problems.

What Edwin Cox conceived was an abrasive pad containing soap that could be used to clean pots and pans. He took small steel wool pads in his kitchen and repeatedly dipped them into a soapy solution. Then he let them dry and dipped them again. He continued the process until the pads were full of dried soap. When he began offering the pads as gifts, his cookware sales increased. Cox also found that housewives started calling him to obtain more pads. Demand for the cleaning pads soon surpassed Cox's ability to make them in his kitchen. Eventually he had to stop selling cookware to cover the growing demand for his new product. Cox's wife called the pads S.O.S. for "Save Our Saucepans," and the name stuck. In 1918 Cox found an investor group to fund his new business. A hundred years later, S.O.S. pads are still a staple of American kitchens.

Consider This: Keep an eye on those sidelines that may point to something that has great potential.

THE STATUE OF LIBERTY

Give me your tired, your poor, your huddled
masses yearning to breathe free.
EMMA LAZARUS

Many Americans didn't want the Statue of Liberty. The giant copper figure, originally known as Liberty Enlightening the World, was a gift from the people of France. But it came with the stipulation that Americans must provide the foundation on which the statue would stand. Donations were first solicited in 1877 but came in slowly. Some people protested. They said the figure would ruin the view of New York harbor. Many other citizens around the US were hard-pressed to contribute to a monument that would stand in New York. Finally, Joseph Pulitzer, the *New York World* publisher, took up the cause. His publications praised the symbolic importance of the statue and encouraged contributions. People responded.

Edouard Rene Lefebvre first discussed the idea for the monument in 1865 in Paris, to keep alive the ideals of French liberty. Lefebvre conferred with sculptor Auguste Bartholdi, who created a 1.25-meter likeness of the statue. For the full-size version, which was constructed in Paris in 1884, Gustave Eiffel designed an inner support structure onto which Liberty's copper skin was affixed. By 1885 sufficient money had been raised to complete the foundation, and the Statue of Liberty was dedicated on October 26, 1886. Today it is a symbol of freedom recognized worldwide. Liberty's image is found in restaurants, shops, and hotels worldwide—anywhere liberty, justice, and freedom are advocated. For example, during Chinese freedom rallies in the 1990s, students made a version of the statue and paraded it through Beijing. Unfortunately, the Chinese government wiped those events from Chinese history.

Consider This: Other countries look to America for freedom and hope. Be thankful for the liberty that allows us to choose the dreams we follow.

LANE BRYANT

Put your knowledge to practical experience and reap the harvest.

A. A. MILNE

Lena Himmelstein left Lithuania in 1885 at the invitation of distant relatives in America. When she learned a marriage was being arranged, she refused and joined her sister Anna, who worked as a seamstress for one dollar per week in a New York lingerie sweatshop. Lena was adept at operating a sewing machine and eventually was earning fifteen dollars per week. Several years later, Lena quit her job to marry David Bryant. Shortly after their first son was born, David died, and the young widow moved in with her sister and began sewing at home for a few customers. Despite tough financial times, Lena's business slowly grew. One day a customer asked Lena to design a maternity dress, an article of clothing that was not available at the time. The result was the famous No. 5 Maternity Gown, named for its place on a price list.

When Anna married, Lena's brother-in-law loaned Lena $300 to help her open a bank account. When the nervous Lena went to the grand Oriental Bank to open her account, she filled out the deposit slip as "Lane Bryant." The name stuck. In 1909 Lena married Albert Malsin, an engineer. By 1910 Albert saw more potential in his wife's business than he did in his career, and he became her finance manager. Lane Bryant's business grew, and Lena opened a store in New York that pioneered the acceptance of maternity wear. Albert began to recognize that customers, no matter how loyal they might be, needed maternity clothes only for relatively short periods in their lives. After researching other women's apparel needs, Lane Bryant began designing attractive clothes for full-figured women.

Consider This: Most men and women do not look like the models in magazine advertisements. So who is going to make everybody else look good?

THE TEDDY BEAR

In any moment of decision, the best thing you can
do is the right thing, the next best thing is the wrong
thing, and the worst thing you can do is nothing.
THEODORE ROOSEVELT

Teddy Roosevelt was a popular president, and his exploits were well covered in the nation's newspapers. One of his adventures took place in 1902 when he went to the South to help resolve a border dispute between Louisiana and Mississippi. While he was in the area, he decided to go hunting. The friendly Southerners wanted the president to take home a nice trophy. So they trapped a bear cub, intending to release it at just the right moment to allow Roosevelt a clear shot at the animal. During the hunt Roosevelt found out about the plan. He refused to shoot the bear. The incident made a great newspaper story and also inspired a memorable cartoon. *The Washington Star* carried a cartoon by Clifford Berryman that showed Teddy Roosevelt, gun in hand, standing with his back turned to the bear cub.

Russian immigrant Morris Michtom was the owner of a small candy shop in Brooklyn when he first noticed the poignant cartoon in the paper. He came up with a plan to use the incident to attract the attention of potential customers. He placed a small stuffed bear in his store's window with a sign saying "Teddy's Bear." The bear attracted attention. Everyone wanted to buy one of the bears. Michtom asked Roosevelt's permission to call his bear "Teddy's Bear." The president responded that he "couldn't see what use my name would be in the stuffed animal trade." As demand for the teddy bear grew, Michtom turned his attention to the toy market and founded the Ideal Toy Company, which has sold millions of the cuddly stuffed critters.

Consider This: You never know what idea may turn into the next national sensation.

JAMES WELDON JOHNSON

"You are young, gifted, and Black." We must begin
to tell our young, "There's a world waiting for
you. Yours is the quest that's just begun."
JAMES WELDON JOHNSON

James Johnson was born in Florida, although his mother was from the Bahamas. She instilled in him and his brothers an appreciation of classical music and literature. After graduating in 1894 from Atlanta University, a historically Black college, James became a schoolteacher and was eventually promoted to principal. In the 1904 presidential race, he helped Theodore Roosevelt's campaign. As a result, he was appointed by the new president as a United States consul, first in Venezuela and then in Nicaragua. In 1910 he moved to New York with a new wife. He became involved in the art and music of the Harlem Renaissance. With growing activism in the civil rights movement, James became a field secretary in the National Association for the Advancement of Colored People (NAACP) in 1917. In 1920 he became its executive secretary.

He always remembered the music training he'd received from this mother. In the early 1900s James and his brother wrote the widely known spiritual "Dem Bones" ("Toe bone connected to the foot bone . . . Hear the word of the Lord"). He also wrote the lyrics to the famous hymn "Lift Every Voice and Sing," as a tribute to the renowned Black educator Booker T. Washington. But his most enduring work was "God's Trombones: Seven Negro Sermons in Verse." This piece captured the fire-and-brimstone preaching style of Black preachers of the era. It was adapted to music by Fred Waring, who introduced Johnson's words to audiences all across the United States. One of the most famous sections is "The Creation," which begins, "And God stepped out on space, / And he looked around and said: / I'm lonely— / I'll make me a world."

Consider This: Circumstances and society's limitations should never hold back your dream. Instead, overcomers push ahead even in the face of challenge and trouble. And they create magic.

THE BROWN PAPER BAG

*The human race is divided into two classes, those who
go ahead and do something, and those who sit and
inquire, "Why wasn't it done the other way?"*
OLIVER WENDELL HOLMES

We tend to take simple things for granted. When we think "invention," we may think of complicated things like the telephone, the automobile, or the cell phone. In fact, our lives are surrounded by thousands of meaningful yet mundane inventions. For example, the brown paper bag. That ubiquitous brown bag is so familiar we overlook its importance. Small versions are used to "brown bag it" to work or school. Larger versions are a necessity in the grocery business. It's excellent as a trash bag. Or as a Halloween mask. Add handles, and it's a shopping bag. We take it for granted, but before 1883 the square-bottomed paper bag didn't exist. For that invention we owe a debt of thanks to Charles Stillwell, born in Ohio in 1845. After service in the Union Army, Stillwell began to invent things. Most of what he devised was forgotten, but not this new type of paper bag.

Unlike the V-shaped bags produced by hand for years, Stillwell's bag had a square bottom and pleated sides. It could be opened with a flick of the wrist. The square base allowed the bag to stand, letting the user fill it quickly without holding it open. The design was not the only important part of Stillwell's invention. His bag was produced by machine, whereas other bags of the period were all hand-pasted. The "self-opening sack" became immediately popular. Still, its real leap to success did not come until the 1930s, when the American supermarket was born. Although some communities fight between the benefits of plastic versus paper, today millions of brown paper bags are sold every year.

Consider This: Simple things that solve simple problems are essential advancements in our lives.

CARRIER AIR CONDITIONING

*There are no rules. That is how art is born, how
breakthroughs happen. Go against the rules or ignore
the rules. That is what invention is about.*
HELEN FRANKENTHALER

Early in the twentieth century, mechanical cooling devices began to come into use; however, most used a highly volatile ammonia refrigerant. Many cities would not allow the operation of devices using ammonia coolant. That was why Dr. Willis Carrier looked forward to a presentation scheduled for May 22, 1922. He was excited about a new cooling device he had developed that was smaller, more efficient, and used a safer coolant called Dilene. Carrier wasn't sure that his five hundred invited guests would be excited enough to come, so he offered a free dinner and a six-round boxing match.

After the meal, a large curtain was pulled aside to reveal a refrigeration machine like nothing anyone had previously seen. Carrier called the device a centrifugal refrigeration machine (or "chiller"). Some of the guests placed orders for the invention on the spot, but there were problems. The New York City building safety chief would not approve the device, calling its coolant untested and unlisted. Finally Carrier decided to take the matter into his own hands. He went to the chief's office, poured some Dilene into an open container, struck a match, and threw it into the can. The chief almost leaped out of the window until it became evident that the substance was simply burning gently. There was no explosion. The safety chief lifted his ban, and the Carrier air-conditioning system was on its way to changing the way Americans lived and worked. Today, the Carrier company continues to produce home and business air-conditioning systems emphasizing energy efficiency and sustainability.

Consider This: Some people won't believe published facts. So you must show them by example—and sometimes in dramatic fashion—that what is purported to be true is actually true.

OVER THE RAINBOW

Words make you think a thought. Music makes you
feel a feeling. A song makes you feel a thought.

YIP HARBURG

In *The Wizard of Oz,* Dorothy sings about escaping from her lonely gray life in
"Over the Rainbow." It became America's most beloved song but was almost
lost to history. E. Y. "Yip" Harburg, the son of Russian immigrants, grew up
on New York's Lower East Side. He and his friend Ira Gershwin memorized
Broadway songs. They were both destined to become lyricists. In 1935 Yip
teamed up with pianist Harold Arlen and wrote songs together. Their tunes
became so popular that they were hired to compose songs for the upcoming
The Wizard of Oz movie. They wrote most of the film's songs but still needed
one for Dorothy. Yip imagined Dorothy's gray and dreary surroundings. Her
only color was a distant rainbow. She "wanted to be on the other side." He tried,
"Over the rainbow is where I want to be," "I'll go over the rainbow someday,"
and "Someday over the rainbow." Somehow . . . Someday . . . Somewhere . . .
The words were close but not quite right. Yip's future wife, Edelaine, helped
by singing Yip's lyrics to Harold's tune. When she sang "Somewhere, over the
rainbow," he knew he'd found the right words.

When Judy Garland, who played Dorothy Gale, first sang "Over the
Rainbow," Yip, Harold, and the entire crew knew it captured the heart of the
movie. Then disaster struck. The producer rejected the song, saying it "slowed
down the picture." Yip and Harold complained, objected, and demanded the
song be reinstated. Luckily, another producer, Arthur Freed, agreed and put
it back. "Over the Rainbow" became an instant hit. It won an Oscar for Best
Song, was declared the number one song of the twentieth century, and was
named the best-ever movie song.

*Consider This: If you know your work is good, fight to get it recognized. Get help
if needed.*

NOVEMBER 2

THE FRISBEE

Who'd have thought the Frisbee would have caught on?

KARL PILKINGTON

It may not be necessary to develop a brand-new idea to make a big impact in the marketplace. There are plenty of examples of businesspeople who have "discovered" something that's been around for years. The trick is to recognize a great idea and find the right way to bring it to the potential market. When Rich Knerr and Spud Melin started Wham-O Manufacturing Co., their main product was a slingshot (hence Wham-O.) They sold them primarily through mail order. One day at the beach, the partners ran into Fred Morrison, who sold disks that would fly through the air when thrown. Kerr and Milin bought the rights to the disk, but it didn't sell very well. Over the next several years, the company promoted the Hula Hoop and several other sports toys. After four years of little success with their "Pluto Platter," they decided to take another look at the flying disk.

Remembering a lesson from the easily copied Hula Hoop, they reengineered the disk to be easy to fly but hard to duplicate. In 1959 they renamed it the Frisbee. The name originated from a tin pie plate imprinted with the name of the Frisbie Pie Company and used by Yale students as a flying disk as early as 1920. To advertise the Frisbee to their target audience, they recruited young people to play with it on college campuses and playgrounds. The promotion worked. Frisbee soon caught on. It became a staple on college campuses and at beach parties and picnics. It even spawned new sports like Frisbee golf.

Consider This: An idea may have the making of a great product, but unless it's promoted correctly, it might never take off.

WALGREENS

*Innovation comes out of great human
ingenuity and very personal passions.*
MEGAN SMITH

Charles Walgreen worked in a Dixon, Illinois, shoe factory until he lost part of a finger in an accident. The doctor who treated Charles liked him and persuaded him to become a druggist's apprentice. In 1893 Charles went to Chicago, where he worked in a drugstore during the day and studied pharmacy at night. After fulfilling the requirements to become a registered pharmacist, Charles enlisted to fight in the Spanish-American War, during which time he contracted malaria. Although the disease left Charles in poor health for many years, he continued to work as a druggist. In 1902 he was able to buy an interest in the pharmacy from a retiring owner for $2,000. The other owner retired in 1909, and Charles acquired the remaining stake in the store, which he renamed the C. R. Walgreen Company.

Charles trained managers and slowly added more stores. By 1927 the Walgreen Company had 110 stores, and when Charles died in 1939, there were 493 stores. Known as the "father of the modern drugstore," Walgreens generated much of its success from innovations made in the areas of the lunch counter, the soda fountain, and the open display of merchandise. His stores were well lit and clean, and Walgreen paid keen attention to small details. He made better quality but less expensive products than those offered by his competition. In 1934 Walgreen introduced display counters that enabled customers to pick out merchandise for themselves. Today such things seem simple and obvious, but it took Charles Walgreen to introduce them to the world.

Consider This: Walgreens' innovative concept of bringing products to the customer in a clean, attractive, and cost-effective way is an idea that still has merit today.

HOW LUCKY WE ARE!

You can wake up every day and make today better than the last.
TOMMY LASORDA

People who grow up in America often have a tendency to discount the notion that ours is the "greatest country in the world" because we have nothing to compare it to. We may see the plight of those in other countries, but somehow it doesn't sink in that America really is different. Listening to immigrants who have discovered the American Dream gives new appreciation for what we frequently take for granted. When veteran baseball manager Tommy Lasorda felt depressed about something, he remembered his dad. "I'm the luckiest man in the world," his dad would say. But when Tommy was a child, he didn't see things that way at all. Tommy asked his dad how he could be happy driving a truck for a stone quarry. How could his dad be happy about getting so cold that he had to massage his feet to get any comfort? How could he be happy when his wife had arthritis? How could he be happy about trying to feed five kids and pay all the doctor bills with hardly any money? Why was he so happy?

His dad told Tommy about coming from the old country. He told the boy how lucky he felt to have a job. He was fortunate to have a loving wife. And having five great kids? That was great. He got to live in a house, drive a car, and live in a great country. "I'm the luckiest man in the world." Later in life, whenever Tommy Lasorda found himself complaining or when things just didn't seem to be working out, he remembered his dad's words. Quickly, his attitude improved. He realized that happiness is all a matter of perspective.

Consider This: Why dwell on the wrong things in your life when there are so many right things? Count your blessings; they will probably far outnumber any complaints you have.

NOVEMBER 5

CHARLES DOOLIN AND FRITOS

Every day is a new opportunity. You can build on yesterday's success or put its failures behind and start over again.
BOB FELLER

In 1932 Charles Doolin wanted a product that would make him some money. He'd operated an ice cream store for years, but the Great Depression killed off that luxury item. So he kept his eyes open for a new opportunity. Nothing he thought of panned out until one day, at lunch, he saw someone crunching a snack called Fritos corn chips. He tried them. He liked them. So he went looking and found the man who had made them. After negotiating, Doolin bought the business—lock, stock, and recipe—for $100. With his mother as his partner, he set up a "factory" in her kitchen. The dough was made from corn and put through a ricer that crushed it into small pieces. Those were formed into strips and cooked. They turned out about ten pounds of Fritos an hour with this setup. Bags of the chips sold for a nickel.

Convinced he'd found a good business, Doolin hopped into his Model T Ford and hit the road. He went to hundreds of cities, visiting grocery stores and cafés. Sometimes he took part-time jobs as a cook to pay his way. Sure enough, his persistence paid off, and the snack sales took off. In fact, they took off too much. He soon had to figure out a way to produce more and more of his tasty chips. With something called a hammer press, he expanded his production and moved to his garage, where he produced one hundred pounds of Fritos an hour. In 1945 Doolin sold a franchise to the H. W. Lay Company. In 1961 the companies merged. Today Frito-Lay, as part of PepsiCo, is the world's largest snack food company.

Consider This: One failure opens a new door of opportunity. Take advantage of the end to start a new beginning.

IN-N-OUT BURGER

*What can I say about [In-N-Out]? It's the only
fast-food chain that I actually like.*
ANTHONY BOURDAIN

Most fast-food restaurant menus are filled with dozens of options. Not so at In-N-Out Burger. It has three: burgers, fries, and drinks. Yet In-N-Out stores typically earn twice the revenue of a McDonald's restaurant. When an In-N-Out store opens, devoted customers come from hundreds of miles. You don't see that when an average fast-food joint opens. But unlike the frozen burger patty used by most franchises, In-N-Out's food is never frozen (or microwaved). It all started in 1948, when Harry and Esther Snyder opened their first burger restaurant. There weren't many to-go hamburger joints in that era, so they made things up as they went along. Their little building, not much bigger than a garage, had a drive-through on the side and soon added something unique. Harry rigged up a two-way speaker system, allowing customers to order from their cars. Plus, burgers and fries were made fresh to order.

Of course, many burger joints started simple, but what's impressive is that In-N-Out stayed that way. Today every patty is made from never-frozen beef and delivered to the store daily. Fries are cut in the store. Everything is served right off the grill. And burgers remain the only food option, along with fries and drinks (although there is a "secret menu"—ask for the burger animal style). Stores are consistently clean, bright, and inviting. Employees are paid more than in any other fast-food franchise. In addition, the company offers benefits that keep employees on the job and happy. So how do they do it? It's all in the family. While most fast-food places become franchises, In-N-Out stayed a family business. They own every store. And more than seventy years after they began, the same family is in charge.

Consider This: "Keep it simple" is more than a clever saying. When any process is kept simple, it gives you a remarkable ability to control consistency and quality.

TOM WATSON, PIANOS TO COMPUTERS

*I guess I have never been much of a complainer. You just take what
is given you, and don't complain about what you can't affect.*
TOM WATSON

Tom Watson was born in 1874, the son of a lumber dealer. After a stint studying business, he worked as a bookkeeper. Later he became a salesman of organs, pianos, and sewing machines. For a while Tom also worked in an ill-fated job selling stocks. He found out the company's dealings were less than completely honest, and the episode resulted in a close brush with the law. After that experience, Tom applied for a job with National Cash Register. The company turned him down, but Tom kept showing up and was finally hired as a salesman. As a new employee, Watson often went weeks without making a sale. But he was determined to learn and improve and soon rose to the top of the sales force.

In 1913 Watson and twenty-five other managers were charged with anticompetitive practices and dismissed. (The allegations were later overturned.) In 1914 he got back on his feet and took another position as a general manager of the Computing-Tabulating-Recording Company. The company was in poor financial shape, and Watson invested money in new products and training for the sales force. He was very picky about who he hired, paid his employees more than the going rate, and rarely fired anyone. In 1924 the company was renamed IBM. During World War II Watson sent parcels to employees serving in the armed forces to let them know that they were still part of the team. He educated everyone, even customers, and encouraged them with slogans such as "Think" and "Aim High." Under Watson's watchful eyes, IBM grew to become one of the most profitable and respected companies in the world.

Consider This: A tough start does not mean you're finished. Pick yourself up, and keep trying. Use your own difficulties to understand others and help them develop into their best.

FANNY CROSBY

*It is not enough to have a song on your lips. You
must also have a song in your heart.*

FANNY CROSBY

Fanny Crosby was born in 1820 and was blind within weeks. But her ears and voice were healthy. She took to music early and started composing her own songs by six. At fifteen she entered the New York Institute for the Blind school, and at twenty-two she became part of their faculty. She married another faculty member, Alexander Van Alstyne, who was a musician. Crosby continued to compose hymns, ballads, and patriotic songs. Sometimes she wrote a song a day. In her lifetime she composed more than eight thousand songs. She often put new words to existing tunes or worked with musicians to fit words into their compositions. Her most famous song was inspired by music written by composer Phoebe Palmer Knapp. Knapp played Cosby the tune and asked what words she would put with it. She replied, "Blessed assurance, Jesus is mine. Oh, what a foretaste of glory divine." Fanny continued singing words, guided by divine inspiration, and the composition became her most famous hymn.

"Blessed Assurance" was first published in 1873 in the *Guide to Holiness* magazine, edited by Joseph and Phoebe Knapp. In 1887 it appeared in *Gospel Hymns, No. 5*, a hymnal used in popular revivals that swept across the United States and Great Britain in the ensuing years. Because of the song's popularity, it was included in the Methodist hymnal beginning in 1889. Many other famous songs composed by Fanny appear in hymnals today, including "To God Be the Glory," "Jesus Keep Me Near the Cross," "I Am Thine, O Lord," "All the Way My Savior Leads Me," and "Praise Him, Praise Him." Because of her popularity, Fanny became friends with several US presidents and even spoke to Congress about education for the blind.

Consider This: Don't let a lack of one ability stop you from achieving greatness. Master your talents and skills with prolific and determined repetition and practice.

VAN CAMP'S BAKED BEANS

Ideas are the beginning points of all fortunes.
NAPOLEON HILL

The recipe for success may be right in front of you. In fact, it may be staring you in the face. Sometimes people move too fast to see the obvious. They are too busy to put two and two together and often can't see the forest for the trees. For example, in 1890 young Frank Van Camp took a little time out, eating lunch at the family cannery in Indianapolis. He may have been daydreaming or relaxing, but his frame of mind allowed him to be susceptible to a new idea. There were cans of pork and beans stacked up all around him, so when he pulled a tomato out of his lunch pail, he set it down on a can of the beans. At that time tomatoes were not used in many canned products. Frank stared intently at the tomato and the beans and imagined them together. What a novel idea! Why not cook beans and tomatoes together? Frank wondered if the idea had any merit. He could have stopped wondering, but he followed through on the thought.

Frank and his father, Gilbert, tested the idea and discovered that beans baked with tomatoes made an excellent combination. So they canned the new concoction and called them "baked beans." They promoted their new product in national magazines. The idea was so good that almost every canner began making beans in tomato sauce. Frank eventually became the president of the Van Camp company, which became the largest producer of pork and beans in the United States.

Consider This: Daydreaming can turn into ideas, and ideas can turn into reality if you follow through. Stop for a moment and think about what you already have. How can it be turned into a new idea?

ARTHUR FIEDLER

A spoonful of sugar makes the medicine go down.
"A SPOONFUL OF SUGAR," FROM *MARY POPPINS*

When the history of the twentieth century is written, it will likely be said that the person who sold classical music to the American public was Arthur Fiedler. Born in 1894 into a musical family, young Arthur took violin lessons but found them a chore. He initially attempted an apprenticeship in publishing but became disenchanted. Finally, at his father's urging, Arthur decided to become a professional musician. By 1915 he took a position with the Boston Symphony Orchestra. There he played almost every instrument at one time or another. His rise as a conductor started in 1924, and in 1930 he was named the director of the Boston Pops.

Arthur had the desire to take music to the public. He reasoned that since people freely enjoyed fine books and paintings at libraries and art centers, they should enjoy fine music as well. He instituted a series of free open-air concerts that soon became the model for other orchestras and bands around the country. He offered the public a variety of music, from current popular music to unknown classical pieces. In addition to Chopin and Wagner, he conducted a work based on commercial radio jingles. His version of "Jalousie," a hitherto unknown tango by a Danish composer, was the first symphonic recording to sell a million copies. Arthur not only appeared on the symphony stage but also appeared on *The Muppets* and *Sesame Street* and even let Big Bird conduct his orchestra. Like a spoonful of sugar to make the medicine go down, for fifty years Fiedler's skillful blending of popular and classical styles had Americans enjoying classical music they otherwise would never have heard.

Consider This: Bring something to the market that people enjoy, package it with excitement, and you will always have an audience.

NOVEMBER 11

DOCTOR MARY

The greater the obstacle, the more glory in overcoming it.

MOLIÈRE

Mary Groda had never been an outstanding student. At first no one was aware that the primary cause of her learning problems was dyslexia. As a result of dealing with a handicap she didn't understand, Mary became a problem student. Making the situation worse, Mary's family fell on hard times. To help with expenses, she spent her teenage years picking berries and living in a house made of cast-off materials. When her family moved to Portland, Oregon, Mary took up with street kids and became involved with alcohol and theft. Finally a counselor recognized that Mary had dyslexia and discovered that she was quite intelligent. Mary entered the Upward Bound program and earned a high school equivalency diploma. At age seventeen she decided she wanted to become a doctor.

Mary's life choices complicated her education. She became pregnant twice during the next few years and had no husband to help support her. The second delivery almost killed her, leaving her unable to walk or speak. Recovery was slow, but with the help of her parents, she made a comeback. She got a job and began attending college while taking care of her two children. In 1974 she married David Lewis. After being rejected by fifteen medical schools, Mary wrote personal letters to each, explaining more fully her circumstances. Finally Albany Medical College gave her a chance. At first the courses were too difficult, and Mary had to enroll in remedial classes. Eventually she was able to complete her medical degree. Dr. Mary ultimately became one of the school's most trusted and capable physicians.

Consider This: Tough times can be overcome if you are willing to set your mind on the goal and persevere when the going is rough.

THE BUSINESS "FAMILY" AT PUBLIX

*The greatest need in the world today is for people of sweet
disposition, good character, and harmonious nature.*

PEARL BUCK

Publix Super Markets are found only in the southeastern United States. Yet they are one of the largest supermarket chains in the country. George Washington Jenkins had grown up in a Georgia retail family. He was seeking his fortune in booming Florida when he founded the company in 1930 with a single small store in Winter Haven. From the very beginning, one of the things that set Publix apart from the competition was the pride employees took in keeping the store immaculate and inviting to customers. Jenkins taught his principles by example and sought to make every detail of his store appealing. As he began opening new locations and refurbishing acquired stores, a tradition began.

The weekend before opening day was vital in getting a Publix store ready. Everything had to be perfect. Without notice, 100 to 150 employees would appear at the store and work without pay to help the crew get ready. After work the employees would stage a cookout. On opening day, the employees would return to hand out brochures about Publix and help customers find their way around. Even the company's top executives would take a turn bagging groceries. If a store suffered a fire, workers from other Publix supermarkets would turn out in force to help repair the damage. Usually the stricken store could reopen within a week. With a tradition of exceptional service, Publix instilled a sense of familial pride in its employees. The result is a profitable chain of stores that makes shopping a pleasure. Today more than a thousand stores produce more than $34 billion in sales annually. Publix also perpetually ranks at the top in customer satisfaction.

Consider This: Everyone likes to be a member of a "family" whose standards are high, whose reputation is respected, and whose accomplishments generate pride.

THE SMARTEST PERSON

If you can't explain it simply, you don't understand it well enough.
ALBERT EINSTEIN

Many people consider William James Sidis the most intelligent person who ever lived, as measured by IQ, a widely accepted measurement of intelligence. His IQ was 250 to 300, whereas an average IQ is 100. Born in Boston in 1898, he read the *New York Times* by age two and entered Harvard at eleven. But his intelligence didn't help him become an influential scientist. He tried being a math professor at Rice University, but that failed. So instead he flitted from job to job for many years. Although he wrote many books (some under pseudonyms), most are obscure and were never taken seriously. For example, one book predicted black holes (in 1925) many years before other scientists accepted the concept. But Sidis lacked emotional intelligence—the ability to give and receive feedback, collaborate with others, and resolve conflicts.

On the other hand, Albert Einstein is often considered the most brilliant scientist who ever lived, yet his IQ was 50 to 100 points lower than Sidis's. Einstein used his genius differently. He influenced the scientific world with his brilliant insights because he knew how to communicate complex ideas, collaborate with others, and defend his ideas. His theories profoundly changed how science understands the universe. What set Einstein apart from other gifted people like Sadis was the ability to understand that intelligence is only part of the genius equation. Einstein said, "I am enough of the artist to draw freely upon my imagination. Imagination is more important than knowledge. Knowledge is limited. Imagination encircles the world." When he conceived the relationship between energy and matter ($e = MC^2$), he described this complex concept with a clarity other scientists could understand.

Consider This: Intelligence is not a ticket to success. To realize the potential of your talents, learn to work with others and navigate the ups and downs of human emotions.

ERIE INSURANCE EXCHANGE

*Fortitude and the power of fixing attention
are the two marks of a great mind.*
FRANCIS BACON

Businesses, especially in their formative stage, must often survive crisis after crisis. Competition can be fierce, scheming, and underhanded. Usually the founders' creativity, hard work, and determination bring a company success-fully through the early, trying years. The difficulties experienced by Erie Insurance during its initial days are examples of the kinds of problems that must be overcome. It all started when two agents, disgruntled with their boss at Philadelphia Reciprocal, decided to form their own insurance agency in Erie, Pennsylvania. They needed a $25,000 guarantee fund to obtain licensure, so they raised the sum by selling $100 shares in the company. Just as things were looking very promising, their former insurance company began promoting a piece of legislation that would raise the ante to $100,000.

Upon hearing of the proposal, the newly formed board voted eleven to four to stop organizing the company at once. The four directors who voted to continue with the company created a special fund to pay all licensing expenses in the event that the company had to fold if the new law was enacted. With that offer, the rest of the board reversed its vote. While lobbying to delay the law, the two salesmen-founders scurried to obtain the minimum number of applications necessary to qualify for licensure. In two days they gathered 150 applications, 50 more than needed. The license was approved on April 1, 1925, just days before the new law went into effect. Today Erie is one of the top prop-erty and liability insurance companies in the US.

Consider This: When a crisis occurs, a cool head (or several cool heads), creativ-ity, and guts can often lead to a solution.

JOHN DEERE

*If we don't improve our product, somebody
else will and we will lose our trade.*
JOHN DEERE

John Deere was born in 1804 and apprenticed as a blacksmith in Vermont. During the 1830s the state's economy was poor, and, like many Americans, John headed west to seek his fortune. Settling in Illinois, he found that his skills were in great demand. The dense midwestern soil often clung to plows designed for eastern dirt, requiring that farmers stop every few feet to clean their plow blades. John studied the problem and came up with an idea to produce a self-polished plow. He fashioned a plow blade that would turn a clean furrow using a broken steel saw.

John Deere knew his invention was good and began producing the plows before receiving orders. When he had sufficient stock on hand, he went into the countryside and sold the implements from farm to farm. At first he had to make the plows from whatever steel he could find. Then, in an ambitious move, he ordered steel from England and paid the high cost of having it shipped up the Mississippi and across forty miles of land. His business continued to grow, and Deere moved to Moline, Illinois, where he opened a factory and convinced an American steel manufacturer to provide rolled steel. Deere prided himself on experimentation and innovation and constantly tried to improve his designs. But he knew that competitors would be breathing down his neck. Deere frequently stated, "I will never put my name on a plow that does not have in it the best that is in me."

Consider This: A good idea and a persistent obsession for quality are two of the most essential factors in creating a successful product or service.

EVERYDAY MILLIONAIRES

Millionaires are risk-takers, and they don't become millionaires until they're 40 or 50. It's a slower process than a lot of people think.
THOMAS J. STANLEY

There are many myths concerning what it takes to be a millionaire. Many people have a misguided conception of what the average millionaire is like. A study by Professor Thomas Stanley of Georgia State University (*The Millionaire Next Door*) dispels some of those images. Although many millionaires inherit wealth, the study found that most were born into middle-class or working-class families. Millionaires do not have to be wheeler-dealers, movie stars, or high-powered corporate executives. The average American millionaire owns a rather mundane business such as a fast-food restaurant or an auto parts store and may have made their money in sales or marketing. Or they have an average job and have been good at investing over their working years. They often drive a slightly out-of-date car, lead a stable family life, have a long-term marriage, and avoid status symbol products.

To clarify, a millionaire does not necessarily have a million dollars in the bank. A millionaire has a net worth of more than a million dollars. Often, a good portion of that wealth is in their home. Potential millionaires save their money, which is often the key to their financial stability. And, they buy a house, which they pay off within fifteen years. But even millionaires with considerable savings often find themselves strapped for cash since much of their worth is frequently tied up in their business or real estate. As unglamorous as it may seem, today's millionaires tend to be the people who live next door. They work hard, save their money, and invest wisely. And when the time comes, they are well prepared for retirement.

Consider This: Glamour is what we often associate with success. But many who have achieved financial success have done so through hard work, frugal spending, and wise investments.

CHARLES LINDBERGH

It is the surmounting of difficulties that makes heroes.
LAJOS KOSSUTH

Few names are so associated with American heroics as Charles A. Lindbergh. His 3,600-mile solo flight across the Atlantic caught the imagination of people on two continents, and his accomplishment has been the model for many young American dreamers. In 1919 Raymond Orteig had offered a $25,000 prize to the first person to make such a flight. No attempt was made for eight years, but by 1927 several pilots wanted to accept the challenge. Lindbergh was one of them, and he worked with a group of St. Louis businessmen to raise $15,000 to build a plane with a specially designed engine and fuel tanks.

The plane was ready on May 12, 1927, the same week that two Frenchmen were lost during an attempted crossing. Weather delayed Lindbergh's departure. But when the clouds cleared, Lindbergh and his crew made final preparations. Everything had to be right. Everything had to be double-checked. By the time Lindbergh crawled into the cockpit, he'd been awake for twenty-four hours. The *Spirit of St. Louis* was so heavily loaded with fuel that getting it off the ground proved very tricky. With every rivet straining, the small plane clawed its way into the air, barely clearing utility wires at the end of the airstrip. Once in the air, Lindbergh faced more challenges, including storms, icy wings, and long hours without sleep. Newspapers had covered his takeoff, and now every American held their breath awaiting word of Lindbergh's fate. After thirty-three and a half hours, the *Spirit of St. Louis* arrived over Paris. Lindbergh circled the Eiffel Tower and landed at a nearby airfield, where he was greeted by throngs of excited Frenchmen. Newspapers the world over proclaimed, "Lindbergh Does It!"

Consider This: Many people try to be a hero. But those who enter that select fraternity do so with more than luck. It also takes precise planning, hard work, and guts.

COMING BACK AFTER LOSS

When you have exhausted all the possibilities,
remember this: you haven't.
ROBERT SCHULLER

Robert Schuller remembers a family tragedy in his book *Tough Times Never Last, But Tough People Do!* It was 1933, some four years into the Great Depression, and things had been difficult on the Iowa farm owned by Robert's father. Besides the poor economy, the family's crops were failing and there had been no rain. Nevertheless, there was a spark of hope as clouds appeared on the horizon one day. But as the clouds approached, an ominous funnel dropped out of the sky and headed for the farm. The Schullers jumped into the family car and made a hair-raising dash out of the tornado's path. When they returned, nothing was left of the farm. It was as if the entire area had been vacuumed clean.

Twenty-six years of backbreaking work were gone in a matter of minutes. The mortgage on the house was due, and the elder Schuller was nearing the age of retirement. When the family examined the spot where the house had been, they found part of a molded plaster motto that had hung in the kitchen. It originally had said, "Keep looking to Jesus," but now it read, "Keep looking." The Schullers took the sign back to the car, and it became their inspiration to continue trying and to not give up. Two weeks later they began rebuilding. Working harder than ever, the Schullers paid off their entire mortgage in five years. That tragedy inspired Robert Schuller, who became a noted evangelist, to believe in the power of "Possibility Thinking"—the idea that, with faith in God, belief in your own capabilities, and hard work, you can make the impossible possible.

Consider This: Circumstances are not your enemy; what is holding you back are your own shallow beliefs and a defeatist attitude. When setbacks occur, regroup and move forward.

WHITEWASHING THE FENCE

Don't let schooling interfere with your education.

MARK TWAIN

It was the 1830s, and young Sam Clemens had disobeyed his mother and taken a dip in the swimming hole near his hometown of Hannibal, Missouri. When his mother discovered the misdeed, she sent the boy to whitewash the fence as punishment. Sam looked down the thirty-foot-long fence and slowly began to paint, all the while trying to think up an excuse to get out of the work. He had painted just half a board when his friend John Robards happened by. "I guess you can't go with me, 'cause you gotta work," said John. "You call this work?" replied Sam. "A boy doesn't get to whitewash every day." Sam continued painting, pretending that he was really enjoying the chore. John watched for a minute, then said, "Let me whitewash for a minute." Sam smiled and said the job couldn't be entrusted to just anyone.

"I'll give you the core of my apple," offered John. Sam "reluctantly" accepted the payment. For the better part of the afternoon, Sam convinced boy after boy to pay for the privilege of whitewashing a portion of the fence. By the time the fence was completely painted, Sam had collected a brass doorknob, a dead cat, a dozen marbles, the handle of a knife, and a kitten with one eye. Years later, after he'd taken the pen name Mark Twain, Sam Clemens recounted the episode in his classic book *The Adventures of Tom Sawyer*. The story has since come to typify the resourcefulness of the American spirit. That is, make the best of a situation and turn one person's chore into another person's play.

Consider This: Work can be unpleasant or fun, depending on how you look at it or the spirit in which it's performed. Make work fun, and you'll attract lots of helpers.

ALKA-SELTZER

Relief is just a swallow away.
ALKA-SELTZER ADVERTISEMENT

Many people overindulge during the holidays and suffer pounding headaches and upset stomachs. Whether the cause of their distress is too much food and drink or the common cold, there's a medicine available that's been around for decades. According to their jingles, Alka-Seltzer's "Plop-plop, fizz-fizz, Oh what a relief it is!" will have you back on your feet in no time. The history of this iconic medicine began with a flu epidemic in December 1928. A. H. (Hub) Beardsley, the president of Miles Laboratories in Elkhart, Iowa, was always looking for new remedies for diseases. So while visiting a local newspaper plant one day, he was surprised to find the entire work crew healthy. Everywhere else in the country, workers were fighting the flu. The editor of the newspaper, Tom Keene, explained why his workplace was different. Whenever a worker appeared to be coming down with a cold, Keene put them on an aspirin regimen with bicarbonate of soda until they were well.

Beardsley returned to his office and didn't waste any time. He instructed his head chemist, Maurice Treneer, to develop an aspirin and soda tablet. And he thought of a name: Alka-Seltzer. He tried out his new concoction on the workers in his own office. He then conducted a field experiment by sharing the preparation with his fellow cruise passengers while traveling to the Mediterranean. The tablets helped with everything from seasickness to the common cold. Alka-Seltzer was introduced to the public in 1931 and was extensively advertised on the radio. When television came along, Alka-Seltzer was also heavily promoted on that medium. For almost a hundred years, Alka-Seltzer has continued to be a common sight in millions of medicine cabinets across America.

Consider This: Family cures, old wives' tales, and legends may have substance. Maybe they shouldn't be dismissed without a trial.

HARRY MULLIKIN OF WESTIN HOTELS

Be an earnest student of yourself. Study your
leading desires and tendencies.
GRENVILLE KLEISER

At age fourteen Harry Mullikin was out looking for a job. He had no particular career in mind. That's when he found a position at the Cascadian Hotel in Wenatchee, Washington. He worked as an elevator operator, bellboy, porter, night janitor, and room clerk. Later, after serving in the US Air Force, Harry tried to get into Washington State College. When his application was rejected, he went back to work at the hotel. One Sunday, while helping a customer check out, Harry noticed that the man's business card said he worked for Washington State College. "You didn't let me into your college. Why should I let you out of my hotel?" Harry quipped. The customer promised to look into the matter, and a few weeks later, Harry received a letter. The man turned out to be the school's director of admissions.

Not knowing that Washington State had a hotel management school, Harry decided to become an architect. One day he ran into the man who had helped him get into school. The man asked why Harry wasn't enrolled in the hotel school. "What hotel school?" Harry replied. Later, Harry confessed that he "never knew you could do something you liked." He liked the hotel business and became manager of one of the Western (later Westin) hotels. Harry Mullikin became known for his excellent judgment and attention to detail. He was given the task of building the Century Plaza Hotel in Los Angeles and was later named chairman and CEO of Westin Hotels and Resorts. During his career, he became known as the guy who got things done and the creator of the megahotel.

Consider This: You really can be in any profession you like. In fact, the one you like is probably the profession in which you will have the most success.

HORATIO SPAFFORD'S SOUL

Trauma creates change you don't choose. Healing
is about creating change you do choose.
MICHELLE ROSENTHAL

Waves lapped against the side of the ship *Ville du Havre* as it crossed the ocean from New York to England. The four daughters and wife of Horatio Spafford were aboard. He'd planned to join them on vacation later. On November 22, 1873, another ship rammed the *Ville du Havre*. It went under quickly, killing 226 people. Of his family, only Spafford's wife, Anna, survived. When she arrived in England, she sent a telegram to her husband in New York: "Saved alone." The news devastated Spafford. He took the next ship to England to be with his wife. As he crossed the sea that had taken his four daughters, he must have cried, been angry, and felt sad. With these emotions haunting his mind, he wrote a poem. His words would fashion one of the Christian church's greatest hymns: "When peace like a river, attendeth my way, When sorrows like sea billows roll; Whatever my lot, Thou hast taught me to say, It is well, it is well with my soul."

Tragedy happens. Almost everyone has lost a loved one in an untimely and perhaps tragic manner. Or we have seen news of an unspeakable atrocity. Such news can throw life into a miserable depression. Disaster devastates plans. It destroys happiness. How then can anyone recover? It creates a dark and lasting effect on the soul. Just as those in the military may experience post-traumatic stress disorder (PTSD), personal tragedy can cause PTSD symptoms such as debilitating flashbacks and despair. There is no easy cure for such things. Stafford found some solace in his faith. As difficult as it was, he trudged through life until he became hopeful again and could say, "Even so, it is well with my soul."

Consider This: Adversity happens. Expecting it or dwelling on a past occurrence will only constrain you and make your life miserable. Do whatever it takes to stand back up, move forward, and take your life back.

ZOOM MEETINGS

*It's being in the right place at the right time and
taking advantage of your opportunities.*

LEE MAJORS

Sometimes it is best to be in the right place at the right time. Of course, that's hard to plan. Nevertheless, the prize sometimes goes to those who are prepared. This is the story of Eric Yuan. He was born in China in 1970. While courting his wife-to-be, who lived ten hours away, he used his engineering education to develop software to allow him to "call" her over the internet. After hearing a Bill Gates talk, he became interested in using his computer expertise in Silicon Valley. He applied for a visa to the United States and was turned down eight times. Finally, in 2006, Yuan succeeded and entered an executive business program at Stanford. From there he joined a call-conferencing startup named Webex. Webex was bought by Cisco, and Yuan became a VP of engineering. Then he had a great idea. He pitched a concept of a smartphone-friendly conferencing system. Cisco said no. So Yuan did what any entrepreneur would do. He started his own company.

Zoom was born in 2011. In January 2013 Zoom 1.0 was released to the marketplace. It didn't take long for consumers to see its potential. Within five months it had more than a million users. Zoom went public in April 2019. Its stock quickly rose from an IPO price of $36 to more than $100 by June. Then, in 2020, the COVID pandemic hit. Zoom was there to help at-home workers teleconference with colleagues around the world. Millions of people developed a love-hate relationship in the next few years with "Zoom meetings." Nevertheless, many people used Zoom because it was the right technology at the right time.

Consider This: You can't predict what will come next. But you can be prepared with your best ideas so you can take advantage of the opportunity when it arrives.

QUAD/GRAPHICS

It's not the big that beat the small; it's the fast that beat the slow.

HARRY QUADRACCI

Quad/Graphics is tucked away in Pewaukee, Wisconsin, but the printing company has often maintained a 30 to 40 percent growth rate in an industry whose average annual growth rate is less than 10 percent. Founded in 1971 by Harry V. Quadracci and a covey of managers from a strike-ridden printing company, Quad/Graphics had little time to establish a formal management style. The founders instead based their new company philosophy on bits and pieces of management theory culled from the works of Kenneth Blanchard, Tom Peters, and a host of other managerial theorists. At Quad/Graphics, a significant part of the company's management strategy is to give each employee the responsibility to make their particular department productive and profitable. The plant itself is a textbook example of participative management.

In the transportation department, truckers were responsible for making profits on their runs. With only an occasional course-correction from management, the truckers worked with the Interstate Commerce Commission to get common-carrier status and then marketed their services to brokers. Other departments were similarly charged with the responsibility to generate profits. At times they experimented with different ways to make their employees happier and more productive. For example, to give employees more time to pursue leisure activities, they instituted a three-day, thirty-six-hour work week. They also created a stock ownership plan and a training program that offered college credit. Quad/Graphics also constructed a $3 million sports facility for its employees. And the entire plant, even the restrooms, were luxuriously appointed. Even in today's challenging printing market, CEO Joel Quadracci said, "We at Quad/Graphics continue to believe in the power of print."

Consider This: People respond to the trust given to them. So give your employees responsibilities in your company's future and watch them step up to the challenge.

WILL ROGERS

Some folks figure it's a compliment to be called broad-minded. Back home, broad-minded is just another way of sayin' a feller's too lazy to form an opinion.

WILL ROGERS

In many ways, Will Rogers epitomizes the character of Americans—at least how we would like to be. Born in Oologah, Indian Territory (Oklahoma), he was five-sixteenth Native American. He would often quip, "My ancestors didn't come over on the Mayflower; they met the boat." Will was a real-life adventurer. Before becoming a star rodeo performer, he learned his cowboy skills roping cattle in Argentina and Africa during the 1920s. In Texas Jack's Wild West Show, Will got his start on stage with a trick roping act. One night during the performance, he made a mistake and found himself ensnared in his lariat. Thinking quickly, Will told the audience, "A rope ain't bad to get tangled up in if it ain't around your neck." The ad-lib got a big laugh, and that was the beginning of his famous off-the-cuff roping routine.

Americans heard Will Rogers talk about the very things they'd say if only they'd thought of the right words. "Our foreign policy dealings are an open book—a checkbook." "Too many people spend money they haven't earned to buy things they don't want, to impress people they don't like." "Everybody is ignorant, only on different subjects." Rogers liked to try new ideas. He told his audiences, "Why not go out on a limb? That's where the fruit is." After he died in a plane crash in 1935, a statue was erected to his memory. It bears an inscription that perhaps tells us more about that insightful American than any other legacy: "I never met a man I didn't like."

Consider This: Americans respond to common sense. Humor is better than hype, and possessing good character is better than being clever.

BILLY GRAHAM

Although hotels, night clubs, and bars in the city were
crowded last night, the largest gathering . . . packed
Mechanics Building to hear Rev. Billy Graham.
BOSTON SUNDAY GLOBE

For decades Billy Graham was known as "America's Pastor." In an age when some evangelists were mistrusted and considered charlatans, Graham maintained his integrity. He met, encouraged, and advised every president since Harry Truman during his ministry. Without words of condemnation, name-calling, or political rancor, he brought a message of God's love and the need for repentance to millions of people worldwide. He was a comforting and inspiring voice during times of both celebration and sorrow.

Power and prominence often destroy men whose original intentions are honorable. Perhaps one reason Graham never succumbed to such forces stems from a 1948 meeting of Graham's team of evangelists in Modesto, California. Graham, Cliff Barrows, George Beverly Shea, and Grady Wilson were all concerned about the poor image of evangelists. The team prayed, discussed the problem, and came up with a list of actions to avoid falling into moral issues. First, they would be paid by salary instead of depending on gifts or offerings. They would work through local churches and not independently. They also committed themselves to maintain integrity in all publicity. Next, they were committed to reporting accurate attendance figures for various religious services. Finally, they pledged to avoid any appearance of sexual impropriety. Graham never traveled with, met, or dined alone with any woman except his wife from that day forward.

Consider This: Integrity doesn't just happen. Sometimes it takes extraordinary efforts. Some strategies may seem overly conservative. But in eras of suspicion and innuendo, it can be difficult for any public figure to protect their reputation.

CHICKEN SOUP FOR THE SOUL

*I believe that people make their own luck by
great preparation and good strategy.*
JACK CANFIELD

Jack Canfield and Mark Hansen had satisfying careers as motivational speakers. In their talks, they often told inspiring stories from their own lives or the lives of others. People asked them if the stories were in a book. They were not. The more they were asked, the more convinced they were of the need for a book. So they collected 101 stories in a book they called *Chicken Soup for the Soul*. The name was meant to describe stories that helped to heal people from anxiety or make them feel warm and cozy like a cup of chicken soup. First they put the stories into a book. Anyone with a word processor can do that. Next they looked for a publisher. Of course, they started with big publishers. They got a resounding no thanks.

When big publishers didn't pan out, they tried smaller publishers. Still no luck. Finally, at a book convention, they talked to Peter Vegso. He liked the stories and decided to give the book a chance. An unlikely publisher of health books in Florida named HCI became their publisher. The final step for their book was the hardest—turning it into a bestseller. Canfield and Hansen marketed their book relentlessly. They promoted it at conferences and seminars. They did hundreds of radio interviews. They gave stories to newspapers to publish for free. They talked gas stations, restaurants, and even a mortuary into selling it. Then, in a stroke of genius, they sent copies to the O. J. Simpson jury (on TV every day at that time). When viewers saw jurors walking into court carrying the book, it created a media sensation. That publicity sent the book soaring onto the bestseller lists.

Consider This: Create your own luck by doggedly promoting yourself or your product. Do what no one else has done. Get known. Get going.

GEORGE EASTMAN

It is indeed astonishing how many great men have been poor.
JOHN LUBBOCK

Poverty can be a prison. But to some, the fear of poverty leads to Herculean efforts of inventiveness. Such was the case of George Eastman. In 1868, when George was fourteen, his father died, leaving the family penniless. Instead of wallowing in his misfortune, George took action. He quit day school and became a messenger boy but continued his education at night. His schooling enabled him to get a position as a junior clerk at the Rochester Savings Bank. It was a good job, and he was frugal with his income. This allowed him to not only rise above poverty but also save money. With a small bankroll in his pocket, he decided to take a long-needed vacation to Santo Domingo. A friend suggested photographing his journey, so George bought a new-fangled wet-plate photographic outfit.

Because wet-plate photography proved difficult and tedious, Eastman looked for an alternative way to process pictures. He spent his nights formulating his own photographic plates using a dry-plate technology. It took Eastman three years of trial and error to develop a superior photographic plate. Finally, in April 1880, he leased a room and began to produce dry plates for sale. Unfortunately, Eastman quickly learned his product had severe flaws. Customer complaints resulting from poor batches almost killed his business. He kept experimenting. By 1888 he'd perfected an innovative photographic idea. This new process enabled photographic chemicals to be placed onto a roll of paper, then inserted into the camera. The camera was preloaded and required only that the user press a button to take a picture. He called it a Kodak. Eastman's revolutionary camera brought photography into a new era.

Consider This: If you're seeking to improve your life, open your mind to new ideas. Try a new hobby. Improve on someone else's idea. Go exploring. You may find the adventure of a lifetime.

BORDEN INVENTS CONDENSED MILK

Many strokes, though with a little axe, hew
down and fell the hardest-timbered oak.
WILLIAM SHAKESPEARE

In the sometimes long road toward success, persistence and determination are your two best travel companions. The tombstone above Gail Borden's grave reads, "I tried and failed, I tried again and again and succeeded." Borden did not have success early in life. Yet after each failure, he began a new quest. He became a schoolteacher, an editor, a real-estate salesman, a customs collector, and a surveyor. He came up with several innovative ideas that had no commercial success. His land and water vehicle nearly drowned the town elders of Galveston, Texas, on a demonstration voyage. Borden experimented with food preservation and won a gold medal at the 1851 London Crystal Palace Exposition for a dried meat biscuit. Still, he was unsuccessful in marketing the product. On the trip back to America, Borden was concerned about the deaths of four children on the ship caused by soured milk. This sparked his inventive thinking. How could milk be stored for long periods?

After a long search, he discovered how the Shakers condensed fruit juice using a vacuum process. With this idea, he developed condensed milk to keep it from spoiling even without refrigeration. Unfortunately, his first attempt to produce the milk was underfinanced and failed. A year later, with more financing, he tried again. Then the Civil War began. Borden received steady orders from the army. He was finally on his way to success. Borden used much of his profits to educate farmers in dairy techniques, organize schools for African Americans, build churches, and support underpaid ministers, teachers, and students.

Consider This: If you think you have the right stuff to make it, keep trying, keep seeking until an opportunity comes, then grab it for all it's worth!

SPACE INVENTIONS

One rule of invention: before you can
invent it, you have to imagine it.
JAMES GUNN

Somehow humans are programmed to explore. And space is perhaps our final frontier. How has Earth benefited from rockets, space shuttles, and Mars landers? Sending a rocket into space and living there for a while is complicated. It takes a tremendous amount of technology, experimentation, and imagination to pull it off. Survival requires innovation. A few Earth inventions have benefited from space exploration. Medical science has been a big beneficiary. Advances in artificial-limbs technology are traced directly to the robotic arms needed in the space program. Tiny bits of space dust collide with their helmets and could quickly cause the glass to scratch or break. Earthlings benefit from scratch-resistant lenses for prescription glasses. Diabetes is a significant health issue here on Earth. And advancements in insulin pumps came from life-support mechanisms used in space. LASIK surgery uses technology initially developed to track astronauts' eye movements. Scanning technology used to study images of the moon improved CAT scans and MRIs.

Everyday technology has also benefited from the space race. The design of rocket launch facilities has helped architects build earthquake-resistant buildings. Power for almost every space vehicle comes from solar cells, whose advancements for space benefit Earth's quest for sustainable energy. And the cameras and lenses on your cell phone? Those high-quality lightweight cameras were developed to take photos in space. The list could go on for pages.

Consider This: The advancement of civilization has always been driven by exploration and experimentation. And putting ourselves on the cutting edge of discovery is a sure way to spur inventions that sustain life.

GENERAL EVANGELINE BOOTH

It is not how many years we live, but what we do with them.
EVANGELINE BOOTH

Every time disasters strike, one group of volunteers jumps into the fray with a helping hand. When homeless people need a place to sleep, food, or support, there is one place they can go. When families struggle to have holiday dinner and provide toys for the kids, one group offers a welcoming hand up. William and Claire Booth started the Salvation Army in England to bring hope to "thieves, prostitutes, gamblers, and drunkards"—souls the traditional church ignored. But one of their daughters would lead the Army's American branch into a powerful worldwide resource for good.

Evangeline Booth was the seventh child of William and Claire Booth. In 1896 she was sent to the US to lead the American (and Canadian) Salvation Army. She eventually became the fourth General in the worldwide Salvation Army movement. She started hospitals for unwed mothers, homes for the aged, and "Evangeline Residences" for working women. In 1917 she gathered 250 Salvationist women to support troops on the war front. Supported by donations, these "donut lassies" brought a cheerful "seven days a week Christianity" complete with smiles, baked goods (donuts for doughboys), and supplies for the soldiers. After the war the Salvation Army provided services and accommodations for returning troops. Evangeline was awarded the Distinguished Service Medal by the US Army. Although many people know the Salvation Army only for its red donation kettles at Christmastime, they do much more. Their relentless commitment is to help people of all beliefs and walks of life find salvation from poverty, homelessness, depression, and hopelessness.

Consider This: Poverty, disasters, and destitution are plagues that constantly afflict the human race. Yet people of goodwill and resources take the responsibility and opportunity to help others as they can: physically, spiritually, or monetarily.

COSTCO

> I think the biggest single thing that causes difficulty in the business world is the short-term view. We become obsessed with it. But it forces bad decisions.
>
> **JAMES SINEGAL**

Costco stores are the grandchild of a series of other stores. In 1954 a lawyer named Sol Price opened a members-only department store called FedMart in an old airplane hangar. The store's customers were federal employees, who paid two dollars to become members. When a West German retailer purchased the company and fired Sol, the company went broke. (Such is often the case when a visionary loses control of a business.) Sol didn't give up. He raised $2.5 million and opened another store called the Price Club. He sold memberships to government employees, credit union members, bank employees, and the like. Each had to pay twenty-five dollars.

Costco founders James Sinegal and Jeffrey Brotman trace their inspiration to the Price Club model. James began working at FedMart at age eighteen and learned every aspect of the business while working his way up to executive vice president. Jeffrey also had retailing experience and became enamored with a large "hypermart" store in France. Jeffrey and James discovered they had a similar moral compass—simply doing the right thing for people, both employees and customers. Taking a cue from Price Stores, Jeffrey partnered with James to blend the hypermart and Price Club concepts. They called the store Costco. Price Club merged with Costco in 1993, creating the stores we know today. Wall Street often presses Costco to charge higher prices and lower employee wages to maximize short-term profits. But so far Costco believes its strategy of having generous compensation and superior customer service is beneficial in the long run.

Consider This: Even in discounting, the secret to success is having people who care about providing top-quality service and merchandise and ensuring that both customers and employees are treated fairly.

THERE'S GOLD IN THOSE HILLS

Gold! Gold! Gold! Gold! Bright and yellow, hard and cold.

THOMAS HOOD

People often have no idea how close they've come to attaining a goal—until they've given up. Nearly all of us have abandoned a goal we wanted to achieve at some point in our lives. Perhaps we had worked for days, weeks, or even years trying to reach our goal but finally found it was too difficult to keep going. We became burned out. We decided to quit. We lost all hope of finding a plan that would make it work. Later we asked ourselves, "Why didn't I hold on for just a little longer?" In *Think and Grow Rich*, author Napoleon Hill tells the story of R. U. Darby, who discovered gold in the Colorado hills. It seemed that the vein of gold ore was massive until it suddenly ran out. Frantically, the drillers searched to pick up the vein again, but to no avail. Finally, Darby gave up and sold the remaining assets to a junkyard dealer.

The junkyard owner called in a mining engineer who was an expert in mineral deposits. The engineer surveyed the situation and calculated that the gold vein would start up about three feet from where the others had stopped digging. The expert had a thorough knowledge of geology and understood how rock formations often shifted. He had the tools and training to determine where the vein would likely be found—and he was exactly right! The mine was reopened, and the junkyard owner took millions of dollars' worth of gold from the previously abandoned vein.

Consider This: Before you give up, cover all the possibilities. Then ask for advice from those who know more than you. Your pot of gold may be only a few feet away.

THE STRATEGY OF LEADERSHIP

The essence of leadership is to get others to do something because they think you want it done and because they know it is worthwhile doing—that is what we are talking about.

DWIGHT EISENHOWER

Leadership is something every organization wants. Everyone agrees that it's good to have, but few people really know how to find it or define it. In researching their book, *Leaders*, authors Warren Bennis and Burt Nanus interviewed ninety leaders from various professional fields to find common threads in leadership behavior. Most leadership gurus agree that there is no decisively correct way to lead. Still, there are underlying leadership principles that can be identified. By analyzing the character and personality traits of the ninety leaders, Bennis and Nanus were able to discern four distinct characteristics that most leaders share:

1. Leaders bring attention to their agenda (vision).
2. Leaders communicate, although not necessarily in conventional ways.
3. Leaders trust people. They put themselves at risk by giving other people the power to act.
4. Leaders believe in themselves and keep their eyes on the positive side of their goals.

A business leader's worth does not necessarily come from the technical knowledge of the industry. A leader must encourage others to act, help them visualize their goals, and cheer them on when things look bleak. A strong leader is part visionary, part cheerleader, and part warrior. No one is born with all of these leadership traits. They are acquired from a combination of life skills and training.

Consider This: How do you measure up as a leader? Are there personal strategies you should change to become a more effective leader?

MARY BLAIR'S FLAIR

*You get an education in school and in college. And then
you start to work. And that's when you learn!*

MARY BLAIR

Walt Disney required a lot of gifted artists to build his empire. Mary Blair was
one of his most talented Imagineers, whose artistic fingerprints are all over
Disney. Mary Robinson was born in 1911 into a poor family in Oklahoma.
After moving to California in 1918, she graduated from high school and
enrolled in San Jose State College, majoring in Fine Arts. There, she had opportunities to study under several prominent artists, including Alfaro Siqueiros
and Pruett Carter. After marrying Lee Blair in 1934, both Mary and Lee
worked with Ub Iwerks, one of Disney's original partners. Later, Mary and
Lee took jobs at Disney Studios. A turning point in Mary's life was a trip with
the Disney team to South America during World War II in a "good neighbor"
tour. The experience heavily influenced her artistic style, making her art more
colorful and vivid. People called it "Mary Blair's Flair." Walt loved her art and
used her talents in several projects, including *The Three Caballeros* cartoons.

Mary was also responsible for color styling in *Cinderella*, *Alice in
Wonderland*, *Peter Pan*, and other projects. She left Disney to pursue her own
career as a freelance designer, but came back in 1964 to help create a new ride
called "It's a Small World" for the New York World's Fair. Its dolls, animals,
and artwork show Mary's distinctive magic. Even the building's unique facade
is her design. She continued working on other Disney projects, including creating Disneyland and Walt Disney World murals. She was honored in 1991 as
a Disney Legend. On The Magic Kingdom's Main Street, you'll find a window
on one of the buildings called the "Center Street Academy of Fine Art." Among
the artists listed is Mary Blair.

*Consider This: People remember flair. So do what you do best, then add some
flair to make it memorable.*

WHITMAN SAMPLER

When it comes to chocolate, resistance is futile.

REGINA BRETT

A good company cannot remain the same forever. It must change with the times. It must retain those ideas and products that continue to be popular while daring to experiment with new concepts and new products. Since 1912 the Whitman Sampler assortment of chocolate candies has been a favorite gift to give and to receive. But it was not the Whitman company's original product. The enterprise's tradition goes back to 1842 when Stephen Whitman opened a small candy shop in Philadelphia. The Market Street store was located near the city's wharves. There Stephen bought exotic nuts and fruits to include in his chocolates. In the early days Stephen sold his customers an empty box that they could fill with candies from the store.

Stephen's candies became popular, and to take advantage of the increasing demand, he began prepackaging them in fancy boxes. By the turn of the century, Walter Sharp ran Whitman's candy business. While visiting his grandmother's house, Sharp noticed an embroidered box that he recognized as a potential candy box. He produced a likeness of the box and put an index of the candies in the lid to let customers choose their favorites. The product instantly became a popular addition to his line. The Whitman's Sampler that can be seen on store shelves today is patterned after that same box. Experimentation and adaptation are the lifeblood of any growing organization. More than a billion Whitman's Samplers have been sold since its inception. Today one is sold somewhere in the world every 2.5 seconds.

Consider This: Keep your eyes open for the idea with the potential to become a legend. Even if what you now have is successful, don't be afraid to experiment with new ideas.

DORIS MILLER AT PEARL HARBOR

A hero is an ordinary individual who finds the strength to
persevere and endure in spite of overwhelming obstacles.

CHRISTOPHER REEVE

On December 7, 1941, Americans were shocked by an attack on its relatively undefended Naval Base at Pearl Harbor, Hawaii. There were many stories of bravery as 353 Japanese aircraft arrived on that otherwise sleepy Sunday morning. The attack sank five battleships, a gunnery training ship, and three destroyers. In addition, many other ships and three hundred airplanes were obliterated. A total of 2,403 Americans were killed and many more wounded. Sailors aboard ships were suddenly awakened to the sound of bombs and torpedoes exploding. Some were killed instantly. Others had to fight through fire, smoke, and heat to fend for their lives. Many went down with the ships. The incident woke the "sleeping giant," and President Franklin Roosevelt asked Congress to declare war.

One story of that morning was the bravery of Doris Miller, an African-American mess assistant on the *USS West Virginia*. While doing laundry below decks, he heard explosions and a call to battle stations. He raced up to the deck, where he carried wounded sailors to places of safety, including the mortally wounded ship's captain. He then found an abandoned 50-caliber antiaircraft gun. Miller fired on approaching aircraft until he ran out of ammunition (although he'd never received any combat training). Finally he was ordered to abandon ship. The *West Virginia* sank as he and other sailors fled to rescue boats. In 1942 Miller received the Navy Cross from Fleet Admiral Chester W. Nimitz, who said, "This marks the first time in this conflict that such high tribute has been made in the Pacific Fleet to a member of his race, and I'm sure that the future will see others similarly honored for brave acts."

Consider This: No matter your station, be prepared to step to the forefront and do your best. Every person counts.

INTEL'S BEGINNINGS

*Talent hits a target no one else can hit; Genius
hits a target no one else can see.*
ARTHUR SCHOPENHAUER

Many pioneers in the computer and electronics fields have been employed
by Fairchild Semiconductor. So many, in fact, they've become known as
Fairchildren. Three of those former employees were Robert Noyce, Gordon
Moore, and Andy Grove. In the mid-1960s, Fairchild went through three
different CEOs in a year. Tension was high, and morale was low. In the meantime, Noyce and Moore, both brilliant research scientists, spent more time
on administrative tasks than on research. They believed their talents were
wasted and didn't want to spend their careers as corporate bureaucrats. So in
1968, Noyce and Moore left Fairchild. They were soon joined by Grove, and
together they formed Intel, named for a combination of the words "integrated
electronics."

Intel set out to make computer memory chips. Unfortunately, many of its
early attempts didn't work well. When one chip finally worked, it called for a
champagne celebration. (It was the 1103 chip, a one-kilobit dynamic random-
access memory—DRAM—chip.) Progress to make the highly complex chips
required patience and ingenuity. In 1981 Intel developed a critical electronic
component that became the primary chip (the 8088) in the successful line of
IBM personal computers. This was followed by the pioneering 80386, a 32-bit
chip, and Pentium. The advancement of chips follows Moore's Law, which
states the number of components on a chip would double every eighteen to
twenty-four months. For example, Intel's chips grew from 2,250 transistors in
1971 (on its 4004 chip) to a hefty 100 billion on its latest three-dimensional
processor chip. Today Intel has more than fifteen thousand employees and
continues to define the computer marketplace with innovative advancements.

*Consider This: Keep geniuses in your enterprise by allowing them to fulfill their
dreams. Otherwise, they may take their dreams elsewhere.*

A CHARLIE BROWN CHRISTMAS

Christmas is doing a little something extra for someone.
CHARLES M. SCHULZ

For more than fifty years, Charles Schulz entertained the world with his *Peanuts* comic strip. Although Schulz knew he wanted to be a cartoonist from an early age, his first attempts were rejected repeatedly. He even submitted a portfolio to Walt Disney and was turned down. Even his proposal to his redheaded sweetheart was rejected. Finally, at the age of twenty-eight, he got a contract for a United Feature Syndicate comic strip called *L'il Folks*. But they made him rename it, so he called his strip *Peanuts*. Soon Charlie Brown, Snoopy, Lucy, and the others became household names. Schulz also significantly influenced American culture with his TV special *A Charlie Brown Christmas*, which first aired on December 9, 1965. But the entire project was almost scrapped.

When *Peanuts* was featured on the cover of *Time* magazine, CBS came courting, wanting a TV Christmas special. A deadline was approaching. Schulz and the producer quickly came up with a story. Then the trouble started. The network didn't like the jazzy music. They didn't like the slowness of the story or the kids dancing or using kids' voices instead of adult voice actors. They didn't like the absence of a laugh track. And they certainly didn't like Linus reading the nativity story from the Gospel of Luke. But it was too late to stop the production. Plus, Charles Schulz had enough clout to stand up for his choices. In the end the sponsors and the network just wanted to get the disaster over with. It turned out Schulz knew what people wanted, and the television moguls had no clue. The show garnered a 50 percent share of the nightly audience. It also won an Emmy, a Peabody Award, and the accolades of audiences (and generations) across the nation.

Consider This: Stand up for what you believe in and what you know works within your area of expertise. Sometimes the top dogs in the big offices are often clueless.

EMILY DICKINSON, UNKNOWN SUCCESS

If I can stop one heart from breaking, / I shall not live in vain; / If I can ease one life the aching, / Or cool one pain, / Or help one fainting robin / Unto his nest again, / I shall not live in vain.

EMILY DICKINSON

As unfortunate as it sounds, sometimes a successful person doesn't live long enough to see their own legacy. An example is American poet Emily Dickinson. Born December 10, 1830, in Amherst, Massachusetts, she was raised in a well-educated family. Unlike the reclusive Emily, Lavinia, her younger sister (nicknamed Vinnie), was popular, active, friendly, and always busy. She was also the family organizer. If there was a task to do, Vinnie did it. Emily was the opposite. She didn't go out unless Vinnie was with her. She was quiet, contemplative, and dependent on her sister. They were inseparable.

Influenced by her Puritanical faith, Emily wrote poems inspired by the book of Revelation and John Calvin. She adored the poetry of Robert and Elizabeth Browning and John Keats. She wrote poems her entire lifetime, often enclosing them in letters to friends. But her poems were rarely seen by others, nor was her talent recognized during her lifetime. Emily died in 1886 with instructions to her sister to burn her personal correspondence. Vinnie did as she promised. But she also discovered forty handbound volumes of Emily's writing that were not letters, so she kept them. They included more than 1,800 poems. With continuing devotion to her sister, Vinnie worked for more than a decade to get her sister's poems published. From 1890 until 1955, various Emily Dickinson poems were published for the first time. Emily Dickinson became known as one of the most influential American poets of the nineteenth century. Thousands of scholarly articles have been written about her legacy.

Consider This: Are you searching for fame and fortune? Or are you creating a legacy that others may benefit from in the future? Fame and fortune are fleeting, but a legacy is lasting.

OLGA'S SLIPS

The country would not be what it is if it wasn't
for the immigrants in this country.
RICK SANTELLI

We are a country of immigrants seeking a better life. Dreams are often conceived in other countries, hoping they may eventually take root in the fertile soil of free enterprise. Olga and Jan Erteszek were married in Poland during World War II. To escape Nazi oppression, they emigrated to the United States and moved to California. Jan was trained as a lawyer but could not practice in the United States, so Olga decided to bring in money using her talent for sewing. Her mother had been a corsetiere, but Olga knew little about the design of women's undergarments. For ten dollars she rented a machine and bought fabric. After spending long hours sewing and modeling in front of the mirror, Olga had made several samples of garter belts. Jan took them to a local department store and received an order for more. The items proved popular, and the stores soon placed additional orders.

The small business grew during the war, and Olga designed new intimate apparel items. Her secret, she claimed, was that she served as her own model. Olga wore everything she made and fit the apparel to live models rather than templates. Her unique feminine touches were original since she refused to look at what the competition was doing. Jan and Olga loved to hear about things that were "impossible" since they enjoyed the challenge of devising ways to accomplish those very feats. Their creativity and drive to do what no one else could do made the Olga Company one of the most successful intimate apparel manufacturers in the United States.

Consider This: Those willing to try to do the impossible are the same people who reap the benefits when the impossible is finally accomplished.

THE LOUISVILLE SLUGGER

I'd have been a .290 hitter without a Louisville Slugger.

TED WILLIAMS

Pete Browning was known as the Gladiator in the American Association baseball league. He holds one of the highest lifetime batting averages in league history at .341. But another aspect of his career is perhaps more lasting. When he broke his favorite bat, Pete was fighting a batting slump during the 1884 season. As it happened, John "Bud" Hillerich was at the ballpark that day, playing hooky from his father's woodworking shop. Hillerich invited the despondent ball player to go with him to the woodshop, promising to make Pete a new bat. The two found a piece of white ash, and Hillerich worked late into the night trying to create a perfect bat.

During the next baseball game, Browning went three-for-three with his new bat. He was immediately enamored with his custom-made slugger. But Hillerich's father saw no future in the bat business, preferring to continue making bedposts, tenpins, and wooden bowling balls. Hillerich thought otherwise. He continued to make bats on the side, with ever-increasing success. His early efforts were known as Falls City Sluggers, but the name was changed to Louisville Slugger in 1894. Hillerich continued to custom-make bats to players' exacting specifications, and they soon became legendary. Players' names were often carved into the handles to identify the bats. Hillerich also came up with a unique marketing idea for bats created for general distribution. In 1905 he signed Honus Wagner to a contract. He included the famous player's signature on his Louisville Sluggers, thus beginning the era of endorsement advertising.

Consider This: Solve someone's problem by giving him a better tool to perform his job. There is always a demand for the best.

JIM HENSON

The only way the magic works is by hard work.
JIM HENSON

Jim Henson begged his parents to get a television. All the other kids' families had them. Finally in 1950, when Jim was fourteen, they relented and bought one. Jim was fascinated with the medium's sights and sounds and wanted to be a part of its magic. He got his first opportunity in 1954, when, as a member of his high school puppet club, he heard that a local TV station, WTOP, was looking for a puppeteer. Jim applied for the job and soon began working on the *Junior Good Morning Show*, but the program was canceled after three weeks. Jim entered college and planned to develop his talents as a cartoonist. Fate intervened. He got a job performing a five-minute puppet show for WRC-TV. He used the opportunity to create new puppet ideas and also learned how to make people laugh.

Jim combined traditional marionettes and hand puppets to make his own creations. He called them "Muppets." In 1956, through his work at WRC, he was given national exposure for his Muppets by appearing on NBC's *Tonight Show*. That led to appearances on such popular programs as *The Ed Sullivan Show* and *The Jimmy Dean Show*. In 1969 Jim Henson's Muppets became part of a new educational show on the Public Broadcasting System called *Sesame Street*. The program was a hit, but the major networks still wouldn't give Jim his own show. Finally, in 1976 an English businessman provided the funding to produce *The Muppet Show*. The series made superstars of Kermit the Frog, Miss Piggy, and the rest. When asked about his secret for success, Henson replied, "Follow your enthusiasm. It's something I've always believed in. Find those parts of your life you enjoy the most. Do what you enjoy doing."

Consider This: Your most creative energy is released when you do what you love the most.

RUDOLPH THE RED-NOSED REINDEER

*Christmas waves a magic wand over this world, and
behold, everything is softer and more beautiful.*
NORMAN VINCENT PEALE

Robert L. May was a copywriter for the Montgomery Ward department store in 1939. During that winter his wife was seriously ill with cancer. When he went to work on a cold winter day, he was glad Christmas was over because he didn't feel festive. But he was assigned to create a Christmas coloring book for the store to give to kids the following Christmas. His only instruction was to make it about an animal. May considered the task and noticed how so many decorations featured reindeer. With that start, he thought about the eight deer in "A Visit from Saint Nicholas" and decided he'd create a new one. He considered the names Rollo and Reginal but settled on Rudolph. The more he got into the story, the more it provided some comfort for his aching heart.

Unfortunately, his wife died that winter. His boss told him to drop the project, but by that time May admitted, "I needed Rudolph more than ever." He buried himself in his writing. His light-bulb moment for Rudolph's nose came as he gazed into a foggy Chicago day and saw glowing lights. The story about the sad reindeer who became happy was inspired by his own favorite kids' story, *The Ugly Duckling*. When he finished the story, he read it to his daughter. He realized immediately it "accomplished what I had hoped." May's brother-in-law, Johnny Marks, turned the story *Rudolph the Red-Nosed Reindeer* into a song sung by Gene Autry. The record blasted onto the American Christmas scene as an instant classic. The song, plus a 1964 stop-motion TV special, made Rudolph a permanent part of the Christmas landscape.

Consider This: Any time of the year, life can be tragic. We can let our circumstances destroy us. Or we can rise above the sadness and create something uplifting that's wonderful and new.

THE SLINKY

The man with a new idea is a crank until his idea succeeds.

MARK TWAIN

Some toys remain fascinating for children of every generation. One such toy is the Slinky. How it came about is almost as interesting as its ability to fascinate kids. Opportunity often knocks at odd times and in strange ways. When the knock occurs, some people answer the door and say, "What a great idea!" but do little or nothing about it. A few people will grab the opportunity and make something happen.

The Slinky, the springlike toy that walks downstairs, essentially invented itself. One day in 1943, Richard James, a marine engineer, was startled by a zero-compression spring that fell off a shelf, proceeded to "walk" across a row of books, and then bounced to the floor. James took the spring home, and his toddler played with it for hours. The spring represented an opportunity. What could be done with it? James decided to test the potential of marketing the spring as a toy. He and his wife Betty made one hundred of the springs and arranged to show them at Gimbels department store. Customers loved Slinky's personality and bought the entire stock.

Manufacture, promotion, and distribution of the Slinky was haphazard at first, but sales soon flourished. Unfortunately, Richard had a difficult time coping with success. By the mid-1950s, he had drained the company of most of its assets. After Richard left his wife and the Slinky organization, Betty continued to run the business herself and returned it to prosperity. After many decades on the toy aisle and with only slight modifications, the Slinky still has the appeal to become a favorite toy of each new generation.

Consider This: Look at simple things, and let your imagination go wild. How can something meant for one purpose be used for another? If the idea is good, then add hard work. That formula often spells success.

FREE PUBLIC LIBRARIES

Surplus wealth is a sacred trust which its possessor is bound to administer in his lifetime for the good of the community.
ANDREW CARNEGIE

If you borrowed this book from a library, thank Andrew Carnegie. For much of America's history, libraries were nonexistent for public use. Those that did exist were subscription-based: you paid a yearly subscription fee for the privilege of using it. Some had books you could read in the building, but you couldn't actually borrow them. Then, in the 1800s, a few American communities opened public libraries. These were initially sponsored by churches and schools. In 1886 that changed because of the philanthropy of Andrew Carnegie. Carnegie worked for a factory as a "bobbin boy" when he was a teenager, filling the bobbins with thread. But he wanted to better himself. He decided that reading books was the way to learn. However, he couldn't afford the two-dollar yearly fee for the library. So he sent a letter to the local newspaper telling of his plight. The paper published the letter, and the library owner opened his library (but only to male factory workers).

Carnegie remembered the "leg up" he got from reading. After he'd made a fortune, he adopted a philosophy that "the man who dies rich dies in disgrace." So even though he became one of the world's richest men, he decided to use his wealth to help others. He built free public libraries open to men, women, children, and people of all races. In many cities they became the only place where African Americans could use public toilets. From 1886 until 1929 Carnegie paid for 1,689 libraries all across the United States. Many of these libraries still exist today. And even if some of the buildings are gone, their legacy lives on. Today almost every American community has free public libraries.

Consider This: How can you give back to your community? Not many have millions to give, but we all have time and talents that can help bring equality and opportunity to people in our city, town, or neighborhood.

TIMEX WATCHES

They take a licking and keep on ticking.
TIMEX ADVERTISEMENT

Norwegian Joakim Lehmkuhl first came to America to study engineering at Harvard and MIT. He returned to Norway in 1919 to apply his newly acquired skills to shipbuilding, but in the wake of Hitler's rise, he fled first to England, then to the US in 1940. Using his engineering background to help in the war effort, Joakim and others bought the Waterbury Clock Company, where they made fuses and timers for munitions. After the war the company began to look at other markets to use the new techniques and materials discovered during the conflict. In 1949 Lehmkuhl helped to design a reliable and straightforward watch mechanism.

When Timex watches were introduced in 1950, they were not runaway sellers. With virtually no advertising, however, sales of the watches slowly increased. But it was a unique advertising campaign that eventually made Timex a success. The legendary golfer Ben Hogan was recruited to test a Timex watch by wearing it while making 100,000 golf swings. During baseball games Mickey Mantle performed similar tests with a Timex strapped to his wrist. Some of the most memorable advertisements in US history involved "torture tests" performed by John Cameron Swayze on live television. The tests were conducted under some of the most challenging conditions imaginable. They always produced a watch that "takes a licking and keeps on ticking." One of the early torture tests seemed to be a disaster when the watch accidentally came free from the outboard motor propeller to which it had been attached. But when the Timex was recovered from the bottom of the test tank, it was still ticking.

Consider This: Inexpensive and built to survive rigors beyond everyday life—that is what consumers are looking for!

TIFFANY

[Tiffany's] calms me down right away, the quietness and the
proud look of it; nothing very bad could happen to you there.
TRUMAN CAPOTE, *BREAKFAST AT TIFFANY'S*

In 1837 Charles Lewis Tiffany borrowed $1,000 from his father and went to
New York, where he partnered with John Young and opened a small store on
lower Broadway. The store carried all manner of interesting items but little
jewelry. Then, in 1848, with a revolution in Europe and jewelry prices falling,
Tiffany decided to enter the market. During the California gold rush of the
following year, the entrepreneur added precious metals to his line. Tiffany pioneered a one-price system and touted the concept in advertising: "Every article
is marked in plain figures, upon which there will not be the slightest variation."

Tiffany & Co. was incorporated in 1868 and continued to grow until
the Great Depression of the 1930s began to erode profits. The company was
rescued in the mid-1950s by Walter Hoving, who owned the Bonwit Teller
& Co. fashion-apparel store adjoining Tiffany. Getting rid of leftover "white
elephants" with a half-price sale, Hoving brought in the best jewelry and china
designers to upgrade the store's merchandise. He also hired the most creative professionals to attractively decorate Tiffany store windows. Unlike the
previous owner, who shunned publicity, Hoving encouraged Tiffany's noto-
riety via ads in the *Wall Street Journal* that blasted poor taste in all its forms,
from tattooing to a "loud and vulgar" Christmas tree on Park Avenue. Tiffany
was back and setting a high standard for good taste. In its first decade under
Hoving, profits increased more than 900 percent. Today, any present in a
Tiffany Blue Box is sure to bring a smile.

*Consider This: No public enterprise can exist in health without a healthy love for
the public.*

POOR RICHARD'S ALMANACK

America is great because America is good. If America
ever stops being good, she will stop being great.
ALEXIS DE TOCQUEVILLE

The book you're now reading, and every American book about motivation, self-help, and personal achievement, can trace at least part of its inspiration to a little forty-eight-page booklet called *Poor Richard's Almanack*. First printed in Philadelphia on December 19, 1732, this yearly publication was well read throughout the colonies. Poor Richard was, in fact, Benjamin Franklin. After apprenticing with his brother James and acquiring a press from England, he set up his own printing company in Philadelphia. Then he looked for a way to expand his business. One idea was to create a yearly publication. He surmised it would make more money than printing a book someone would purchase only once. So he came up with an almanac filled with helpful information. Some people compare his *Almanack* to today's internet. It had a little of everything, including household tips, personal advice, poems, calendars, weather predictions, advice for farmers, political opinions, news stories, and even the occasional mathematical puzzle. But perhaps its most memorable inclusion was Richard's pithy sayings.

These short sayings account for more English language maxims than any other writer except perhaps William Shakespeare. Some of them include "Early to bed, and early to rise, makes a man healthy, wealthy and wise"; "A friend in need is a friend indeed"; "God helps them that help themselves"; "Haste makes waste"; and "No gains without pains." The advice found in twenty-five years of the *Almanack* created a culture of frugality, responsibility, and independence that continues to influence all Americans today.

Consider This: Pithy sayings are cute and memorable. But it is only when we take their wisdom to heart that we can genuinely contribute to the betterment of our own life and the world.

JESSICA MCCLURE'S RESCUE

I was in need, and you helped me.
THE BIBLE

It was a warm day in Midland, Texas, and Jessica McClure and her friends were playing in the backyard. As the children ventured into an overgrown area, eighteen-month-old Jessica suddenly disappeared down a hole. The hole proved to be an abandoned water well, and the youngster had become trapped some twenty feet down an eight-inch pipe. Jessica's story quickly became international news and a national obsession. Everyone wanted to help. Oil drillers from the area arrived and began to dig a hole nearby in order to reach the toddler. Not far down, however, they hit super-hard caliche rock, which shattered drill bits and slowed progress to just inches each hour. Twenty-four hours passed, then thirty-six, then forty-eight. Every newscast carried the story, and special newsbreaks updated people about progress, new hope, or new problems.

Midland's economy was depressed due to falling oil prices. Still, the rescue attempt seemed to spark new life in the city's residents. Drillers donated $1,200 bits, knowing that they would last only a short while before breaking. Experts flew in from all over the country to donate their time, and people throughout the region did what they could: they prayed. Fifty-six hours after the ordeal began, Jessica was pulled from the hole and carried to safety as throngs of people cheered. Shouts and celebrations were repeated in homes, restaurants, football stadiums, and almost everywhere else as word spread that little Jessica had been saved. So many people cared. So many people worked, hoped, and shared. It was America at its best.

Consider This: The American Dream is opportunity for all people. From helping one little child to helping an entire community in need, America is bent on giving every person the chance to make their life count.

PHILO FARNSWORTH

If it weren't for Philo T. Farnsworth, inventor of television, we'd still be eating frozen radio dinners.
JOHNNY CARSON

Philo Farnsworth may be the most famous person you've never heard about. He's even listed in *Time* magazine's "100 Most Important Persons of the Twentieth Century." Chances are, you use his invention every day. Farnsworth is the inventor of electronic television. Born in 1906 in Utah, young Philo was an avid reader. In particular, he liked to read science magazines. One invention that fascinated him was the mechanical television. This device used a rotating disk full of holes to capture and transmit crude images across a wire. He imagined that an electronic scanner would be much faster and produce a better image. So by 1922 (while still in high school), he worked out the basic theory for how such a television could work.

His father's death in 1924 meant financial struggles for the Farnsworth family, and Philo had to put his plans on hold. But by 1926 he had found a partner to help with expenses, and he and his wife moved to Los Angeles to work on his idea. On September 7, 1927, he filed a patent for this invention. That's when more troubles began. RCA was also developing an electronic television. They offered Farnsworth $100,000 for his patent, but he refused. Farnsworth and RCA fought about patent rights in court for years. Sometimes he won; sometimes he lost. Finally, in 1939 RCA bought Farnsworth's patents. Unfortunately, World War II prevented television from becoming commercial until 1947. Although Farnsworth tried to create his own television brand, he was outspent and outmarketed by more established players like RCA. As a result, his name vanished from the public's eye for many years until history remembered his contribution and recognized him as television's true inventor.

Consider This: Ideas don't mean a thing unless they can be successfully sold in the marketplace. So make sure your idea gets teamed up with someone who can appropriately market it.

THE CLOSE SHAVE

I always entertain great hopes.

ROBERT FROST

Until the turn of the century, shaving was performed with a straight-edged razor (which could be dangerous in unsteady hands). King Gillette changed that. In 1901 Gillette introduced the safety razor, which proved successful and came into particular prominence as a standard issue for American soldiers during World War I. After all, the doughboys had to be clean-shaven for their gas masks to fit correctly. After the war many soldiers kept using their safety razors. But Jacob Schick was not satisfied with his wartime experience. The razor worked well enough when hot water was available, but Schick was stationed in Alaska. Every morning he had to crack a layer of ice to get to the water to shave. Then the wheels of invention began to turn.

After his discharge from the service, Schick decided to invent a dry razor. His biggest problem was the lack of a small electric motor sufficient to power his invention. Schick worked for five years to develop a workable motor, which he patented in 1923. But that success did not solve all of his problems. Schick could not find any financial backers. After all, who needed an electric shaver when the safety razor was so good? Schick mortgaged everything he owned to bring his razor to the marketplace in 1931. The twenty-five-dollar price tag seemed high, particularly during the Great Depression, but he managed to sell three thousand of the devices. His novel razor began making money, and Schick reinvested all of his profits in advertising. As a result, by 1937 Jacob Schick had sold almost two million electric razors.

Consider This: Few people find instant success. For most people, success comes after commitment, hard work, and determination to see the project through to completion.

MACY'S

It is easier to go down a hill than up, but
the view is best from the top.
ARNOLD BENNETT

Macy's department store is an American tradition. When people visit New York, they go to the Statue of Liberty, the Empire State Building, and Macy's. It is doubtful that Rowland Macy could have conceived the full extent of his venture. In fact, he failed quite a few times before finding any success in the retail business. The Nantucket Quaker left home as a teenager and spent four years aboard the sailing ship *Emily Morgan*. In 1844 Macy started a needle-and-thread shop in Boston, but it failed. He went to California during the gold rush, tried to make a go of another store in Massachusetts, and eventually tried again by selling ribbons and lace from a small store on Sixth Avenue in New York. Macy subscribed to the Quaker principles of one price, true value, and cash-only transactions. Macy's New York store made a profit, and he began a policy of expansion that has never stopped.

By the modern era, Macy's store was so big that small problems were magnified a thousandfold. Most customers believed that Macy's carried everything. Once, when Macy's advertised a book entitled *One Million Islands for Sale*, the sales staff had their hands full explaining that the store did not actually sell islands. To handle the problem of occasionally misdelivered baby furniture, Macy's kept an emergency supply of standard products in stock. They also kept a truck ready to quickly deliver them. A staff of writers answered letters, a laboratory tested thousands of potential items, and an army of secret shoppers compared prices to ensure Macy's prices were lower than the competition's. And the customers showed appreciation with continued store loyalty.

Consider This: Rowland Macy could have quit after his first failure. Or his second or third. A dreamer continues his quest until the dream is in hand.

IT'S A WONDERFUL LIFE

*Every time you hear a bell ring, it means that
some angel's just got his wings.*
CLARENCE ODBODY

Jimmy Stewart and Donna Reed starred in a post-World War II movie about the life of George Bailey, a struggling young man searching for his own American Dream. *It's a Wonderful Life* opened in 1946 and promptly lost more than a half million dollars. It lay virtually forgotten in film vaults until the video and cable revolution sparked an interest in older films. It quickly became a beloved classic when the film sprang back to life as a Christmas television film.

In the movie George Bailey dreams of traveling the world and seeing mysterious, exotic places. Unfortunately, his plans always seem to be thwarted by circumstances. George postpones his travels to help his family's small savings and loan bank protect townspeople from a greedy banker. When George falls in love with Mary Hatch, they plan an elaborate honeymoon, only to have their plans shattered when there's a run on the bank. Then, when his Uncle Billy misplaces an $8,000 deposit just as bank examiners arrive, George faces certain ruin and humiliation. He wishes he'd never been born. An angel second-class, Clarence Odbody, grants his wish and lets George see what his hometown would have been like if George had never been born. In that vision, George finds formerly pastoral Bedford Falls filled with mean, poor, and unhappy people. He desperately begs to return to his family, even if it means he must face the grim consequences. When Clarence grants his wish, George returns home and learns that his friends have banded together to replace the missing bank funds. He realizes that true wealth is not measured in possessions but in faith, family, and friends.

Consider This: Wealth and power are fleeting. Faith, hope, and love are the true building blocks of a wonderful life.

CHRISTMAS

Maybe Christmas, the Grinch thought, *doesn't come from a store.*
DR. SEUSS

The Christmas lights, music, and decorations that fill our homes, workplaces, and stores celebrate the birth of a baby who contributed more to our culture and societal beliefs than any other. Two thousand years later, the spiritual lessons he taught continue to inspire billions of his followers. In fact, the stories of many of the people in this book indicate that Jesus's teachings set the bar for how they choose to live and lead. As D. Michael Lindsay states in *Faith in the Halls of Power,* "It is a way of life that has gripped the hearts and minds of leaders around the country, and it is not likely to go away anytime soon."

Jesus defined the moral underpinnings of civilization worldwide. Perhaps his best-known maxim is the Golden Rule (treat others like you want to be treated). His parables, such as the Good Samaritan, taught us to love our neighbors as ourselves (no matter a person's class, beliefs, or origins). He modeled a plan of leadership that guided his organization (the church) for two thousand years (even if it has often deviated from his standard of morality). He showed anger toward those who took advantage of the poor. And he praised those who shared their wealth with those in need. And finally, he warned followers to beware of false spiritual leaders and charlatans. Christmas is more than a celebration of a baby's birth. The material gifts we exchange at Christmas are symbols that represent Jesus's gifts of life, hope, love, and purpose. We only need to tear open the package and claim the wonder that's inside.

Consider This: Take time to discover the priceless gifts given to you—inspiration, imagination, and determination. Celebrate! Throw a big party! Then get to work.

SELF-AFFIRMATION

The only thing we have to fear is fear itself.
FRANKLIN D. ROOSEVELT

People who are successful need to believe in themselves. But often, life circumstances don't automatically give us the capacity for self-affirmation. In that case it's something we can work to acquire. We must change our beliefs from "I can't do it" to "I can." William Danforth was a sickly schoolboy and a weakling until a teacher challenged him to become the class's healthiest, most muscular boy. Danforth took the challenge, changed his life, founded Ralston Purina Company, and devoted much of his time and fortune to helping youngsters "take a dare."

Teddy Roosevelt came out of the same "weakling" mold as Danforth. Recognizing the need for change, he decided to do everything he was afraid of doing. He thus developed a strong belief in his own capabilities. It was clothing that "made the man" in the case of Bill Zanker, who founded the successful Learning Annex. His agent refused to work with him unless he looked the part. Zanker was told to buy a $1,000 suit of clothes, a challenge that cost him just about everything he could muster. But when he put that suit on, his whole concept of himself underwent a significant change. Zanker looked like a success, he thought like a success, and he became a success. Bernie Kopell was a door-to-door vacuum cleaner salesman trying to break into acting. At the end of a frustrating day, his boss turned on some positive-thinking records—and their message began to soak into Kopell's brain. His attitude about his own capabilities changed, which enabled him to become a successful actor in *Get Smart, The Love Boat*, and many other shows.

Consider This: The first key to success in any enterprise is believing in yourself— forging ahead in the face of opposition, circumstance, fear, and frustration.

THE IMPORTANCE OF OTHERS

Do unto others as you would have them do unto you.
THE GOLDEN RULE

When James Cash Penney began his Golden Rule stores, the business's name reflected his commitment to serving his customers. Various restatements of this rule are the guiding force behind many successful enterprises, from Digital Equipment Corporation to Mary Kay Cosmetics. Although "the customer is always right" is a familiar concept in our society, it is frequently paid only lip service. Organizations that actually adhere to that principle find themselves establishing a long list of loyal customers. The Sears guarantee is the cornerstone of the company's initial success. Mail-order services such as Amazon, Land's End and L. L. Bean would find it challenging to exist if they didn't offer a firm guarantee. The "world's most successful salesman," Joe Girard, admitted that customers occasionally take advantage of service. Still, the willingness to trust the customer pays dividends in the long run.

The entire excellence movement begun by Tom Peters and Robert Waterman Jr. hinges on the powerful word *listen*. Levi Strauss listened to the needs of miners and invented blue jeans. Bette Nesmith listened to the complaints of secretaries trying to correct typing mistakes and invented Liquid Paper. Procter & Gamble listened to customers and began to promote Ivory as "the soap that floats." Kleenex was marketed as a cold-cream wipe until Kimberly-Clark listened to customers who said the tissue was also a convenient handkerchief. Arthur Fiedler became the most popular orchestra conductor in America because of his ability to give people the music they wanted to hear.

Consider This: Serving people should be the motivating concept behind every organization. People are drawn to those organizations with a high desire to serve.

FOLLOWING YOUR DREAM

We all have dreams. But in order to make dreams
come into reality, it takes an awful lot of determination,
dedication, self-discipline, and effort.

JESSE OWENS

What good is having a dream if you never follow it? Many people dream and dream, but they never act. There must be a conscious action plan for dreams to become a reality. In a 1986 *Reader's Digest* article, Barbara Bartocci listed six points to consider while searching for your dream. It seems that many people have a dream but are content to accept whatever comes along. Bartocci said that we must take our goals seriously. Age and lack of education or experience can all be overcome. Never believe that you are too old to accomplish something. Colonel Harland Sanders began selling his chicken recipe at age sixty-five, and his new career lasted twenty-five years. Take on your dream in stages. Make plans to move closer to reality, one step at a time, breaking each step into small, attainable goals.

People often think multitasking is good. Instead, it leads to mediocrity in everything you do. Focus on one big thing at a time. Pick and choose to do only things that lead to your goal. Drop unproductive chores. Change yourself into a person who pursues a goal relentlessly. Then, when obstacles come (as they will), refuse to be sidetracked. Keep going. As George Lucas summed up the concept, "You simply have to put one foot in front of the other and keep going. Put blinders on and plow right ahead." Gary Keller and Jay Papasan summarize the concept in their book *The ONE Thing*, "People who achieve extraordinary results don't achieve them by working more hours. They achieve them by getting more done in the hours they work."

Consider This: You must dream your own dream and then follow it. No one else can do it for you. If you do not take hold of your future, you'll never experience the best that life can offer.

CONQUERING THE MOUSETRAP SYNDROME

> No man is great in and of himself. He must touch the
> lives of other great men who will inspire him, lift him,
> push him forward and give him confidence.
>
> **A. A. MILNE**

Why can two people have the same idea, but only one can turn it into a success? Many people have the misconception that products and services sell themselves. Some call this the "build a better mousetrap" syndrome. Literally millions of small businesses have started and failed because they could not sell their "better idea." Some entrepreneurs develop a service or product and enjoy an initial burst of success. Then they can only watch as their business spirals out of control and fails. It is a rare individual who can start a business and bring all the skills necessary to succeed through consistent and controlled growth.

On his gravestone Andrew Carnegie claimed that his success resulted from surrounding himself with people smarter than he. More than fifty people had "invented" the typewriter. But it never made it to the marketplace until businessman and promoter James Dunmore took the idea to Remington, which had the marketing expertise to sell it to the public. Mo Siegel had a sound idea when he started Celestial Seasonings. He was smart enough to hire experience from the nation's biggest food companies to catapult the company to national success. In the fierce microcomputer wars, companies like Dell, Compaq, and Apple became successful partly because they reached out to experts. They filled their top ranks by hiring away the best and brightest people from such successful companies as Revlon, Pepsi, and IBM.

Consider This: The most intelligent people are the ones who know when to seek the help of others. So how can you multiply your own capabilities by using the skills of others?

DO IT ANYWAY

The sluggard craves and gets nothing, but the
desires of the diligent are fully satisfied.
PROVERBS 13:4

There can be no doubt that formal education plays a role in success. There are basic skills that you must possess to succeed in any venture. But there is a point at which schooling does not provide the tools for success. No one believed a housewife who knew nothing about engineering could invent an automated dishwasher. Josephine Cochrane did it anyway. Almost everyone scoffed at Elon Musk's idea of landing and reusing rockets until he did it. The signers of the Declaration of Independence essentially signed their own death warrants. Their desire for freedom overcame their fear. No one would give an old man with a chicken recipe much chance for success, but Colonel Sanders kept selling his idea until someone listened.

How can a person ignore reality and cling to the vapor of a dream? How can personal drive overcome the fear of failure? What drives people to work eighty hours a week for a vision when they would balk at working such hours for a boss? Why do some people quit when others continue? The answer lies in the age-old conflict between self-determination and the realities of the world. People are endowed with the ability to envision great things. But circumstance, education, personal doubts, and the ridicule of others challenge those dreams. Unwavering determination, some say obsession, is paramount in realizing your goals. In the end you must listen to yourself and filter out the cynics and naysayers. You alone must take responsibility for your life and what you do with it.

Consider This: What you make of your life is entirely up to you. So choose carefully to spend your energy only on those dreams that thrill you the most.

THE JOURNEY OF SUCCESS

Success is not final, failure is not fatal: it is the
courage to continue that counts.
WINSTON CHURCHILL

The end of the year is a time many assess past accomplishments. Yet many quests for success are difficult to measure or even define. Is it accumulating a certain amount of wealth—a few million dollars, for example? Will winning the lottery bring success? Most people who win the lottery are dead broke and depressed within a few years. Perhaps your life's goal is having power over other people through politics or as a high-ranking bureaucrat or CEO. Or it could be the attainment of a certain status, such as the title of doctor or professor. Notable business successes include Bill Gates, Warren Buffett, Oprah Winfrey, Zhou Qunfei, and Elon Musk. Or perhaps success is measured by fame and fortune, for example, Shaquille O'Neal, Beyoncé, Gal Gadot, or Tom Hanks. Finally, success might be counted as service to others. This might include Mother Teresa, Florence Nightingale, or Oskar Schindler. There's nothing wrong with any of these kinds of success. You can be happy in any of these situations. But whatever your station in life, it's clear that for most people ultimate success is not measured in money, titles, or fame.

One of America's greatest philosophers, Ralph Waldo Emerson, described success this way: "To laugh often and much; to win the respect of intelligent people and the affection of children; to earn the appreciation of honest critics and endure the betrayal of false friends; to appreciate beauty; to find the best in others; to leave the world a bit better, whether by a healthy child, a garden patch, or a redeemed social condition; to know even one life has breathed easier because you lived; this is to have succeeded."

Consider This: It is good and noble to seek success in whatever you do. But it is better to know precisely what will make your life fulfilling, honorable, and satisfying.